W9-CAO-448

A View from the Campidoglio
Selected Essays 1953–1984

A View from the Campidoglio
Selected Essays 1953-1984

Robert Venturi and Denise Scott Brown

Edited by   Peter Arnell   Ted Bickford   Catherine Bergart

Icon Editions

HARPER & ROW, PUBLISHERS, NEW YORK
Cambridge, Philadelphia, San Francisco, London
Mexico City, São Paulo, Sydney

A VIEW FROM THE CAMPIDOGLIO. Copyright ©1984
by Robert Venturi and Denise Scott Brown. Foreword
copyright ©1984 by Peter Arnell and Ted Bickford. All
rights reserved. Printed In Japan. No part of this book may
be used or reproduced in any manner whatsoever without
written permission except in the case of brief quotations
embodied in critical articles and reviews. For information
address Harper & Row, Publishers, Inc., 10 East 53rd Street,
New York, N.Y. 10022. Published simultaneously in Canada
by Fitzhenry & Whiteside Limited, Toronto.

FIRST EDITION

LIBRARY OF CONGRESS CATALOG CARD NUMBER: 83-49206

ISBN: 0-06-438851-4
ISBN: 0-06-430139-7 pbk.

Printed and bound by Dai Nippon Printing Company

Set in Simoncini Garamond by Circle Graphics, Washington,
D.C.

The editors would like to extend a special thanks to Vincent
Scully for providing inspiration, to Mark Uhlig, to Cass
Canfield Jr. for his continual support, and to the office of
Venturi, Rauch and Scott Brown, most notably Steve Estock
for his patience and efficiency, and, of course, Denise Scott
Brown and Robert Venturi.

Grateful acknowledgement is made for permission to reprint:
p. 46, "A Reaction to Complexity and Contradiction in the
Work of Furness," published by permission of The
Pennsylvania Academy of the Fine Arts, Philadelphia; p. 110,
"Diversity, relevance and representation in historicism or plus
ca change...," reprinted from *Architectural Record* 1982 ©
1982, by McGraw-Hill, Inc. with all rights reserved; p. 24,
"Leading From the Rear by Venturi and Scott Brown," ©
Architectural Design Magazine, London. Volume 40, July
1970; p. 64, "Learning the Right Lessons from the
Beaux-Arts by Venturi," © *Architectural Design* Magazine,
London. AD Vol. 49, No. 1 1979 'Rob and Leo Krier.' In
addition we would like to thank *The Architectural Review,
Architectural Forum, RIBA Journal, Casabella, Prospectus
13/14: The Yale Architectural Journal, A + U, Allen Memorial
Art Museum Bulletin, Arkkitehti, Oppositions 8,* and *Gran
Bazaar.*

Executive Editors:
Peter Arnell
Ted Bickford

Associate Editor:
Catherine Bergart

Design:
Holly Jaffe
Arnell Bickford Associates

Contents

Vincent Scully, in his introduction to *Complexity and Contradiction in Architecture,* wrote "This is not an easy book." At that time, eighteen years ago, Robert Venturi and Denise Scott Brown were struggling to get people to listen, see, and share their vision. With this book, listening and seeing are easier for us and sharing their vision is easier for the Venturis. They can point to thirty-one years of work that is consistent with their first vision and has clearly withstood the test of time. With the buildings—a real-life embodiment of that vision—the words re-emerge.

The ideas, since their first appearance, have been admired, disputed, adopted, misrepresented, but never forgotten. To many of us they are now part of our lives as Americans. Rather than jarring because they are new, they are taken for granted and their origin is forgotten. This compendium of words and buildings should take us back to the source of so much of what we believe in architecture today: the work of Venturi and Scott Brown.

As philosophers, writers, and architects—as two people who each play three roles—they have given us a new way to examine and study, a new way to see. The result is that, after many years, our fear of the past is gone, and so is our still more debilitating fear of the future. The Venturis have a profound and complex involvement in the American landscape and its symbols. By bravely embracing this unexplored world, they have derived concepts through which it may be understood. As a result, a new spontaneity now enlivens old traditions and we have regained an old but new architectural language. Venturi and Scott Brown focus on specific problems until they yield, then communicate the results to all of us.

This book appears at a time when the firm, Venturi, Rauch and Scott Brown, is receiving more attention than ever before. With the presentation of more buildings, writing, drawings, decorative arts, and furniture, there is now an intense interest in and support for their work, and their ideas are being disbursed throughout our culture from many platforms. This book is one platform; perhaps one of the most important, not only for the access it provides to the work, but also because it traces the initiation and development of an idea. By delving backward in the journals to recover these articles, we give that idea its history and define its place in the intellectual growth of our time. Such a collecting of thoughts is needed, on occasion, as an aid to understanding the present and as a prelude to going further. "If ancient books were lost or ceased to be, then lost would be the key of memory."

P.A. T.B. C.B.
New York City
Fall 1984

Introduction

Writing was important to us as younger architects before we had the opportunity to express ideas through building. However, as our practice has grown, we have continued to pen essays with some frequency, for the same reasons we, and other architects, sketch while designing: to clarify ideas about architecture. It seems that mixed media—opera, words with pictures, buildings with writing—is our medium. Writing, for us, is part of a cycle of development that results in both theory and building: we look, analyze, synthesize through writing, synthesize through design, then look again. Sometimes design results from writing, sometimes writing from design; and both are at once cause of and caused by the swivel-head learning from the environment that we do.

These essays, selected from the body of our writing between 1952 and 1984, span our careers to date. They are subsidiary words, set down on the way to defining broader ideas, written in times of search to help clarify an argument or assert a position. For this reason they have an element of urgency, like letters from a battlefield. In some, an extra force is generated by disagreement with colleagues or by a desire to come to the aid of an admired predecessor.

The essays are presented with little alteration (although several titles have been changed). I have made a few small additions and, in a couple of places, cut, to avoid repetition; but I have allowed repetition where the second version shifts its reference points or is more detailed than the first. I have not attempted to alter or explain time-bound phrases. For example, the frequent references to "urban renewal," designate specifically the United States federal Urban Renewal program, boon to architects in the fifties, bane of social critics in the sixties, bereft of funds in the seventies, and bypassed in the eighties. I have left in, as well, references to the architect as "he." That too is part of history. In later essays we try to achieve language without gender, elegantly and unnoticeably.

The sequence of essays starts with a view of the Campidoglio, which has given its name to the book. Here, a young architect has seen Rome. His response contains the seeds of what he has stood for since: architecture as context—the subject of his MFA thesis at Princeton; historical continuity within which the architect acts; a complex vision, even the possible joys of "the grotesque." The style is spare and eloquent, proving Bob could write on his own. This is the last essay in that category. Every work written since has received comment, usually editing, from me.

Between the first and second articles is a gap of fifteen years. In that time, Bob returned to Rome to the American Academy. We met as faculty members at the University of Pennsylvania, forming a friendship and eventually an academic collaboration, when I taught the tutorials for his course on theories of architecture. Out of this course grew Bob's book, *Complexity and Contradiction in Architecture.* Not long after it appeared we married, I joined Venturi and Rauch, and our joint teaching continued at Yale. We also started to write together, describing our work, defending our theories, and developing our ideas.

At that time, having collaborated for nearly ten years, our ideas were so inextricably intertwined that there was no way to assign individual authorship to our work. We therefore arranged that the writer of the larger portion of the first draft would place his or her name first in the attribution. *Learning From Las Vegas,* published in 1972, was a collaboration of this type. However, by the early seventies I had learned that, wherever my name was, material with both names on it would be attributed to Bob alone. Therefore, I have since written articles on my own and, for the same reason, have contributed only three articles to this volume. But Bob and I remain avid users of each other's ideas and edit each other's writing; close readers will note considerable cross-fertilization and some cross-reference in our work.

After another brief gap in the sequence, while we wrote *Learning From Las Vegas,* the essays continue almost year by year. One way or another, the span of our ideas and the developing sequence of our thought over this period is set out. Some essays help initiate an idea. For example, our defense of Sir Edwin Lutyens, written in 1969, is an elaboration on the first Postmodernist discussion of this architect, which appeared in *Complexity and Contradiction in Architecture.* "Learning From Lutyens," is one of my favorite essays, partly for its word play, which is used to salute Lutyens' love of puns (architectural and verbal) and also to deflate the pompousness of his critics.

Several essays continue a line of thinking initiated elsewhere. For example, in "Diversity and Relevance etc., etc.," the Vanna Venturi house is reassessed for its Classical qualities, which were always present but which, in the sixties, were less important to note than its Mannerist leanings. This house contained in miniature, so to speak, all the elements developed later in a sequence of houses and institutional buildings. It has become an icon of Postmodernism and is now part of history. That is why it needs reassessing on occasion.

Learning From Las Vegas answered an unasked question, "What did you learn from *Complexity and Contradiction in Architecture?*" The later essays of this book attempt to answer the much-asked question, "What did you learn from Las Vegas?" As both books recede in time, so our view has gained perspective and our main themes in architecture stand revealed in the body of our work. What we learned in Las Vegas has become evident through the subsequent development of our architecture and ideas.

But perhaps we have had only one idea. One person in one lifetime is lucky to have one idea. We took ours to Rome, matched it against Las Vegas, brought it back to Rome, and then polished and burnished it over a set of demanding projects, through words and designs, and in reaction to societal movements and intellectual currents that followed the social turmoil of the sixties.

At the outset of this book, Le Corbusier had produced some unexpected, postwar buildings, Mies van der Rohe was the major source of inspiration for architects, and the New Brutalists were about to begin questioning Modern architecture. By the end of the period, our words and what was on our boards had played a major part in bringing the profession around. The issues that we confronted personally at the initiation of our careers have become the issues of architecture today. Now everyone learns from the Campidoglio.

Because our work was initially strange and unfamiliar, we have struggled as architects during most of our working life, and in the world of practice, our ideas have brought more opportunities to others than to ourselves. Now many buildings are built in accordance with our philosophies and, although most are a misinterpretation of what we stand for, some achieve more aplomb than we might have managed.

Given this new context, notions in this book that once raised hackles may now seem obvious or unarguable; buildings that were daring when designed may look tame today. For example, the thin line of white brick at cornice level on the Guild House appears modest indeed when compared with the strident stripes and dashes of much Postmodern work, but it took courage to do in 1965. In 1984 we find most Postmodern architecture brash, brittle and not really related to what we intended. We also believe some of our buildings have not yet had their day: the Brant house in Greenwich, Connecticut, for example. There is, nevertheless, a satisfaction in seeing that time has proved us more or less right.

What next? Developing our idea has recently taken us in new directions. Although our interests and practice have always stretched from urban planning to interior design, we are, at the moment, bemused to find ourselves designing a teapot (for Alessi in Milan) and an urban region (for Westway in New York). In between are plans for downtown Austin and downtown Memphis, two art museums, a series of buildings for Princeton

University, furniture, fabrics, china, and glassware. The wide span of these projects has helped further our interest in symbolism and representation at different scales. While we have continued to investigate the use of pattern and appliqué for architecture and objects, we have also broadened our study of urban relationships beyond architecture, into areas where city and regional economics act as muse.

In order to make this diversity work professionally, our architectural interests must now include the structure and organization of our office. We must consider how best to maintain an alchemist's den on Main Street, bulging with signs, fabrics, sculptures, buildings, maps, and books—yet also meet the deadlines and production requirements of the larger-scale architecture we do. What is the best use of our own span of attention? Can we keep happy and fulfilled our group of mainly chiefs and few Indians, of people who are mostly like ourselves?

The questions we face at the end of this book concern the doing of architecture and our effort to do it well; they stress quality over polemic, being good over being new. They derive from our opportunity to put theory to practice. Are they the same questions dogging the world of architecture today? We don't know.

Our words have been written primarily to help us, as architects, to learn from our own experience. The lessons are homely and down-to-earth ones, pursued mainly in the interest of improving our own art.

Denise Scott Brown
Main Street, Manayunk
September 1984

The Campidoglio: A Case Study
Robert Venturi

This essay formed part of Robert Venturi's MFA thesis at Princeton University. It was first published in **The Architectural Review,** May 1953, pp. 333–334.

The architect has a responsibility toward the landscape which he can subtly enhance or impair, for we see in perceptual wholes, and the introduction of any new building will change the character of all the other elements in a scene. The Campidoglio in Rome has been injured through ignorance of this principle. A study of maps and drawings of its changing setting shows a group of buildings in themselves not significantly altered, but nevertheless revealing variations in expression and quality.

Michelangelo's design of the Campidoglio can itself be considered as an enhanced setting for the Senatorial Palace which was in existence in the mid-sixteenth century (figs. 1, 2). This he modified almost negligibly by the application of the pilasters, entablature, and window architraves. It was by means of the form and position of the flanking buildings (fig. 3) that the Senatorial Palace acquired new value. The contrasting elements of their color and texture and the neutral, even rhythm of their columned facades gave emphasis to the palace. Their unique positional arrangement created direction and an illusion of increased size; moreover, it gave a controlled approach to the palace (fig. 4) which contributed to its monumentality. The piazza which they form created an enriched space for the palace.

Since the end of the nineteenth century one has had to approach the Campidoglio group with eyes straight ahead, preferably equipped with blinkers. At the left, and always influencing one's image, looms the Victor Emanuel Monument, ludicrous in itself, but catastrophic in its effect on the neighboring Campidoglio. In fact, adverse criticism of the shiny monster should concern itself not so much with its form (which can appeal to one's sense of the grotesque), but with

its effect on its architectural neighbors. By its size, scale, and color, it makes the Campidoglio a weak anticlimax. Furthermore, the monument's direction (fig. 5) creates for the Campidoglio a backstage position and causes it to lose any meaningful relation as a capitol to the city plan.

Similarly drastic in effect was the substitution during Mussolini's era of big boulevards and unenclosed spaces of monumental parks (fig. 6)

for the intricate small-scale neighborhoods composing the original setting. The complex formerly afforded views tantalizingly interrupted with rich, unaffected architectural foregrounds. The experience of small spaces achieved, by contrast, an effect of power for the Campidoglio piazza when it was reached. The removal of the congested areas was of doubtful social advantage, and the substitution of the fragmentary highway of no real value in the overall circulation system

1

12

of the city. The vast Parisian spaces and other trimmings have robbed the buildings and their immediate exterior spaces of force. The modern planners' scrupulous respect for a Michelangelo design has caused them to leave the Campidoglio untouched physically, but they have, nevertheless, obscured its meaning and significance. A wrecking crew could hardly have damaged it more.

13

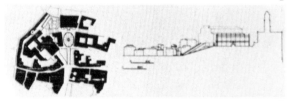

2

4

6

3

1 Perspective drawing, the Campidoglio in the mid-sixteenth century
2 Plan and section
3 Drawing, the Campidoglio with modifications and flanking buildings
4 Plan and section with modifications
5 Aerial photograph, the Campidoglio and Victor Emanuel Monument
6 Plan and section with changes made during Mussolini era

5

A Billdingboard Involving Movies, Relics, and Space
Robert Venturi

This essay was first published in **Architectural Forum,** April 1968, pp. 74–79.

1 Section-perspective, proposal for FDR Memorial, Washington, D.C., 1960[1]
2 Photomontage, proposal for fountain for J.F.K. Plaza, Fairmount Park, Philadelphia, 1964
3 Axonometric, proposal for Copley Square, Boston, 1966
4 Model, proposal for a billdingboard, National Football Hall of Fame, New Brunswick, New Jersey, 1967. Side and front
5 Side and back

Most of the competitions our office has entered have had something in common: they were hybrids. Our scheme for the F.D.R. Memorial (fig. 1) was architecture *and* landscape; our fountain for the Philadelphia Fairmount Park Commission (fig. 2) was architecture *and* sculpture; our design for the Copley Plaza (fig. 3) was architecture *and* urban design. Our latest submission, the National Football Hall of Fame, is a building *and* a billboard.

The program for this competition was restrictive in the maximum cubage permitted, in the precise and elaborate relationships stipulated for administrative, research, library, and dining facilities, and in the requirement for banqueting one thousand people within the exhibition spaces. But it was unrestrictive concerning the main function of the building as a museum for the masses, and concerning methods of exhibition.

1

2

The unique characteristics of the program, the displays and their content, were based on the policies of the sponsor, the National Football Foundation. The Hall of Fame was described by its president in the program literature as *an Ideological Center, serving our social and education structure and our competitive economy—to the end the power of decision is kept with the people. Honoring [football heroes] . . . brings into focus, at a time of the long hair, beard, beatnik revolt on the campus, the conviction of the Foundation that the disciplines of football make it the biggest and best classroom in the nation for teaching leadership.*

The structure of the organization to be reflected in the displays was particularly interesting to us. The program stated:

The Hall of Fame is devoted to the players *who*

3

have been elected to its ranks (some 150 are presently included; five or six elected every year); the coaches *who have been elected (some 50 with one or none added annually to the ranks);* The Men Who Made the Game *(Walter Camp, Alonzo Stagg, William Heffelfinger and others);* The Gold Medal Winners, *men who symbolize in the nation the qualities that are inherent in football (one is elected yearly; Eisenhower, MacArthur, Hoover, Kennedy, Whizzer White, Stagg, Lourie, Trippe, and Roger Blough have thus far received the Gold Medal);* The Scholar Athletes, *college seniors (of whom 75 have been elected so far, and another nine to 11 are picked yearly); and the* MacArthur Bowl, *an annual award of major significance to a great team. The Gold Medal Winners and the players elected to the National Football Hall of Fame are the most important groups to dramatize.*

After this description of a hierarchical order—recalling to us the subtle rankings of the beatified and canonized in the medieval Kingdom of Heaven—suggestions were elaborated for displays, which included relics (*sic*) of football history, reminiscent again of medieval theology. The program further provided a rich catalog of suggestions for the content of the exhibits, covering historical, topical, theoretical, and technical aspects of the game and biographical material on the players. It encouraged as well imaginative and advanced techniques of display sympathetic to some of our ideas on an architecture of communication for moving masses. Their peculiar message suggested particular media: movies, relics, and space.

The basis for our design is the accommodation of the relic on one hand and the wide-screen on the other: of Knute Rockne's sweater displayed in a little case *and* his forward pass projected on a big surface. In the Czech Pavilion at Expo '67, real

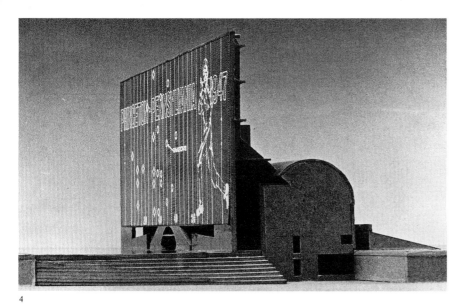

4

5

lace work and sophisticated cinematography complemented each other. Here Knute Rockne's sweater—or trophies like the MacArthur Bowl—satisfy the individual's thirst for the immediacy of the real thing, and big movies absorb the masses' attention through changing illusion: the one involves extensive detail, the other simple impact. These contradictions of scale and space (big and little, individual and mass), of movement (stopping and going), and of light (bright and dark), satisfy the need for contrast in an architecture of communication. Our original idea was to make the building the shape of a football on the outside. For impact in the vast spaces and before the vast crowds at the Rutgers Stadium, this building should be both symbolic sculpture and architecture. But the limitations on cubage in the program precluded a sculptural outer shape which did not conform closely to the inside architectural space, so we devised a sign instead of a sculpture: an essentially two-dimensional billboard (fig. 4), big in size but economical in cubage, which is also a building. Our "billdingboard" conveys impact beyond that too subtle kind of expression which is derived from pure architectural elements. Space, form, and structure, *the* traditional architectural elements, mean little in the vast parking spaces that are the context of this building and most other buildings that architects can't force into their megastructural fantasies.

You just can't see space, form, and structure across a teeming parking lot without a mixture of other media. Our mixed media include symbolic and representational elements, that is, billboards and words, along with the abstract elements of space, form, and structure. Symbols with architecture enrich meaning. They can evoke the instant associations crucial for today's vast spaces, fast speeds, complex programs and, perhaps, jaded senses which respond only to bold stimuli.

The front of our building, which is billboard, inflects toward the big parking spaces and the stadium. The back (fig. 5), which is building, relates to the exhibition field in the rear and, in fact, turns, like Aalto's Otaniemi Technical Institute, into a quasi-grandstand (fig. 6). The enormous billboard, one hundred feet high and two hundred and ten feet long, needs buttressing in the back. These buttresses integrate the building with the sign. Parts of the interior display are niches—static spaces along a long gallery: these fall within the buttresses as do the chapels along the nave in a Gothic cathedral (fig. 7). Outside, the billboard, which is several feet thick, is backed by maintenance catwalks which interlace with the buttresses. The giant screen has the approximate proportions of a football field. On it, two hundred thousand electronically programed lights produce moving sequences of naturalistic images, words, and phrases, and

diagrammatic choreographies of famous football plays (fig. 8). These displays can be viewed from the parking lots, the picnic green in front, and the Rutgers Stadium beyond.

From nearby, the billboard corresponds to the largely false west facade of a Gothic cathedral, especially an Italian one like Orvieto, teeming with glittering mosaics and niched statues, whose main function is to communicate information toward the piazza. From a distance the analogy with the billboard on the highway is obvious. Immediately in front of the screen, where the seats are bad at a movie, is a moat. Below the screen are various ways to enter the building.

Since the public access to the museum is from the parking which is at the sides, the main entrances to the building are from the sides. Two symmetrical ramps lead to a single, hidden entrance at the center of the facade. They ape the monumentality of the double, symmetrical stairways which approach the door of a terraced, Baroque villa. The big, low spans of the ramp openings in front increase the monumentality. But narrow stairways at the center eat out of the ramps and superimpose sharper diagonals upon them. Below, at ground level, an opening goes through the building to the field beyond and contains doors to nonpublic staff, research, and service areas on the ground floor. The shape of

6

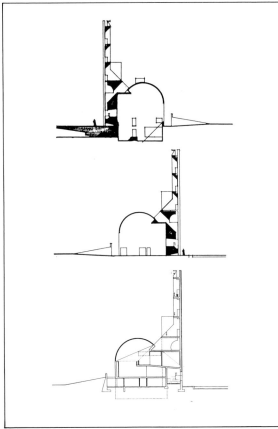

7

this opening is a partial football.

There are contradictions in the facade of the billdingboard. The top, which is mostly billboard and mostly seen from afar, is scaleless, perhaps more so than a real billboard because it is bigger than usual and of slightly different proportions: you might not be sure how big it is or how far away it is. A little ominous perhaps.

But the bottom, which is mostly building and seen closer-up, is less ambiguous in scale. Its combination of contrasting ramps and stairs suggests a human scale. The top is not monumental, except perhaps through its size, but certainly not through its associations, which are commercial; the bottom, through its symmetrical form as well as its associations (with the central building of the Campidoglio, for instance) is almost pompously monumental.

I have mentioned that the sets of ramps and stairs lead to no door, or at least to a partially hidden door behind the lower part of the billboard. The focus on no-door in turn reinforces the ambiguous scale. The top, the billboard, is a consistently flat surface, but the bottom, although it maintains the billboard's surface and silhouette for the sake of the scale of the whole, is violently punctured with big openings containing deep shadows. The lower entrance is a positive and symbolic shape, while the others are negative, residual shapes resulting from the diagonal ramps and stairs at the bottom and the boundary of the sign on top.

The flat, high easel of the front elevation contrasts with the busy profiles of the side elevations. This disunity as the building turns the corner reflects the contradiction between the front and the back, between the behind-the-

scenes mess, including the semi-exposed buttresses which support the facadism of the front, and the front itself.

A similar tension occurs in a Gothic cathedral between the inside and the outside: from the inside you are "fooled" because the unseen buttresses outside make the spindling, vaulted nave seem magically light. Our side elevations are essentially cross sections of the interior, and therefore correspond to orthodox Modern practice, where design proceeds "from within outward." They imply, since the building is merely cut off at each end, an open-ended system along the long axis. If the architecture in between becomes a pictorial easel toward the front, it becomes earth-sculpture at the back to accommodate the abortive grandstands which face the field (fig. 9).

The main floor of our Football Hall of Fame contains three zones parallel with the front. In the first zone are the outside ramps and auxiliary stairs which approach the entrance. Because they are contained within the perimeter of the building, they appear uneasily big in juxtaposition with the other, interior elements. Like the ramps in the Villa Savoye, they are outside scale inside. Flying buttresses span this zone and sometimes rooms within buttresses bridge it at the balcony level, modifying the degree of top light.

The second and third zones interact closely in plan. The second zone, the niches between the buttresses along the gallery, resembles the chapels between the buttresses along the nave. This contains the services and all the vertical circulation except the elevator. The spacing, and therefore the rhythm of the buttresses, varies slightly to accommodate specific functions. But

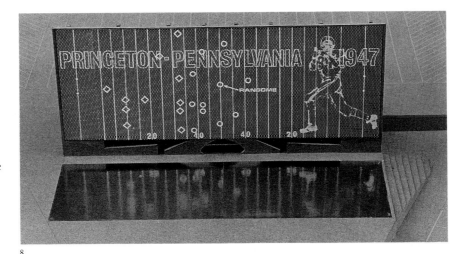

8

the niches' main function are to contrast with the gallery. This is the small space off the big space, the low space off the high space, the static space off the directional space, the protected space off the expansive space, the focused space off the continuous space, the bright or dark space off the medium-lit space. It is the place, open but secluded, for the little relic or the specialized movie; for concentrated detail rather than general impact. It parallels the niches in the facade at Amiens, each with its own story to communicate, alone and in series.

The constant, vaulted space of the gallery is like the gallery space in Tintoretto's *Finding of the Body of St. Mark*, where the quality of light is all that varies along the exaggerated length. But the directional pull of our long gallery is contradicted by the cross axes of its niches (fig. 10). Its balcony almost fills it up, and its even lighting is bisected by a solitary shaft of light from a narrow window directly opposite the entrance, which permits the sole glimpse of the practice field beyond. The ceiling is vaulted to act as a screen for continuous and huge movie projections from the parapet of the balcony, as shown in the section. The figure of Adam from the Sistine ceiling is inserted among the flying football players in our collage to suggest the qualities, both spatial and iconographic, of a ceiling fresco, but the simulated movement of the dynamic angels of a Baroque ceiling might better parallel the real movement of our reflected images of charging players.

A mosaic of rear-projecting screens complements the niches on the opposite wall of the gallery. This continuous bank of images is programed by a computer like the diapolyeran of the Czech Pavilion. Used as individual screens or in larger ensembles, it could be an extensive source of

detailed material on members of the Hall of Fame and Gold Medal winners. It represents a smaller-scale, two-dimensional version of the spatial niches opposite: a triptych screen perhaps, in comparison with the aedicula portal in Medieval architecture.

Revolving panels flip mechanically from the niches in the balcony like those in Grand Central Terminal and generate further movement to complement the cinematic reflections on most other surfaces. I forgot to mention the movies on the sides of the balcony parapet. Movies, in fact, are almost all over. They spill over the surfaces, essentially independent of the architectural forms they smother; like Giotto's frescoes in the Arena Chapel, or the rocaille ornament which indiscriminately suffuses walls, fixtures, and furnishings in a Rococo interior; or the ubiquitous and independent patterns on the tattooed man in the circus, or the camouflage patterns on a military tank, whose purpose, significantly, is to render its surfaces ambiguous. The message dominates the space.

9

6 Alvar Aalto's Otaniemi Technical Institute
7 Billdingboard, side elevations and section
8 Model, front
9 Model, rear

18

10 Billdingboard, interior perspective, gallery and niches

Learning from Lutyens: Reply to Alison and Peter Smithson

Robert Venturi and Denise Scott Brown

This essay was first published in the **RIBA Journal,** August 1969, pp. 353–354. ·It was written in response to "The Responsibility of Lutyens" by Alison Smithson, and "The Viceroy's House in Imperial Delhi" by Peter Smithson, both published in the **RIBA Journal,** April 1969, pp. 146–151 and pp. 152–154.

The centenary celebration of Sir Edwin Lutyens' birth should be a celebration: an occasion not for condescension, but for learning from Lutyens—a celebration of his skill and the particular relevance of his work now.

Le Corbusier's tribute in the fifties in his introduction to the work at Chandigarh is well known: "New Delhi, capital of Imperial India, was built by Lutyens over 30 years ago with extreme care, great talent and true success. The critics may rant as they will but the accomplishment of such an undertaking earns respect"; and it is said that the Memorial Volumes were open in the drafting room at Taliesin. Recently Allan Greenberg has discovered significant parallels between Wright's and Lutyens' plans and between the planning at New Delhi and Chandigarh ("Lutyens' Architecture Restudied," *Perspecta 12*, 1969). Greenberg prefaced this thoughtful analysis with a brilliant study of the houses and gardens themselves, and of New Delhi. Earlier, one of us, in the context of an architecture of complexity and contradiction, discussed the qualities of paradox, ambiguity, and accommodation in Luytens which have been so stimulating to us as architects. We now go beyond these characteristics of form, space, and program because we are beginning to learn as well from the symbolism of his eclectic architecture. Commercial strip architecture *and* Lutyens' houses are relevant to an architecture of meaning.

The arguments against Lutyens in the April 1969 *RIBA Journal* are condescending and irrelevant. To hold Lutyens "responsible" for "the look of housing in England from 1934 to 1956"—that is, for suburban housing—is like blaming Le Corbusier for the equally prevalent travesties of the Ville Radieuse during the same twenty-one

years. But more to the point, are we still so sure that "the house on a plot, with roses and a hedge as the accepted dream" perpetuated under the influence of Lutyens—from Lutyens to Levittown—is bad, and the opposite, as implied, good? Are architects still so condescending about the "dreams" of the occupants of Levittown, and cavalier about the complex social and economic, as well as symbolic, bases of residential sprawl? The argument is no longer simply low rise versus high rise, suburban sprawl versus megastructure, or even "anonymous" architecture versus Georgian (or other) styling. Rather, there is no longer an argument. Some battles don't end, the ground merely shifts and they become irrelevant.

The ground has shifted under Alison Smithson. Her comparisons of Lutyens with Charles Rennie Mackintosh and C.F. Annesley Voysey come from a good guys versus bad guys view of recent history. The polemic was effective in the Heroic period of Modern architecture as a basis for simplistic and moralistic slogans, but is irrelevant today. The argument however goes something like this: Lutyens was a gifted architect who lived at the wrong time ("an enviable talent . . . caught in the box of his times," Peter Smithson puts it). He took "the wrong path" at the turn of the century, or rather in 1901. (We envy the historical precision of English critics: Los Angeles, we have read elsewhere, was first discovered in 1961 by Cedric Price.) Before 1901 Lutyens' houses were "good"—with a strong "sense of material," of course. Thereafter his work became "retrogressive," and fell outside the "mainstream of architecture flowing from Mackintosh and Le Corbusier." On top of that came his "complete Americanisation most visible in 1906." Leaving aside the question of whether national hostilities go very well with rational criticism, let us consider whether mainstreams do

not lie in the eye of the beholder. In other words, whose mainstream? Sigfried Giedion's? Away with doctrinaire history, especially if outmoded. We should learn from any source we can.

Forgetting mainstreams and looking at work, we think Lutyens, as an architect, was at least the equal of Mackintosh and Voysey. But more important, we can learn from him perhaps more than we can from Mackintosh and Voysey. For Mackintosh and Voysey everything had to match: the saucer the table, the table the mantel, the mantel the cornice, the cornice the doorknob, the doorknob the dormer, the dormer the massing of the whole house; not to mention the matching border—designed by the architect too—on the mistress's gown. So much for *their* "sense of material." This form of easy unity—paralleling that of contemporary Art Nouveau—is not a useful exemplar. The purist, motival consistency of their forms and patterns, derived from simple programs and craft-like, individualistic techniques in limited environments, has an undeniable, archaeological charm, but it is not pertinent for architecture today since architects patently cannot exert this type of control over the environment. But it is the prototype for our continuing obsession with—to use Mrs. Smithson's words—"total environment," with the search for "our cultural betterment" through "a more consistent object/container culture"—and with the myth of architectural control through the megastructure, as the answer to the "chaos" in our landscape. (We do not hold Mackintosh or Voysey responsible however, for *our* architects' superficial, reformist urbanism, their compulsion for neatness, or their dreams of power.)

The complexities and inconsistencies of Lutyens' forms appear valid and poignant when matched against our attempts to accommodate to the richness as well as the problems of our own environment and culture. Mrs. Smithson admits as an "aspect of his growing skill as a manipulator of forms" an "increase of expertise" inexorably woven into which is "the 'Americanisation' synonymous with the perfected look of an admixture of styles." But this "admixture of styles," the symbolism of Lutyens' forms, comes in for even more criticism and more clichéd criticism, beyond their characteristic condescension, than does his complexity of forms: "He came imaginatively to assemble pieces derivative of past styles [but] assemblage of styles was a dead end." The good guys' "original" forms presumably did not bring about "the debasing of the language of architecture."

Lutyens is blamed for his lack of "unselfconscious form." Must one still apologize for the element of planned association to enrich meaning in architecture? Alan Colquhoun's article on the place of association in the perception of form (*Arena*, June 1967) should have laid to rest this boring ghost. Stylistic eclecticism was part of the tradition which included the iconography in Medieval, symbolism in Renaissance, and association in Romantic architecture, and continues in the bold advertising symbolism of commercial architecture suited to the roadside environment. A "debased" admixture of styles and symbols has been attractive in the past to pluralist and expanding societies such as Imperial Rome, the Venetian Republic, and Victorian England. The method, if less so the content, of Lutyens' historical eclecticism is valid again in our own pluralist, mobile, pop, mass culture and post-heroic period of Modern architecture.

It is the post-heroic period for criticism too. To empathize with the heroic period involves us in false and useless polemics: "Lutyens' 'floodtide' . . . represented a retrogressive step by an architect which because of his plentiful talent probably cannot be forgiven by any who fought for the heroic period of modern architecture, or even, as some did, only caught a whiff of the powder." Faint whiffs they must be in '69. We have our own battles to fight—different ones, real and relevant.

The heroic stance makes for simplistic interpretations of history by architects. For instance: "The post-1901 Lutyens style was neither what the situation wanted nor what the art of architecture called for. . . . The buildings of an architect can be an anchor in the mess. To jump over the mess, be ahead in some way of the ensuing problems . . . is what Le Corbusier taught architects to recognise as genius." But genius includes infinite variety, as did Le Corbusier's own genius, and it can evolve by engaging "the mess" as well as transcending it. Indeed, the jumping ahead by architects of late has produced the diagram. That architectural genius can lead us beyond the mess is a proposition open to question today. We suggest that such an architectural genius, if he exists for our time, will illuminate the mess rather than jump over it, and will do so by first participating in it. As Mrs. Smithson says, "no artist is secure from some deeply instinctive reaction to the *Zeitgeist*." But the zeitgeist argument, the case for relevance, cuts two ways. Perhaps Lutyens' architecture was not what either the situation or the art called for, post-1918; but are the Smithsons sure they are not themselves in the same position, assuming a 1920s-heroic-Modern stance when the shifting zeitgeist has boomeranged, making Lutyens seem apt in 1969 and leaving them where Lutyens was in 1919?

Lutyens can perhaps be faulted for not "proposing new forms to meet new social needs." But the traditional role of the architect as a doer who is only incidentally a philosophical visionary has almost always aligned him with an existing and conservative establishment. Michelangelo and Mansart faced this problem as do Russian architects today. Programs for Edwardian manor houses and capitalistic office blocks were no more or less obsolete or wrong than those of Blenheim, St. Peter's, Chartres, the Pantheon or others we look at and learn from.

Our argument with "The Viceroy's House in Imperial Delhi" by Peter Smithson is similarly based on its irrelevant polemicism, an unnecessary condescension, and on the gratuitous supposition that "it is probable" that Lutyens, who was "not a bookish man," was shown Bramante's plan for St. Peter's by some one "obsessed by Bramante" at the British School in Rome, and "he took in Bramante's design at a single glance as his own." Mr. Smithson goes gung ho for Bramante as a heretofore-ignored source for the Durbar Hall. But there may be hundreds of different sources for Lutyens' Classical forms. The mention by Christopher Hussey of a predominant Palladianism certainly doesn't exclude Bramante, although—to play the same dubious game—we think as good a case can be made for St. Paul's or for other densely poché, Baroque plans. Mr. Smithson says "what is unique [about the Durbar Hall is] a deployment of the dense encysted plan-form devised but never built by Bramante for St. Peter's. . . . The Delhi central block is not like Bramante's plan in detail; it is just that it is an embedded dome in a generally square plan mass with a certain balance of void to wall, and that none other than Bramante's has quite this quality." Perhaps, but what is vividly unique about the plan of the Durbar Hall is what makes it closer to St. Paul's—the eight piers supporting the dome rather than the conventional four, niched piers, and the penetration of the side aisles into the area of the dome. (The section of the Durbar Hall where each quadrantal niche evolves into a species of squinch is different from the St. Paul's section with its complex and ambiguous pendentives, but less different than it is from St. Peter's. A direct simulation of Wren is the adjacent room for the State Library based on the interior of St. Stephen Walbrook.)

We disagree that the quality of the Viceroy's house is unusual for Lutyens, "quite outside the range of its architect" and "an inexplicable leap from the ordinary sort of banal mixture of styles and poorish [sic] English Palladian planning" (we pore over his plans) which was his norm. He had never been given a Viceroy's palace to design before; of course the vocabulary changed, just as it did for that other challenge and perhaps his greatest design, his post-1901 Liverpool cathedral. But all his work, the Durbar Hall as much as the houses, shares a quality defined by Greenberg as a qualified monumentality, and by Sir John Summerson as Lutyens' wit.

Let us come to the aid of two other maligned buildings: Tigbourne Court, "nothing but the tricky screen wall to the road" to Mrs. Smithson, but to us an intriguing and amusing handling of two axes perpendicular to each other, one for the private, garden-viewing family life, and one for the road; and the Pantheon. One's enthusiasm for the dome of the Durbar Hall shouldn't preclude liking the First Dome: it is hard to imagine an architect standing within its interior light and finding it "banal and obvious," except perhaps in the good sense of those words. But the authors appear to relish rejecting the norms,

for Mrs. Smithson refers to "that particularly dead hand the English can lay on Classicism as seen from this side of Mansart." May we uphold the Anglicanization of Classicism in the land of Wren, Hawksmoor, Vanbrugh, Archer, Adam, and Soane as seen from this side of Bunshaft?

But the most disturbing aspect of these articles for us is the hollow-heroic stance of the savior-architect, contemptuous of the mess and sure of the answers: "We [presumably we architects] have not knocked this sick culture on the head yet [sic, so help us]." Our greatest lesson from Lutyens is perhaps his tolerance and wit.

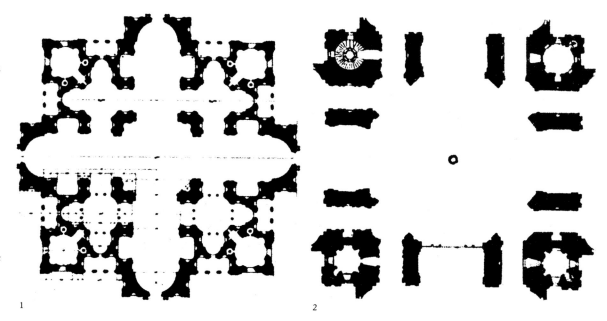

1

2

3

1 Bramante's plan for St. Peter's
2 Wren's plan for St. Paul's
3 Lutyens' plan for Durbar Hall

"Leading from the Rear": Reply to Martin Pawley

Robert Venturi and Denise Scott Brown

This essay was first published in **Architectural Design** Magazine, London, vol. 40, July 1970, pp. 320, 370. It was written in response to "Leading from the Rear" by Martin Pawley, published in **Architectural Design** Magazine, London, January 1970, p. 45.

On the subject of imperialist atrocities, it is a moot point who is pot and who is kettle, England or America; but, as we remarked recently in the *RIBA Journal*, emotional evocations of national animosities do not engender rational discourse. National prejudice and architectural criticism do not make good bedfellows. While acknowledging your reviewer's skill in working the My Lai massacre into the first sentence of a review on American architecture, we believe his prejudice has muddled his content, and he has by no means muddled through.

It is a bad reviewer who confuses his author's interpretations of the subject matter with the subject matter itself, as Mr. Pawley has done by criticizing us for what Robert Stern said about Las Vegas. And it is a tiresome architect who, gleefully appropriating Vincent Scully's anguished criticism of his country, disdaining the life's work distillation of history from which it springs, and learning no nuances from Scully, indulges in the simplistic rhetoric of the heroic twenties to approach the "disasters of urban America."

We can tell your reviewer things wrong with this country he never dreamed of. And we suggest that the architect who starts with what *is*—admittedly pathetic as his impact seems to be—is more aware of "nonsensical planning and zoning laws, archaic financial practices and absurdly restrictive and elitist goals," and will be less harmful and more effective than the petulant rhetorician grandly and dryly continuing to evoke "the impact of technology on Western civilization" and "the relationship of the nascent science of design to human goals and aspirations." We are in favor of science in architecture but not of science-voodooism, twenties *or* sixties style. There is no evidence yet that the offerings of the present generation of aspirant architectural scientists will be more useful than the European CIAM rationalist philosophy upon which the United States federal program, Urban Renewal, was based, with disastrous social results in the American city. On the contrary, it appears that Operation Breakthrough will be the purview of some of the largest corporations in the country, although it is the answer to your reviewer's dream since it is designed to produce "mass" housing by overcoming all those "irrationalities," economic, legal, and technological, of the present system. With his major support from the chamber of commerce and the largest corporations, where does this put the gentleman architect of the Modern movement, CIAM or Computer Style? Who is in the cultural elite and who is leading from the rear?

We tend to agree with the social planners who see architects' environmental megalomania as a curse on the city. We don't think we should play that game, or as Mr. Pawley would put it, "lead that team"—we don't know enough. But Mr. Pawley can't have it both ways, i.e., recommend leaving Las Vegas alone and rationalize the total environment. (He must know Las Vegas will not be left alone: even now a "Strip Beautification Committee" of local owners plans to convert it to a desert Champs Elysées. Is this what "ought to be"?)

We are grateful to our swinging, Jewish, Pop Art clients whose little houses, alterations, sympathy, and promotion have helped us weather nine years of almost unsuccessful practice. We are grateful to our black clients on South Street who can't pay, but give us the best work there is in Philadelphia. We are grateful to one or two architects who have helped us get the small amount of institutional work we have. Do they constitute a cultural elite? We suspect architects define the cultural elite as "the other architect's clients." Meanwhile we, like other architects, continue to look for work along the line of our sympathies and interests without, we hope, having to sell our souls. Does the system work better in England?

As for who is leading and from what direction, this is a basically uninteresting question. But we feel our pathetic, imperfect, expedient, limited, immediate, activist approach is more useful (or at least less harmful) for the near future than is your reviewer's arrogant, authoritarian, sensational, simplistic, indulgent, condescending, apocalyptic, heroic, meaningless, easy, disastrous utopianism. Time will tell who is right. At present, rears lie in the eye of the beholder.

Martin Pawley replies:

Why can't you people leave us science-voodooists alone? We try to make a decent living reviewing books in an arrogant, authoritarian, sensational, simplistic, indulgent, condescending, apocalyptic, heroic, meaningless, easy and disastrously utopian manner and all we get are letters of protest practically as long as the reviews we write. The architectural dispute system thrives on this kind of footnoted footnote.[1] In my review I did not mean to belittle "nine years of almost unsuccessful practice"—indeed why not take encouragement from the fact that not only were you mentioned in three books in one week (with a whole chapter in one), but in the reviews as well! What I really said was that architecture doesn't seem to make much difference. It's time (as Scully said) for something else, and it's not much use any of us pretending to be it unless we are prepared to come across pretty quickly. The trouble is that good and bad architecture are only distinguishable at the level of social irrelevance—so now tell me how you would define nine years of *successful* practice.

Learning from Pop
Denise Scott Brown

This essay was first published in **Casabella,** December 1971, n. 359–360, pp. 15–23.

26

Las Vegas, Los Angeles, Levittown, the swinging singles on the Westheimer Strip, golf resorts, boating communities, Co-op City, the residential backgrounds to soap operas, TV commercials and mass mag ads, billboards, and Route 66 are sources for a changing architectural sensibility. New sources are sought when the old forms go stale and the way out is not clear; then a Classical heritage, an art movement, or industrial engineers' and primitives' "architecture without architects" may help to sweep out the flowery remains of the old revolution as practiced by its originators' conservative descendants. In America in the sixties an extra ingredient was added to this recipe for artistic change: social revolution. Urban renewal, supplier of work for architects for two decades and a major locus of the soft remains of the Modern movement, was not merely artistically stale, it was socially harmful. The urgency of the social situation, and the social

critique of urban renewal and of the architect as server of a rich narrow spectrum of the population—in particular the criticism of Herbert Gans—have been as important as the Pop artists in steering us toward the existing American city and its builders. If high-style architects are not producing what people want or need, who is, and what can we learn from them?

Needs, plural
Sensitivity to needs is a first reason for going to the existing city. Once there, the first lesson for architects is the pluralism of need. No builder-developer in his right mind would announce: I am building for Man. He is building for a market, for a group of people defined by income range, age, family composition, and life style. Levittowns, Leisureworlds, Georgian-styled town houses grow from someone's estimation of the needs of the groups who will be their markets.

The city can be seen as the built artifacts of a set of subcultures. At the moment, those subcultures which willingly resort to architects are few.

Of course learning from what's there is subject to the caveats and limitations of all behavioristic analysis—one is surveying behavior which is constrained, it is not what people might do in other conditions. The poor do not willingly live in tenements and maybe the middle classes don't willingly live in Levittowns; perhaps the Georgian-styling is less pertinent to the townhouse resident than is the rent. In times of housing shortage this is a particularly forceful argument against architectural behaviorism since people can't vote against a particular offering by staying away if there is no alternative. To counteract this danger one must search for comparison environments where for some reason the constraints do not hold. There are

1 Pico Boulevard, Santa Monica, California
2 Newspaper advertisement, with annotations
3 Millionaires' Row, Miami Beach, Florida
4 Caesars Palace, Las Vegas, Nevada
5 Television soap opera
6 Society Hill urban renewal area, Philadelphia,
  Pennsylvania, 1963
7 Merchant builder's advertisement

5

6

environments which suggest what economically constrained groups' tastes might be if they were less constrained. They are the nouveau riche environments: Hollywood for a former era, Las Vegas for today, and the homes of film stars, sportsmen, and other groups where upward mobility may resemble vertical takeoff, yet where maintenance of previous value systems is encouraged.

Another source is physical backgrounds in the mass media, movies, soap operas, pickle and furniture polish ads. Here the aim is not to sell houses but something else, and the background represents someone's (Madison Avenue's?) idea of what pickle buyers or soap opera watchers want in a house. Now the Madison Avenue observer's view may be as biased as the architect's, and it should be studied in the light of what it is trying to sell—must pickle

architecture look homey like my house or elegant like yours if it is to sell me pickles? But at least it's another bias, an alternative to the architectural navel contemplation we so often do for research, i.e., ask: What did Le Corbusier do? Both Madison Avenue and the builder, although they can tell us little of the needs of the very poor, cover a broader range of the population and pass a stiffer market test than does the architect in urban renewal or public housing, and if we learn no more from these sources than that architecture must differ for different groups, that is a great deal. But an alternative to both is to examine what people do to buildings—in Levittowns, Society Hills, gray areas, and slums—once they are in them. Here, costs and availability are less constraining forces since the enterprise is smaller. Also, changes tend often to be symbolic rather than structural, and aspirations can perhaps be more easily inferred

from symbols than from structures.

Attention to built sources for information on need does not imply that asking people what they want is not extremely necessary as well. This is an important topic, as is the relation between the two types of survey, asking and looking; but it is not the subject of this enquiry, which is on what can be learned from the artifacts of pop culture.

Formal analysis as design research
A second reason for looking to pop culture is to find formal vocabularies for today which are more relevant to people's diverse needs and more tolerant of the untidinesses of urban life than the "rationalist," Cartesian formal orders of latter-day Modern architecture. How much low-income housing and nineteenth-century architecture has been cleared so some tidy purist architect or planner could start with a clean slate?

8 Decorated suburban home
9 Precedents of suburban symbols
10 Space and image in the suburbs

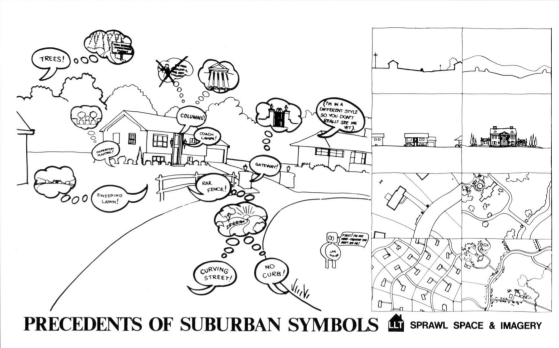

PRECEDENTS OF SUBURBAN SYMBOLS 🏠 SPRAWL SPACE & IMAGERY

Modern architects can now admit that whatever forces, processes, and technologies determine architectural form, ideas about form determine it as well; that a formal vocabulary is as much a part of architecture as are bricks and mortar (plastics and systems, for futurists); that form does not, cannot, arise from function alone, newborn and innocent as Venus from her shell, but rather that form follows, *inter alia*, function, forces, and form. Formal biases, if they are consciously recognized, need not tyrannize as they have done in urban renewal; and formal vocabularies, given their place in architecture, can be studied and improved to suit functional requirements, rather than accepted unconsciously and unsuitably—an old hand-me-down from some irrelevant master. The forms of the pop landscape are as relevant to us now as were the forms of antique Rome to the Beaux-Arts, Cubism and Machine Architecture to the early

Moderns, and the industrial midlands and the Dogon to Team 10, which is to say extremely relevant, and more so than the latest bathysphere, launch pad, or systems hospital (or even, *pace* Banham, the Santa Monica pier). Unlike these, they speak to our condition not only aesthetically, but on many levels of necessity, from the social necessity to rehouse the poor without destroying them to the architectural necessity to produce buildings and environments that others will need and like. The pop landscape differs from the earlier models in that it is also the place where we build; it is our context. And it is one of the few contemporary sources of data on the symbolic and communicative aspects of architecture, since it was untouched by the Modern movement's purist reduction of architecture to space and structure only. But formal analysis presents a problem. First, since form has for so long been an illegitimate topic, form has for so long been an illegitimate topic,

we have lost the tradition of analyzing it, and second, the forms we are dealing with are new and don't relate easily to traditional architectural or planning techniques of analysis and communications. Orthographic projection hardly conveys the essence of the Stardust sign, and, although this sign is a block long and has an overpowering visual impact "in situ," it doesn't show well on a land use map. Suburban space, being automobile space, is not defined by enclosing walls and floors and is therefore difficult to portray graphically using systems devised for the description of buildings. In fact, space is not the most important constituent of suburban form. Communication across space is more important, and it requires a symbolic and a time element in its descriptive systems which are only slowly being devised.

New analytic techniques must use film and

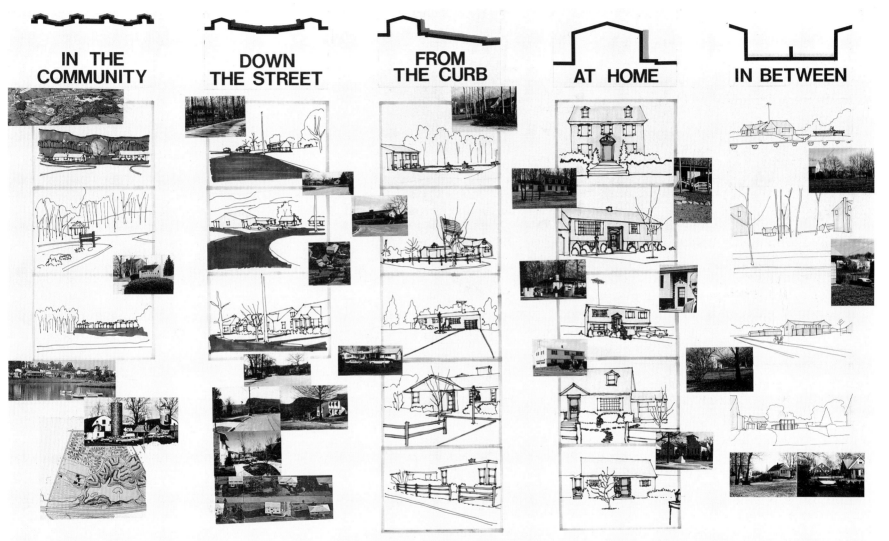

IN THE COMMUNITY

DOWN THE STREET

FROM THE CURB

AT HOME

IN BETWEEN

SPACE & IMAGE

SPRAWL SPACE & IMAGERY

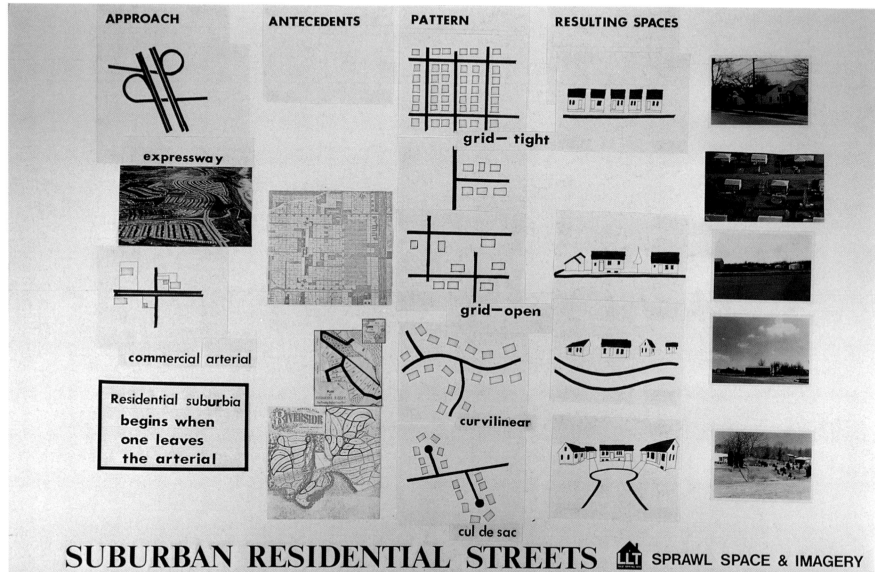

APPROACH

expressway

commercial arterial

Residential suburbia
begins when
one leaves
the arterial

ANTECEDENTS

PATTERN

grid—tight

grid—open

curvilinear

cul de sac

RESULTING SPACES

SUBURBAN RESIDENTIAL STREETS SPRAWL SPACE & IMAGERY

11 Suburban residential streets
12 Collage, Nolli's Rome and Las Vegas
13 Aerial view of Las Vegas Strip

12

13

videotape to convey the dynamism of sign architecture and the sequential experience of vast landscapes; and computers are needed to aggregate mass repeated data into comprehensible patterns. Valuable traditional techniques should also be resuscitated by their application to new phenomena; for example, when Nolli's mid-eighteenth-century technique for mapping Rome is adapted to include parking lots, it throws considerable light on Las Vegas. It could also lend itself fairly easily to computer techniques.

Formal analysis should be comparative, linking the new forms, by comparison, to the rest of the formal tradition of architecture thereby incorporating them into the architectural discipline and helping us to understand our new experience in light of our formal training. By suggesting that form should be analyzed, I do not

imply that function (the program), technologies, or forces (urban social processes or land economics) are not vital to architecture, nor indeed, that they too can't serve as sources of artistic inspiration to the architect. All are necessary and they work in combination. The others are merely not the subject of this particular enquiry.

The soup can and the establishment
There is an irony in the fact that the "popular" culture and the "popular" landscape are not popular with those who make the decisions to renew the city and rehouse the poor. Here is John Kenneth Galbraith, an important and influential liberal, quoted in *Life* magazine:

For the average citizen there are some simple tests which will tell him when we have passed from incantation to practical action on the environment.

Restriction of auto use in the large cities will be one. Another will be when the billboards, the worst and most nearly useless excrescence of industrial civilization, are removed from the highways. Yet another will be when telephone and electric wires everywhere in the cities go underground and we accept the added charge on our bills.

My own personal test, for what it may be worth, concerns the gasoline service station. This is the most repellent piece of architecture of the past two thousand years. There are far more of them than are needed. Usually they are filthy. Their merchandise is hideously packaged and garishly displayed. They are uncontrollably addicted to great strings of ragged little flags. Protecting them is an ominous coalition of small businessmen and large. The stations should be excluded entirely from most streets and highways. Where allowed,

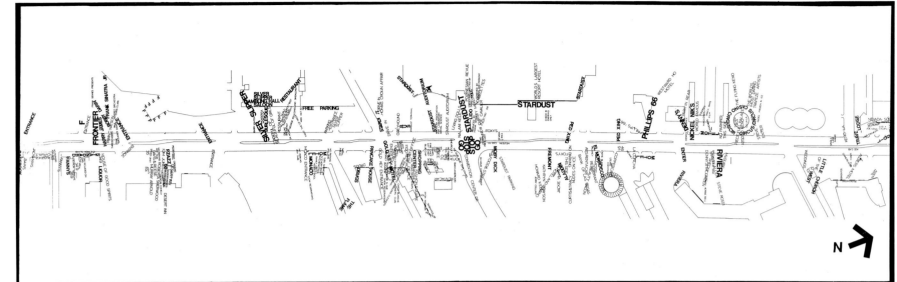

14

15

they should be franchised to limit the number, and there should be stern requirements as to architecture, appearance and general reticence. When we begin on this (and similar roadside commerce), I will think that we are serious.[1]

He does not even mention the need for low-income housing as an urgent environmental problem, and in my opinion he should stick to economics. But the conventional wisdom which Galbraith expounds is shared by his colleagues, the elderly architectural radicals who man America's fine arts commissions, the "design" departments of HUD and the planning and redevelopment agencies, who plan and build for the larger public and private corporations and have the ear of the city makers. If the public is to be well served by their decisions, these members of the architectural establishment must learn to separate out for a different type of scrutiny their

aesthetic preoccupations from other concerns with "environmental pollution." Fouled water and billboards are not of the same magnitude or order of problem. The first cannot be done well, but the second can; particularly if we are given the opportunity to study them for awhile, nonjudgmentally.

When "blighted" neighborhoods are swept away together with billboards and gasoline stations in the name of the avoidance of "visual pollution," the social harm can be irreparable. However, an old aesthetic formula, even though it is shown to be obstructive, will not be relinquished until it is replaced by a new one, since, as we have seen, form depends on form for its making. And, for the architectural establishment, the new vocabulary must have a respectable lineage. Hence, if the popular environment is to provide that vocabulary, it must be filtered through the

proper processes for its acceptance. It must become a part of the high-art tradition; it must be last year's avant-garde. This is another reason to submit the new landscape to traditional architectural analysis: for the sake of its acceptance by the establishment. They can't learn from pop until Pop hangs in the academy.

Hop on pop
I have recommended an investigation of the forms of the new, existing city on both social and aesthetic grounds for architects who hope to hone their skills to a sharp new edge. High art has followed low art before and vice versa; in fact, where did the McDonald's parabola and the split-level rancher come from in the first place?

In the movement from low art to high art lies an element of the deferral of judgment. Judgment is withheld in the interest of understanding and

14 Strip signs, a map in words
15 Tanya billboard
16 Las Vegas Strip
17 McDonald's drive-in

16

receptivity. This is an exciting heuristic technique but also a dangerous one since liking the whole of pop culture is as irrational as hating the whole of it, and it calls forth the vision of a general and indiscriminate hopping on the pop bandwagon, where everything is good and judgment is abandoned rather than deferred. Yet artists, architects, actors, must judge, albeit, one hopes, with a sigh. After a decent interval, suitable criteria must grow out of the new source. Judgment is merely deferred to make subsequent judgment more sensitive.

17

Pop Off: Reply to Kenneth Frampton
Denise Scott Brown

This essay was first published in **Casabella,** December 1971, n. 359-360, pp. 41–45. It was written in response to "America 1960–1970 Notes on Urban Images and Theory" by Kenneth Frampton, published in **Casabella,** December 1971, n. 359-360, pp. 24–38.

Frampton:

▾ misses the agony in our acceptance of pop
▾ squeezes us and others into pigeonholes
▾ confuses pop sources ("consumer mass and folk culture") with Pop Art
▾ sees manipulation in the "city of Kitsch" but discounts it presumably in Chartres and Versailles
▾ seems to suggest that Kevin Lynch allowed urban renewal to happen
▾ suggests architects be radical about the wrong thing: not about using their skills to serve social innovation, but about revolutionary architecture, an easier task since we won't come within fighting distance of getting any
▾ nowhere suggests what he, Ken, stands for.

He distorts:

▾ Tom Wolfe's essay on Las Vegas by omitting quotations which demonstrate his fascination with the city. Wolfe's tone is ambivalent rather than derogatory
▾ our argument on subway redesign. We did not advocate the "creation" of the New York subway spaces, but the acceptance of their existence as they are. Nor did I say their squalid conditions are "what the poor need." The tenor of the article was in the opposite direction: how to make these spaces welcoming and civic while accepting them as they are, because they're all we'll get. We recommended facing their challenge realistically rather than dreaming up Piranesian fantasies (and by "Piranesian" Ken means the opposite of what we mean), since these fantasies will be used by the establishment to put off doing anything, saying, "Of course we'd love to renovate the subways, but it would be too expensive." Besides, I'd rather see the money which radical reconstruction would require spent on housing, not subway palaces
▾ my statement that we can learn about what people want from looking at the environments they use; and also learn about what people would like but can't afford by looking at what others like themselves but richer have chosen. He interprets this as "under-employed design talent" (us) suggesting to Levittowners that "they might prefer the extravagant confines of the West Coast Nouveau-Riche." A 180° turnabout: from learning what people want to suggesting to them what they ought to want
▾ our approach, by suggesting that we consider objects independently of their relationships. Our point is that architects tend to oversimplify relationships in the city; that Las Vegas is an object lesson in complex relationships.

For the record:

▾ I started thinking the way I do now in the early fifties at the Architectural Association
▾ that's why I found Gans so "simpatico" when I first studied with him in 1958
▾ and Venturi in 1960
▾ Ken should have mentioned Davidoff and Mitchell, who with Dyckman and Webber have been pressing the social and political responsibilities of the planner for much longer than he realizes. And, of course, the tradition in architecture of "liking what you hate" goes back further than he suggests too, to the early Moderns and their appreciation of the industrial vernacular.

But my main argument with Frampton lies in what he deems to be socially relevant or socially irresponsible in architecture. Our statement that we were analyzing Las Vegas for its physical form and not for its social or economic values has raised the hackles of several critics, as did our request to the Las Vegas studio jury not to criticize us for lack of social concern since we were trying to focus on making our architectural skills more relevant: relevant, we should have added, to present social needs and physical form; we should have added, from the point of view of the purposes—functional, perceptual, and symbolic—that it serves. But Modern architects and critics seem to equate analysis of physical properties with lack of social concern. This is a non sequitur. The separation for closer study of one variable (Las Vegas's physical form) does not imply irresponsibility to the others; it is approved scientific and humanistic behavior. Frampton should criticize if the pieces are not resynthesized in design. This, no doubt, has been the case in urban renewal, where architects well-trained in the art of coordinating have not (and often could not—we can't blame all the faults of society on the architects) included important social requirements in their coordinations. What looked like CIAM "social housing" excluded the poor. These architects were often not so much "value-free" as value-unaware; unaware of the needs and values of people unlike themselves. The dubiously "value-free" scientists or technicians of the early sixties cannot be compared, as Frampton compares them, with Ed Ruscha. Ruscha is not nonjudgmental, he is deadpan. You don't have to be expressionistic to prove you have values. That he is far from value-free I would have thought was apparent from his choice of material and techniques of

representation. What poses as "scientific" or "anonymous" setting out of facts is Pop Art satire. Nor can we be tarred with the same brush. We have taken a stand on values, architecturally and socially, and try hard in our professional lives to keep formal and social concerns together.

Although Frampton criticizes urban-renewal architecture, he is value-unaware to the extent that he believes "consumer folk culture" to have been manufactured by Madison Avenue, and the "silent majority's" preferences to be "the engineered fantasies of mass taste." Architects have used this argument, i.e. "be uninfluenced by Madison Avenue, see things my way," for many years now, but have been unable to sway "the masses" (this in itself is an unsophisticated formulation; even Madison Avenue separates them out). The majority of the population may not like what Levitt offers, although there is no proof of this, but they support even less the architects' alternatives. The critique of Madison Avenue is old now and a bore. I thought we were on a better wicket asking, "To what extent are peoples' choices constrained, and can we examine them where they have been more freely made?"

Why must architects continue to believe that when "the masses" are "educated" they'll want what the architects want? Why do we turn to exotic folk cultures, as interpreted by other architects (Frampton recommends Nitschke's, Thiel's and Domenig's studies of Japanese traditional space making—not Japan's present patterns), rather than learning directly from the cultures around us? A Scandinavian architect, working in an eastern United States office,

produced a public housing project of single-span roofs and vertical-timber siding. It was impeccable in a clearly Scandinavian idiom and much admired by his colleagues. Unfortunately, to the recent southern migrants who occupied it, the timber sidings and lean-to roofs spelled out something nearer to home: southern outhouses.

And why should the concept of the "silent majority," hostile to liberal beliefs and, ergo, to "good" architecture, be taken up with avidity by critics as different as Ulrich Franzen (*Progressive Architecture*, April 1970), Roger Montgomery (personal altercation with Robert Venturi), and Frampton? First, why should the fact that one disagrees with the silent majority's political and social beliefs (to the extent that there is a silent majority that shares beliefs) make one arrogant about their architectural preferences? Second, I feel the test of a true liberal will be, increasingly, how he reacts to the notion of a silent majority. One can be totally committed to civil rights, social progress, and the needs of the poor without having to hate the lower middle classes who face injustice too. But the concept of a hard-hat majority to be scorned will legitimize and expose a lot of now repressed upper-middle-class prejudice.

Although Frampton implies the opposite, we have been involved, both theoretically and practically, with the relation between architectural formalism and social concern, in teaching and writing, in our work, and particularly as architects and planners to a Philadelphia low-income citizens' committee fighting an expressway. From the point of view of the ghetto community, the architect has often been among the villains, planning for "the people" from the lap of the chamber of commerce. Poor Lynch, although harshly judged by Frampton, has caused far less harm than the Gropius-Miesian school in this respect. And, although I am convinced Ken will not understand our work if he tries to box us with the English Townscape movement, he must admit that it was not their vision but the Ville Radieuse which has been the antecedent of our most socially harmful urban renewal. The megastructure revolutionaries continue this same unintended betrayal.

On South Street, Philadelphia, the highway department and chamber of commerce, intent on ramming the Crosstown Expressway through the ghetto, have used the work of an idealistic young architect to prove you could cover the expressway with a megastructure of oh-so-socially beneficial uses. The community asks pardon, but would rather not risk losing what it has in return for flimsy promises to build two miles of cover which would make South Street the most expensive roadway in America. It wouldn't be built. If it were, it wouldn't be for them. Enter a powerful local realtor, self-styled city father: "You say it can't be done! Where is your faith, Mrs. Venturi! America can do it! Remember the Bauhaus!" Thus are our best architectural ideals used against us. Because the social and economic impact of their physical solutions are insufficiently thought through, the social concern and moral values which lie behind them, though worthy in a naive way, are unattainable through them. Physically, the poor are out on the streets before all the "good" changes happen. But the social aspirations, incongruously attached, serve as a rhetoric for getting the scheme past city council.

(From the above it is clear that I don't agree with Webber either in his negation of the importance

36

of physical concerns—although I find his arguments highly instructive. In fact I look forward to a generation of young social planners less hung-up on architecture than their elders and more open-minded about working with architects. Webber however, for the record, admits that he exaggerated his antiphysical emphasis in his early writing in order to present his argument in its strongest form.)

Ken must pardon us for believing that learning to like Las Vegas for its body will help us to understand how to be gentle with the body of South Street and hence with the lives of its occupants. From its soul too we can learn—or, to put this in the jargon Frampton prefers: from its psycho-socio-politico-economic structure we may derive analytic insights into the form-content interface variables which parameterize its temporal conjoints.

But we as architects and planners don't presume to pass on souls, either to criticize Las Vegas's or to dictate South Street's. Architects shouldn't play God.

Advice to socially concerned architects: keep your ire for social evil, not the "degradation" of taste of the "masses," and your energy for the difficult task of finding ways to put your skills where your heart is. Try to help people live in houses and cities the way they want to live. Try to do what will satisfy you and them. When you disagree, do so honestly and without a tone of "injured-expert." Lose some battles because their needs are greater than your aesthetics; win some because you say so and they have learned to trust you; compromise mostly; sometimes, but rarely, ride out on a white horse but not because "their" values have been "perverted" by the mass media, yours have been brainwashed by the elitist

culture. Irony may be the method that allows all these cultures and values to fit together. Ironic (not cynical) comment on the "status quo" is the artist's gentle subversion. It hurts no one, except self-appointed architectural prophets, but it helps to keep perspectives focused. (For us, not the least of ironies is that our applications for funds to support our Las Vegas and our South Street projects were both turned down; the Las Vegas because we "lacked social concern" and the South Street because we were "too political.")

There now, if I was misunderstood in the first place, it will surely be worse now. I feel Frampton is caught midway between two social critiques of America, a European and an American. On one hand he suggests "our urban society is organized toward self-defeating ends on a socio-economical base that is totally invalid," and "the architectural, planning and sociological disciplines are now semi-derelict through inept and trivial use"; on the other he denounces the failures of authoritarian, idealistically-based "social architecture" as it actually turned out here in urban renewal, and to some extent in Europe as well. In other words, Marcuse is up for Frampton, but Gropius is down. Yet Gropius and Marcuse sound extremely alike (not surprisingly, since they are of the same generation, nation, and social tradition). You can't have it both ways.

I personally find the broad-gauge, European-based dismissal of the entire American society over easy and not useful for several reasons. First, to tell a real social activist that the whole thing stinks invites the response: "What else is new?" to be followed by the question Allard Lowenstein asked the students: "After you marched in Washington what else did you do?" If your response is not to join the bombers but to get involved in strategic change at a local level, then you need a finer-grained, more focused critique that takes the bombast as given and goes from there. Of this type there is a long American tradition from the early muckrakers through the *New Republic* to the *Southern Patriot* and, for architects, it includes the work of Charles Abrams and other social planners and some of the student journals, especially Harvard's *Connection*. Much European criticism is based, at some remove, on these American sources. As Norma Evenson said to Aldo van Eyck, "I know things wrong with America you haven't even heard of."

Second, in view of the results of architects' having the power to translate their flip, value-unaware social prescriptions into physical form, I distrust the presumption behind the social critique that a society which gives freer rein to its architects and planners will find its life improved. American planners and urban designers may lack the power to do more than "discuss without acting" as Jerzy Soltan says (though this is owing, to some extent, to the nature of their discussion), but some of them view with dismay the naive way in which their European counterparts use their power.

Third, America is different from Europe; more different than most visiting European architects realize. United States traditions diverged from the European four hundred years ago, and the immigrant groups, particularly those that left their stamp on American culture, were deviants from their homeland cultures in the first place. European-based prescriptions useful from the Dardanelles to Denmark may not apply here and the harassed American planner may have difficulty explaining why, since, when the gap is great, there is no basis for comparison.

Finally, there is something distasteful about sitting in a plush American university with enough financing to do one's thing full-time instead of part-time, as most European based architectural scholars must, and taking superior armchair-revolutionary pot shots at the capitalists that support you there.

I think I have made it abundantly clear that this is not an "America, love it or leave it" statement. Rather it says, "People who really want to change things here think more deeply." In the same way I feel there are real caveats and pitfalls to be watched for in our approach, although Frampton has not found them. First, there is the generic criticism by revolutionary thinkers of evolutionary thinkers, by theoreticians of pragmatists, by prescribers of describers: there are times when stiff-backed resistance, generalized schema, or normative models are necessary in the lives of men; and I would agree that these times are upon us in our social, economic, and political lives. But in architecture we have had a surfeit of them, and for the moment they are doing us no good.

Second, mannerist we are (for reasons we have given elsewhere), and we are part of a high art, not a folk or popular art, tradition. We use these other traditions, as others have before us, for an artistic reason; but for a social reason as well. Here we differ from the Pop artists: they are socially interpretative; we are, and should be, socially constrained. There is a social need for architectural high art to learn from and relate to folk and pop traditions if it is to serve its real clients and do no further harm in the city.

Third, Thomas Maldonado is right (in *La Speranza Progettuale*): Las Vegas communication happens at high speed and cannot cover the contemplative

aspects of human nature. Although it appeals to deep drives and motivations (sexuality, feelings of adequacy), its message to them is superficial. We cannot find this bad in and of itself; but the challenge to us is to use this source to convey more profound, interpretative, perhaps ironic messages which do reach the contemplative and introverted in the perceiver. We should be commentators, not imitators.

Fourth, what do we do, having learned from Las Vegas? This is basically the question: "How do you move from analysis to synthesis?" and it applies to whatever you learn from. What do you do after you've seen the Parthenon? At a prosaic level you've learned some perceptual tricks of the trade. Beyond this the process of assimilation is unconscious at its most fruitful level, although its results may be evaluated in the work you do. Facing the implications of Las Vegas in our work is proving much more difficult than describing Las Vegas.

Finally, we have left the whole question of judgment and nonjudgment in the air since we have not defined when we defer judgment and when we reassert it, but merely suggested (in "Hop on Pop") that the problem exists. Here again, we are in the realm of the unmeasurable, and a priori rulings will take us so far and no further; beyond that you prove your point by what you do.

Some Houses of Ill-Repute
Robert Venturi and Denise Scott Brown

This essay was first published in **Prospectus 13/14: The Yale Architectural Journal,** 1971, pp. 259–267.

38

Housing is good, but houses are bad. This has been a maxim of Modern architecture. While it is true that concentrating on individual houses is socially irresponsible and technologically irrelevant in the context of the continuing housing crisis of our time, within the circumstances of architectural practice as it is for the individual architect, the little house should not be scorned. It is still the first job for most architects, for obvious economic and social reasons: architecture is an expensive medium, therefore conservative clients award big commissions to old architects or big firms. (Ironically, big responsibilities often go to young planners and to young architects in big firms.) The little house for a close friend or relative is usually, therefore, a first opportunity for the young architect to test and expand theories. If his practice is slack, this at least allows him to put his heart and soul and a full work week into developing this one small idea, which is always a deepening experience. And if the client is poor, the years spent refining the plans while waiting for the financing to be arranged can be in the nature of a personal odyssey for the architect. Of our earlier houses, our beach, mother's, and frug houses were, to some extent, odysseys. The Lieb house was an early, not altogether successful attempt to use a home builder's vernacular in a not-altogether vernacular way.

Norma Evenson has described how in the twenties the young Le Corbusier theorized about the Ville Radieuse while doing nice little houses which he considered the formal prototypes for later urban-scale work of social and technological significance. However, although Le Corbusier saw his individual villas as prototypes for industrial housing, his models, and those of Modern architecture in general, have only slightly influenced mass housing—at least developers'

housing in America—and American architects are still significantly uninvolved in housing. This we believe is due to the unreal outlook which Le Corbusier and his followers brought to the problems of housing; but it does not preclude the possibility that the individual architect, working sympathetically with the merchant builder's real needs and constraints, his real media and symbols, cannot fulfill today (or at least share with others) the paradigmatic role that the architect has, perhaps arrogantly, claimed for himself.

Designing a house may also be the only opportunity for the architect to deal with a real user-client, as opposed to a corporate committee or representatives of a public agency, and therefore to deal with the irrationalities of emotional needs and values. The richness of this experience is what he has later to depend on (although in the context of different value systems) to eke out his statistical data when working on housing—at least for most projects, and until recently when "community architecture" brought representatives of user groups into architectural decision-making. However, situations are still rare where more than lip service is paid to community participation, or paid at a level which gives architects real information on users. So depending on individual rich clients' emotions to tell you something about collective poor clients' emotions, although imperfect, is often better than nothing.

For an architect no longer starting out, a project for a house can serve as a punctuation in his career as well as a point of departure—an opportunity, literally, to seclude himself in order to focus his thinking; to be able to control the whole in a way that distills and clarifies and

informs the bigger work at hand. The five houses illustrated here were just such exercises.

Our brief descriptions will rely a good deal on historical analogy because the heuristic use of historical models was important in the development of their designs and is therefore helpful in describing them (but not because we think it is necessarily the right method for all architects or for seeing all issues and solving all problems). We unashamedly lift our analogs out of their historical context—picking out for study perhaps only one aspect of their makeup—to create new comparisons, aid analysis, and goad invention. This is a traditional methodological device which seems to bother some architects but few historians.

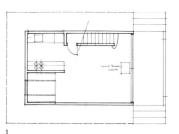

1

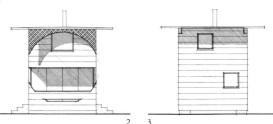

2 3

1 Hersey house project, Hyannisport, Massachusetts, 1968. Plan
2 Front elevation
3 Rear elevation
4 Model
5 Elevation and plan, D'Agostino house project, Clinton, New York, 1968

The Hersey house, 1968

This is literally what we have designated elsewhere as a "decorated shed" and as an appropriate stance for most architectural problems today. To explain, a decorated shed city hall would be a conventional loft building designed for the flexible interior uses of present-day bureaucracies, with rhetorical meaning applied on its outer surfaces in the form of a big sign blinking "This is a Monument"; and it stands in contradistinction to what we have called a "duck"—that is, a nominally undecorated building, itself distorted into a vast decoration through the contortion of structure and function, to serve an unadmitted decorative aim.

To return to our house: it is a summer beach cabin for a small family on Cape Cod. To satisfy the budget, it is a simple box of asbestos shingles with a flat roof and the proverbial Mary Anne behind. We applied ornament to the front porch to increase the scale of the facade: the circular opening, suggested by the curve of the lattice above and the rail below, extends beyond the sides of the facade and includes both stories— like the giant order on a Classical porch. We hoped to achieve, thereby, a poignant shed, both

little *and* big, and dumb *and* sophisticated—after all, it was to be a cabin for a Yale professor. It is hard for an architect to design a dumb building, but we think we succeeded. Unfortunately it was not dumb enough (or we were not clever enough) to meet the budget, and it didn't get built—the fate of many an architectural house of ill-repute.

The D'Agostino house, 1968

This is an admitted duck for a unique program, a rural site, and a generous budget. It is for a couple who want to enjoy the varied views surrounding a beautiful plateau in northern New York State. The main floor is therefore raised half a level above grade with opportunities to see out all around. The house is made of gray glazed brick to match the color of the weathered planks of a nearby barn. The facade toward the long approach forms a bold silhouette with a stepped

parapet reminiscent of Dutch architecture. The bold scale must accommodate the automobile as well, since the garage is the usual entrance in this snowy climate. You enter into a "beautiful" garage (white glazed brick with black headers) onto a "grand" stairway and up to the *piano nobile,* as if from the carriage-way of an eighteenth-century Neapolitan villa, rather than via a mean garage into a back door to the kitchen. The sunken auto court has sloped sides to facilitate snow plowing; and the swimming pool, sunken too, to protect bathers from prevailing winds, is on a side axis, recalling the sunken gardens of a George Howe Norman house. The pavilion at the end of the pool is a little parody of the big house. The bedroom on the top floor is vaulted in wood—Polish synagogues of the eighteenth century. We hope this one gets built.

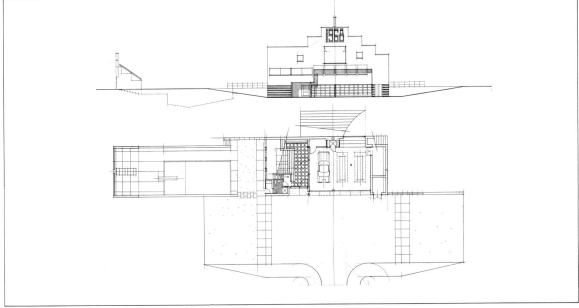

4

5

The Wike house, 1969

Another duck that significantly won't get built because the housing market in suburban Philadelphia abounds in good, old, big houses. Our clients found a beautiful Queen Anne manor on twelve acres, circa 1931, about the time we firmed up the estimate of our schematic design, and they naturally bought the manor because it was twice the size of our design and one-third the price. The program for this family with three small children and a live-in children's nurse was Lutyens-like in scope: a central hall for entertaining, only a little narrower than the gallery at Syon (but considerably shorter), one-and-a-half stories high, shallowly vaulted, and spanning the long way, with a window facing the central exterior stairwell. There is a library remote from the children, a breakfast room with a southeast exposure for plants, and a kitchen which, despite the Edwardian complexity of the plan, was to control the entrances and dominate the main floor almost in the manner of a Usonian "work space." The clients wanted a "formal" setting for their eighteenth-century antiques and therefore the plan starts out symmetrically. Note particularly the venturi effect of the exterior stair which splits the house from the lower loggia in the front to the upper entrance in the rear. (You have to fight your way into this house.) We made the front of the house like a bold Vanbrugh manor with deep shadows, to be read from the road down the hill. The auto entrance facade, with its rectangular geometry of big, frequent windows, is like an Elizabethan manor house, but without the symmetry, and the back, with its functional accommodations to inside needs and the swimming pool-play area outside, is pre-TAC Gropius. Facades were to be yellow brick like Holkham Hall. The porch side and the back were to be frame construction clad with flush boards painted the same color as the brick.

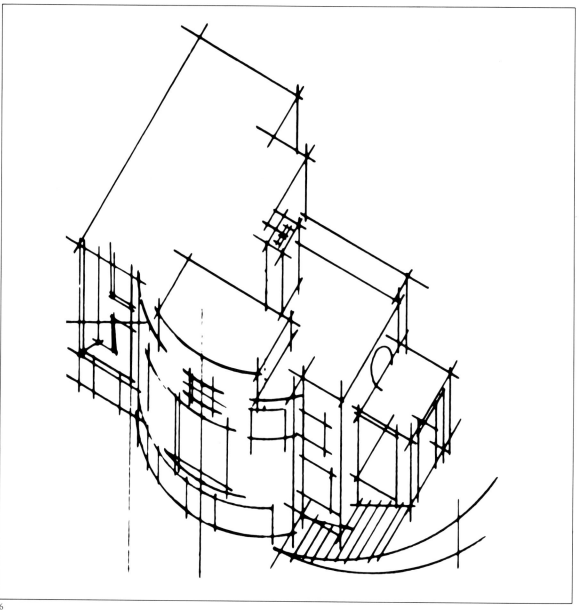

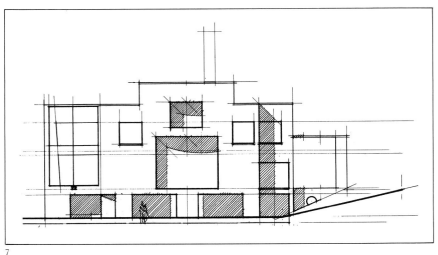

7

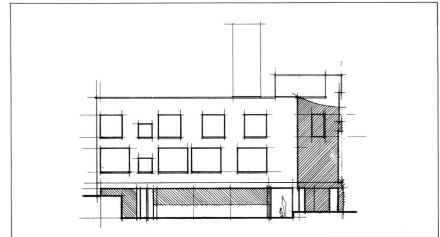

10

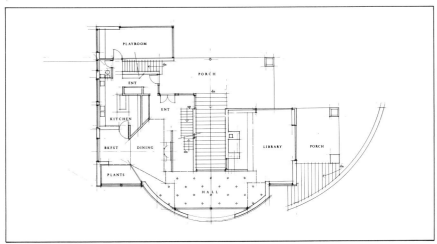

8

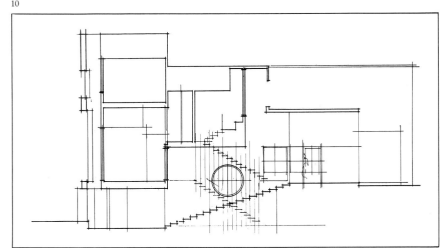

11

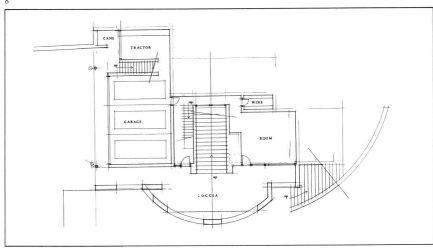

9

6 Wike house project, Devon, Pennsylvania, 1969. Sketch
7 Front elevation
8 First floor plan
9 Ground floor plan
10 Side elevation
11 Section

12 Trubeck and Wislocki houses, Nantucket Island,
   Massachusetts, 1970. Trubeck, front elevation
13 Side elevation
14 Section
15 Plan

The Trubeck and Wislocki houses, 1970

Two summer houses for another Yale professor,
his family, and a related family. The position of
the smaller house blocks the sight of a neighbor's
house to the west. The side elevations of the
larger house have windows like the other
windows in the house but much bigger: their sills
are four feet, three inches high to enhance and
obscure the scale. These are Siasconset
fishermen's cottages with some Shingle style and
Art Nouveau complexities inside. They are also
two little temples on the plain by the sea at
Selinunte, with three bigger than usual porch
steps in front to sit on.

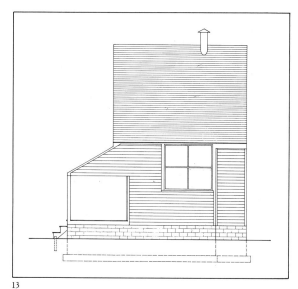

13

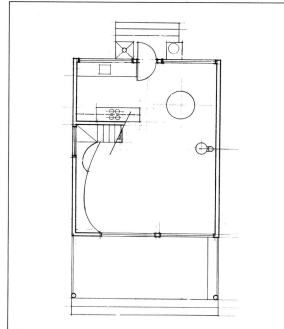

16

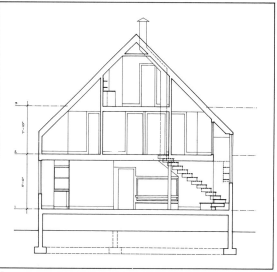

12

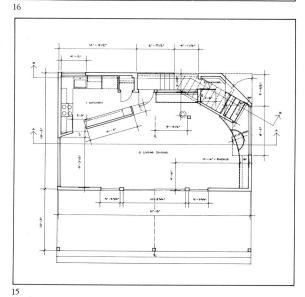

15

14

16 Wislocki, plan
17 Front elevation
18 Trubeck and Wislocki houses. Model, ocean side
19 View, land side

17

18

19

Functionalism, Yes, But...
Robert Venturi and Denise Scott Brown

This essay was first published in **A+U,** November 1974, pp. 33–34.

The great Functionalist architecture of the early part of this century promoted the primacy of program, industrialization, and social goals. But Functionalist architecture was more symbolic than functional. It was symbolically functional. It represented function more than resulted from function. It looked functional more than worked functionally.

This was all right because architecture has always been symbolic, and architects' creativity has come from adapting known symbols more than from inventing new forms. The content of Functionalist architecture was all right too because function was a vital symbol in the cultural context of the twenties.

But the symbolism of Functionalist architecture was unadmitted. It was a symbolism of no symbolism: the functional image of a building was to result from the automatic and explicit expression of the program and structure. By ascribing primary importance to function in architecture, Functionalists twisted the Vitruvian definition of "commodity, firmness and delight is architecture" into "commodity and firmness is delight in architecture." Aesthetic qualities, if ever mentioned, were said to derive from the easy resolution of the never-contradictory functional requirements of program, structure, and at a later period, mechanical equipment. Even Louis Kahn was a functional determinist when he said an architect should be surprised by the appearance of his building after he solved its design. The art in architecture was to come from the expression of original functional forms, rather than from the meaning of familiar decorative symbols. But when architects demoted the aesthetic element of the Vitruvian trio to an incidental by-product, they made of their work fragile tours de force built on shaky theoretical bases.

Functionalist architects rejected picturesque Romantic architecture, but they adopted asymmetrical compositions almost universally to symbolize sensitivity to functional program. Functionalist architects were indeed sensitive to new ways of living and working which they reflected in their plans. But their symbolic asymmetries eventually gave way to the symmetrical and generalized plans of Mies and Kahn because the forms of buildings could not fit, like a glove on a hand, over the complex, unpredictable, and sometimes intangible elements of realistic programs.

Functionalist architects renounced architectural formalism, but they accepted the formal vocabulary of vernacular industrial architecture, a grammar of forms and symbols derived from an idealized industrial style. Their adaptation was no different from Bramante's Renaissance translation of the Classical orders of the Golden Age of Rome. Mies adapted the forms of industrialization more than the techniques; Le Corbusier mastered the forms of a painterly Cubism, and his construction was as much handicraft as industrial.

Functionalist architects denounced eclectic historical styles, but they promoted an International Style. And by eschewing formal vocabularies, they became subject to the dangers of unconscious formalism.

Functionalist architects condemned ornament, but substituted articulation. Articulation in the late phase of Modern architecture evolved into structural exhibitionism and spatial expressionism. When architects rejected applied ornament, they twisted the whole building into one big ornament—an ironic irresponsibility on the part of Functionalists.

Functionalist architects promoted reformist and visionary goals for mass housing through social planning and industrial process, but the expressive forms of socialist housing have become the universal symbols of corporate architecture and beachfront luxury. Symbolic representation of the nonarchitectural goals of the Functionalist movement might have been less easily subverted than were its pure and abstract expressions.

Functionalist architects forgot the iconographic content of early Christian, Byzantine, and Gothic architecture in their exclusive search for pure architecture and abstract expressionist space. Painting and sculpture in architecture were permitted only as abstract articulations at the service of space. Until recently, these architects noticed the "electro-graphic" architecture on the commercial strip only in their condemnation of urban sprawl as "God's Own Junkyard," etc. Signs on architecture were as bad as decoration on architecture. The commercial vernacular, as a vital source for architecture today, shocks our traditional Functionalists in the same way the industrial vernacular shocked the academicians of fifty years ago. But the instructive mosaics and frescoes and sculptural relief which were the fine art of the past and the persuasive commercial signs which are a folk art today both add essential dimensions to architecture.

Great architecture may be based on wrong theory; this perhaps happened in the Renaissance. But we think the ironic deterioration of the Heroic period of the Modern movement and the continuing sterility of its manifestations today come out of architects' misunderstanding of the inevitability and the inherence of symbolism and ornament in architecture, as well as of function in architecture.

Today we are beyond defining a house as a machine for living in, but we may well define architecture as shelter with decoration on it.

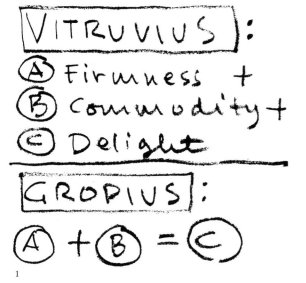

VITRUVIUS):
(A) Firmness +
(B) Commodity +
(C) Delight

GRODIUS):
(A) + (B) = (C)

1

2

1 The Functionalist twist to the Vitruvian definition of architecture
2 Long Island Duckling from *God's Own Junkyard*

45

Complexity and Contradiction in the Work of Furness
Robert Venturi

This essay was first published in **Pennsylvania Academy of the Fine Arts Newsletter,** Spring 1976, p. 5.

I have been asked to write my reaction as a practicing architect to Frank Furness's building for the Pennsylvania Academy of the Fine Arts on its hundredth anniversary. Like other Philadelphians, I might rather write of reactions in the plural because my appreciation of this masterpiece has varied.

46

Every Philadelphian must have noticed, in traveling the city, at least one or two Furness buildings, though possibly without being able to identify them. And any middle-aged Philadelphian—no matter how sophisticated—must remember a time when he or she loathed one of Furness's buildings. James F. O'Gorman, in *The Architecture of Frank Furness*, has brilliantly described the ups and downs in the evolution of the taste for Furness's work. In my case, I remember as a child looking out for those squat columns as my father drove past the Provident Life and Trust Company on our way to the Benjamin Franklin Bridge, almost enjoying the loathing and condescension I felt as an intolerant Colonial Revivalist who doodled dream-house plans on the backs of school books. My conversion to Furness in college, augmented by reading William Campbell's article in the *Architectural Review* in 1951, convinced me that one could change one's mind in matters of taste; in fact, one better had.

Ours is a time prone to revisionism in almost all fields, to a catholicity of taste and a camp tolerance for the taste of the recent past. The experience I describe seems almost routine today. But my conversion to the despised Victorian was a significant revelation for me because, through it, I learned that progress and originality in architecture could come from seeing old things in new ways and not necessarily, as the aesthetic of Modern architecture prescribed, from creating

1

original and radical forms and using advanced techniques. This learned sensibility to the familiar led later to our learning from Las Vegas and Levittown; that is, learning from the everyday environment of urban sprawl and from commercial symbolism.

But the first lessons I learned from Furness had to do with mannerism: architecture could be complex and contradictory. I wrote then in admiration of Furness's architectural complexity: "The main stair in Frank Furness's Pennsylvania Academy of the Fine Arts in Philadelphia is too big in relation to its immediate surroundings. It lands on a space narrower than its width, and faces an opening narrower than its width. Furthermore, the opening is bisected by a post. But this stair is ceremonial and symbolic as well as functional, and it relates to the hall immediately beyond the opening to the whole building, and to the great scale of Broad Street outside." I have recently had the privilege of working in Furness's masterpiece in a small way during its restoration, and seeing the building reemerge as the architect designed it has been yet again a joyful revelation.

47

1 Main stair of the Pennsylvania Academy of the Fine Arts, Philadelphia, Pennsylvania

Plain and Fancy Architecture by Cass Gilbert and the Additions to the Allen Memorial Art Museum by Venturi and Rauch, at Oberlin
Robert Venturi

This essay was first published in **Allen Memorial Art Museum Bulletin,** vol. 34, no. 2, 1976–1977, pp. 83–104.

1

2

3

48

Two aspects of Cass Gilbert's architecture[1] at Oberlin College interested me as I tried as an architect to follow in his footsteps there: one is his combination of plain and fancy styles of architecture, and the other is the contrast between the front and the back in his buildings.

Three of Gilbert's four buildings facing Tappan Square are Romanesque—a simplified but explicit version of that style with buff limestone walls and overhanging terracotta roofs. The Allen Memorial Art Museum (1915–1917), although stylistically Tuscan Renaissance, is similarly explicit in its ornament and symbolism, and it is almost identical to the other buildings in scale, profile, materials, and color. This historical eclecticism is to be expected in important buildings conceived in the tradition of the Ecole des Beaux-Arts in the early part of this century. But Gilbert's architecture also contains elements of a contemporary vernacular vocabulary. In the Cox Administration Building (1913–1915) (fig. 1), for example, the materials, and the columns, pilasters, lunettes, stringcourses, and other ornaments are derived from southern France or northern Italy of the twelfth century, and its proportions and profiles—its form as a whole and its atmosphere—are Romanesque too. But it is also midwestern. It looks like the Winslow house by Frank Lloyd Wright in River Forest, Illinois (fig. 2).

I refer to the Winslow house less as an example of the Prairie style which Wright invented and promoted and more as a manifestation of a contemporary vernacular architecture. Wright was the original genius he himself described in his writings, but his early work was enriched by the conventions and traditions of his place and time, like that of any great artist, and his genius lay in the enhancement of the ordinary, as much

as in the creation of the original. Examples of the ordinary that Wright adapted still exist in houses and civic buildings in most midwestern towns. They are a vernacular architecture of horizontal proportions, low-hip roofs with big overhangs, plain surfaces punctuated by arched openings and double-hung windows, simplified ornament, and buff and terracotta hues—perhaps a reaction at the time against the verticality, ornateness, and deep hues of mid-Victorian architecture, and certainly a derivation from the Richardsonian Romanesque. This is not to say that Gilbert's Romanesque revival at Oberlin was influenced by Wright's Prairie style, but rather that it paralleled and contained elements of a midwestern vernacular of the time, and that, incidentally, Wright's almost contemporary Prairie style did the same thing. On the other hand, one can say that Oberlin comes by its Romanesque in two ways: as a revival via the Beaux-Arts tradition, and as a survival via the Richardsonian Romanesque turned vernacular.

Gilbert combined the plain and the fancy in the Cox Administration Building among its architectural elements and within the single form of a small building. In the more complex form of the School of Theology (Bosworth Hall, 1930–1931), he distinguished high art from low art in the separation of the front of the building from the back (fig. 3). The front wing containing the classrooms and chapel of the School of Theology is Romanesque revival; the dormitory in the back is midwestern vernacular (fig. 4). Both wings of this complex have terracotta tile roofs with overhang, but the front wing is buff limestone with dormer windows, while the back wing is red brick with double-hung windows, though arched on the first floor. The front wing contains a picturesque roofline with tower, a porch at the entrance, and an apse at the rear.

The back wing is a simple block forming a "U," with no protrusions in plan or section, and minimal, flat, only vaguely Romanesque articulation in the brick (fig. 5).

The front's explicitly Romanesque hierarchies of arches, pilasters, lunettes, corbels, stringcourses, and parapets are not exotic, however; they look at home next door to the First Congregational Church, because this symbolic ornamentation is generalized, simplified, flattened—almost a little dry—like the nineteenth-century Greek Revival decoration of the church next door; it even looks a little Art Deco. Also, it is concentrated as symbolic gestures on otherwise plain wall surfaces (fig. 6). The building as a whole is intimate in scale, and even its symmetry generalizes and simplifies its effects, so that the fancy is itself plain in the School of Theology, and a symbolic abbey is at home across from Main Street in an Ohio town (fig. 7).

The Finney Memorial Chapel (1907–1908) is more fancy than plain, perhaps because its function fits the Romanesque symbolism neatly, but even here the demands of the Protestant service prescribed an auditorium rather than a nave, and although Gilbert managed an apse in the back and a tripartite composition of entrances in the front, it remains a Protestant auditorium (fig. 8).

Gilbert's Allen Memorial Art Museum is an exception to the rule. It is not a mixture of plain and fancy. Although it maintains proportions, scale, and profiles similar to those of the Cox Administration Building in particular, and the midwestern vernacular in general, it is a quite literal adaptation of a Brunelleschi villa both as a whole and in its details (fig. 9). And, although it has front and back wings connected, like those of

4

5

6

49

7

8

1 Cox Administration Building, Oberlin College, Oberlin, Ohio
2 Winslow House by Frank Lloyd Wright, River Forest, Illinois
3 School of Theology
4 Side view
5 Rear view
6 Facade
7 View of College Street from Tappan Square
8 Finney Memorial Chapel

the School of Theology, by an arcaded cloister intended to distinguish interior functions (galleries from studios), the architectural difference between front and back is one of scale and form rather than style. Nor does the museum have the analogous harmony with the town, described above. This architecture is high Art with a capital "A." Was the difference due to the fact that this building is an art museum, the repository of what must have been even then an outstanding collection of art, a symbol of high culture in the midplains: no midwestern vernacular here? Or, was the architect's budget bigger? Perhaps the combination of the plain with the fancy in the administration building and the School of Theology was merely a response to low budgets, although to an architect of the seventies, the quality of the materials and workmanship is enviable.

In any case, the art museum is not high art with a vengeance. If it is a symbol of high art midst mid-America, it forms a poignant rather than a condescending image, not a separation between great art and everyday life, but a contrast. As an architectural gem in an ordinary setting, it achieves its own harmony on the corner of Main

and Lorain—a Quattrocento villa symbolizing the greatest decades of Western art—in a gridiron plan; off a village green; and among a Congregational church, a Citgo Service Station, and those somewhat threadbare bungalows, nondescript but universal in the American town (figs. 10, 11). The Cox Administration Building and the School of Theology achieve harmony through their analogous relationships with a small town setting; the art museum achieves harmony through contrast, heightening the quality of its context through jarring juxtapositions such as terracotta friezes with moulded plastic signs;

10

11

della Robbia *tondos* with Citgo *logos*; decorative wrought-iron grilles with gingerbread wooden trellises; pilasters and urns with gas pumps and signs; and a front porch completing a Classical axis (figs. 12, 13). Diverse elements provide context and enhancement for each other, such as Pop Art beer cans in a white-walled gallery. One Allen Memorial Art Museum does not a Fiesole make; on the contrary, it makes Oberlin more what it is.

These impressions and theories are based on what one can see in Oberlin today. As an architect rather than a historian, I have not gone into Gilbert's intentions, other than to note in his letters a recommendation for Romanesque at Oberlin because it is "pliable" and because of its play of plain and fancy: "it permits a great concentration of ornament at some focal point and great simplicity throughout the rest of the building." Nor have I seen, or referred to, Gilbert's master plan, only part of which materialized in the four buildings I have discussed. Perhaps that document would show his desire to change Oberlin into a Fiesole or a Caen. However, although he could not have anticipated the petrol station across the street, and he could have blotted out of his mind's eye those little wooden houses that were there at the time, and if his plan *was* for a simple and total unity between town and college for an ideal future, I think his aesthetic allowed, for the short run (and the short run has become the long run), a complex and contradictory unity including hierarchies among ordinary and ideal elements, and plain and fancy styles, because that aesthetic has worked so well.

Adding to a building by Cass Gilbert is difficult because his architecture is very good and comparisons are inevitable. Adding to the Allen

9

12

13

14

Memorial Art Museum is particularly difficult because you are tampering with what has become an icon at Oberlin: adding a wing to the art museum is like drawing a mustache on a Madonna. It is difficult, too, to add to a completed composition—a wing on a symmetrical Renaissance villa, like a bowler hat on a Venus, will never look correct. Worse still, we had to add to the side of the building, because the back, the logical place for an addition, was extended in 1937 by Clarence Ward (fig. 14). In the end, we extended our villa as a Quattrocento architect might have added to a real villa in Fiesole two generations after it was built; we juxtaposed a workable new block in an architectural style current today (fig. 15). Our addition, in some ways contrasting with, in other ways analogous to, the original block, is inevitably awkward perhaps, and shows a not too obvious respect for the past. In Italian piazzas similar juxtapositions developed over time in the dense architectural complexes that we admire so much; those complexes make up in guts for what they lose in composition. But our impulse to juxtapose the new with the old in this way came primarily from particular determinants of the site and the program, not from an aesthetic preference. The only site for the new wing was a narrow sloping strip of land between the museum and the adjacent Hall Auditorium; there was no room for extension on the north side or in back.

The program was complex: to extend the Allen Memorial Art Museum by the addition of a large gallery; to augment the facilities of the art department; to rehouse the art library and the laboratory of the Intermuseum Conservation Association (ICA); and to renovate the existing museum, adding a print display space in the upper gallery, increasing storage facilities, providing air conditioning and humidity control, and designing a shipping and receiving area to be shared with the new wing. We had thus to modify the program and layout of the existing building and the 1937 extension, and then to consider these and the intended new wing as a whole.

Site restrictions and functional relations dictated that the new addition be a long building that closely paralleled the old complex, with the new gallery in front to connect with the old museum. The new gallery could be entered from the old museum only, for reasons of security. The remainder of the new facilities had to be accessible from the front lawn. We soon found that for economy and simplicity everything should be in one wing (figs. 16, 17).

Our clients saw the new gallery, the Ellen Johnson Gallery of Modern Art, as a room neutral enough in character to be a background for various and changing exhibits and general enough in shape to adapt to various and changing exhibitions; yet they disliked the pure black box popular today. The black box—sans natural light and with a universal system for artificial lighting in the ceiling; sans architectural

51

15

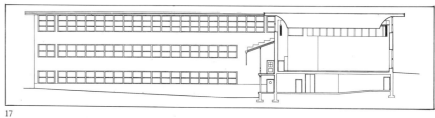

17

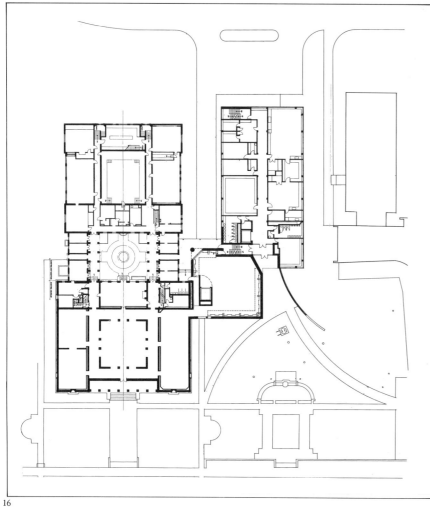

16

18

15 Drawing, Allen Memorial Art Museum, with addition by
   Venturi and Rauch, 1973. West elevation
16 Plan
17 Section
18 Ellen Johnson Gallery of Modern Art, interior
19 Interior

19

character and with a universal system of floating panels to articulate space—answers the requirement of absolute flexibility of spatial and lighting effects. It is a theatrical approach to the display of art objects; the museum becomes a stage, the exhibition a stage set. We wanted a traditional gallery with natural light and a continuing and particular architectural character, a room rather than a stage, a sense of place as well as space. Of course, contradictory goals like neutrality and flexibility *and* natural character and natural light are impossible to achieve in an art gallery without compromise. And they inspire a design that is not pure (figs. 18, 19). To satisfy the goals of neutrality and flexibility, we employed current conventional systems and materials for the interior of an art gallery: track lighting, although on a gypsum plaster ceiling rather than a bold structural grid ceiling; flexible panels for display and spatial articulation (we left their future construction to their users, the museum staff); oak floors; plywood-backed gypsum plaster walls for economy and ease of repair, repainting, and replacement; and flush, recessed bases to accommodate electrical outlets, air returns, and elements of the security system. Our client designated about thirty-two hundred square feet for the new gallery. Its almost square plan was, in large part, determined by the limitations and character of the site. But we liked this shape because it contrasts nicely with the rectangular gallery preceding it in the old building, and because of its neutrality and ease of subdivision.

(On the other hand, we worried about its shape in relation to its size: would the room, if left unsubdivided, be too big for the scale of most paintings?) The square is somewhat distorted to accommodate pressures in the plan from beyond. We liked this because it promotes a sense of

53

scale in a big generalized shape *and* it reflects the asymmetrical attachments to the symmetrical gallery *and* suggests the academic complex this gallery is in. A window in an angled corner of the gallery looks onto a decorative "Ionic" column and down an axis through the rose garden in the Gilbert complex (fig. 20).

The unusual height of the gallery is also determined by the extraneous requirements of its linkage to the old building. The section of the gallery comes largely from requirements of natural lighting (fig. 21). In the very advantages of natural lighting lie its disadvantages: its qualities of chromatic richness and dynamic variety are the result of mobile rays that destroy pigments, distract the eye, and don't conform to museum hours. Therefore natural light had to be indirect and supplemented and balanced by sophisticated artificial illumination. Our preference was to avoid dramatic architectural combinations of space and light—sawtooth clerestories, etc. As advocates of symbolic and ordinary rather than heroic and original architecture, we wanted light to come through recognizable windows rather than innovative modulators.

We are also against skylights in the gallery, partly because they leak, partly because there have been so many electrical simulations of overhead skylight that our eyes tend to interpret the natural as artificial, and the hard-earned effect is lost except when a cloud passes. So the main source of natural light for this gallery became simply strip windows high in the wall to deliver a general, even light at eye level, and to save wall space for paintings.

The light entering these windows is baffled by three elements: a roof overhang outside, the

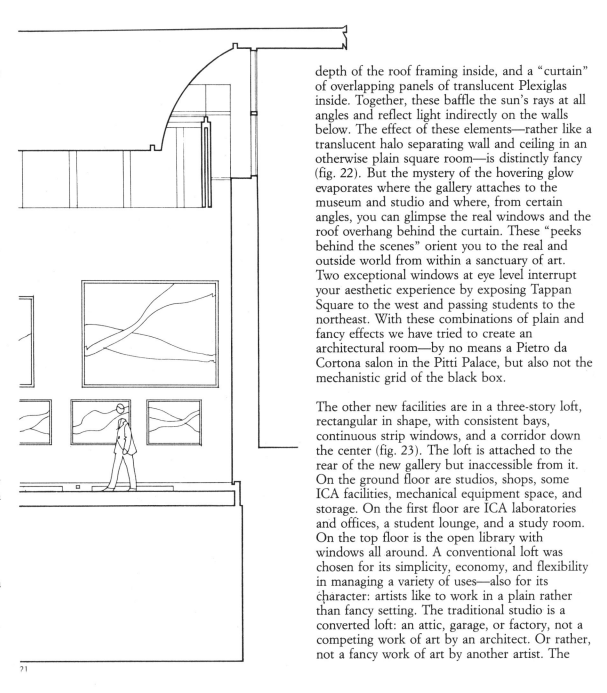

21

depth of the roof framing inside, and a "curtain" of overlapping panels of translucent Plexiglas inside. Together, these baffle the sun's rays at all angles and reflect light indirectly on the walls below. The effect of these elements—rather like a translucent halo separating wall and ceiling in an otherwise plain square room—is distinctly fancy (fig. 22). But the mystery of the hovering glow evaporates where the gallery attaches to the museum and studio and where, from certain angles, you can glimpse the real windows and the roof overhang behind the curtain. These "peeks behind the scenes" orient you to the real and outside world from within a sanctuary of art. Two exceptional windows at eye level interrupt your aesthetic experience by exposing Tappan Square to the west and passing students to the northeast. With these combinations of plain and fancy effects we have tried to create an architectural room—by no means a Pietro da Cortona salon in the Pitti Palace, but also not the mechanistic grid of the black box.

The other new facilities are in a three-story loft, rectangular in shape, with consistent bays, continuous strip windows, and a corridor down the center (fig. 23). The loft is attached to the rear of the new gallery but inaccessible from it. On the ground floor are studios, shops, some ICA facilities, mechanical equipment space, and storage. On the first floor are ICA laboratories and offices, a student lounge, and a study room. On the top floor is the open library with windows all around. A conventional loft was chosen for its simplicity, economy, and flexibility in managing a variety of uses—also for its character: artists like to work in a plain rather than fancy setting. The traditional studio is a converted loft: an attic, garage, or factory, not a competing work of art by an architect. Or rather, not a fancy work of art by another artist. The

55

22

22 Ellen Johnson Gallery of Modern Art, interior
23 Addition, from east end
24 Addition, facade

23

scientists of the ICA also need the scale and
flexibility of a loft for their laboratories.

From the outside the addition is a box-like form
with flat surfaces of varying materials, some with
patterns. It recedes from the old buildings via
jogs in its plan. It has asymmetrical strip
windows and a big overhang, and it is directly
attached to the old building without a connecting
link. This overall form suits the needs of the
gallery and the uses behind. Its flat surfaces are
in harmony with the simple proportions and low
relief of Gilbert's Quattrocento ornament. On
the other hand, the almost consistently flat
surfaces of the new wing appear recessive in the
context of the bold deep entrance arcade in the
center of the museum facade. The pink granite
and rose sandstone of the new facade are
analogous in color but contrasting in overall
pattern with the polychromatic but hierarchic
panels and ordered bays of the old building; our
facade does not even have an architectural base.
In relating these textures, colors, and patterns,
we thought of a Medieval banner hanging from a
Renaissance balcony during the Palio. The rear of
the addition is in buff brick, appropriate for a
loft and matching the brick on Hall Auditorium

next door. This plain material shows from the
front on the last jog and contrasts with the fancy
materials and pattern on the gallery (fig. 24).

The jogs in plan between old building, gallery,
and loft, distinguish the gallery from the loft,
permit a front entrance for the loft and admit
natural light at the end of its corridor, diminish
the bulk of the big addition in relation to the old
museum, lessen the effect of duality between old
and new, and preserve as much of the front lawn
and trees as possible. However, having broken up
the plan for these reasons and having articulated

the jogs through changes in materials, we kept
the elevation of the addition at a constant height
to counterbalance this diversity. The sloping site
allowed this in section. The continuous strip
windows and constant roof overhang are also
common to both gallery and loft and they
enhance the unity of the otherwise diverse
addition. The big roof overhang that protects the
gallery windows in a crucial way also
conveniently shades the library windows in the
loft.

In the beginning we attached the addition to the

old museum in the way we did because it worked and because every other way we tried looked worse. In the end we liked jamming an independent new pavilion onto the old pavilion without a transition—or rather, with a transition at the scale of detail—through placing a flush, ten inch, vertical strip of gray granite on the new wall at the joint meeting the contrasting patterns of each pavilion and receiving the Classical mouldings of the old one; and with careful adjustment of the height of the new wing and its roof overhang to the roof of the old. Although a low and narrow link, perhaps with glass walls, between the old and the new would seem the most respectful and recessive solution to this problem of transition, it neither worked well nor looked good. The link took up space on the limited site, pushing the gallery south, constricting the entrance to the loft, and diminishing natural light at the end of the studio wing corridor. It made elevator access to the mezzanine of the old building problematical. Furthermore, it looked fussy and diminished the scale and unity of the complex vis-à-vis Hall Auditorium. Finally, a connecting link made the addition too independent and therefore architecturally competitive with the old museum.

While our pavilion is independent of the old museum in form and silhouette, it inflects toward the old building in plan and in the asymmetrical composition of its windows. In fact, there *is* a transitional link—within the new pavilion, and inscribed on its face. The strip windows stop near the old building, and the lower window near the old building suggests a glass-walled link. Inside too, although the new room is a big cube immediately juxtaposed on the old gallery, this lower window and the elevator block suggest a transitional vestibule.

The scale of the new pavilion is generous like that of the Gilbert building, but it contains, also like the Gilbert building, elements relating to the size of the human figure around the entrance; a lattice fence made of steel straps at the retaining wall leading to the entrance and a built-in bench are convenient and they add a touch of lace to the whole fabric.

The design of the addition as a whole fits our predilection for the decorated shed—that is, plain architecture with a fancy appliqué. The play between contrasting and analogous harmonies and between plain and fancy elements in the forms of this complex is echoed by a similar play in its symbolism. Our squarish gallery with strip windows and big overhang recalls, on the outside, a high school gym of the forties. But the decorative pattern on it evokes other associations, fancy rather than plain. And the loft with its big proportions and flush windows is a fancy representation of a plain style. From the front, therefore, our complex is meant to be a succession of forms and symbols, juxtaposed and receding: a Quattrocento monument, a decorated shed, and then an enhanced loft (fig. 25).

25

25 View of Allen Memorial Art Museum with addition

Alvar Aalto
Robert Venturi

This essay was first published in **Arkkitehti,** vol. 73, no. 7-8, 1976, pp. 66–67.

Alvar Aalto's work has meant the most to me of all the work of the Modern masters. It is for me the most moving, the most relevant, the richest source to learn from in terms of its art and technique. Like all work that lives beyond its time, Aalto's can be interpreted in many ways. Each interpretation is more or less true for its moment because work of such quality has many dimensions and layers of meaning. When I was growing up in architecture in the forties and fifties, Aalto's architecture was largely appreciated for its human quality, as it was called, derived from free plans which accommodated exceptions within the original order, and from the use of natural wood and red brick—traditional materials introduced within the simple forms of the industrial vocabulary of Modern architecture. These contradictory elements in Aalto's work connoted—rather paradoxically it seems now—qualities of simplicity and serenity.

Aalto's buildings no longer look simple and serene. Their contradictions now evoke complexity and tension. Aalto himself has become an Andrea Palladio of the Modern movement—a mannerist master, but in a low key. Among the complexities and contradictions I see in his work are its conventional architectural elements organized in unconventional ways, its barely maintained balance between order and disorder, and its effects of plain and fancy, of the modest and the monumental at the same time.

Now that we can survey Aalto's whole oeuvre, the conventionality and consistency of his work is very apparent. There is little change in the direction or development of his work over the years in comparison with the varied evolutions in Le Corbusier's work, or even in comparison with those changes between early and late Mies van der Rohe. Moreover, the elements of Aalto's architecture—the windows, hardware, columns, light fixtures, furniture, materials (except for the wood and brick)—are conventional in their forms and associations. They are derived from the industrial and Cubist forms and symbols of the Modern style: in a textbook on classic Modern architectural elements, Mies's pure steel sections and travertine slabs, and Le Corbusier's idiosyncratic, if now almost universal, forms in beton-brut would be included, but Aalto's diverse yet conventional elements would predominate.

The quality of Aalto's elements comes not from their originality or purity, but from their deviations—sometimes very slight, sometimes gross—in form and context. And their power comes from the tensions these deviations produce. The handrail on the stairway of the offices for the *Turun Sanomat* looks conventional, but on second glance you see it as slightly unusual in form and application and highly special in the refinement of its design. The concrete windows in the Enso-Gutzeit Building resemble those in the rather dry and correct grid of a passé SOM office building, but they are slightly off the norm in their proportions and scale, and highly "incorrect" in their application on the rear facade.

The order of Aalto's architecture is also full of tensions. A comparison again with other Modern masters might clarify my point: Mies is well known for his simple and consistent order to which program and human activities serenely conform; Le Corbusier is known for his Classical order with dramatic exceptions and complex juxtapositions involving touches of *terribilitá*; Frank Lloyd Wright for his rich but highly motival order. Aalto's order is not based on serenity or drama or consistency but on tension, derived from exceptions within the order as in the rear facade of the Enso-Gutzeit Building, or in distortions to the original order as in the plan of the high-rise apartments in Bremen, or from an ambiguous order just on the verge of disorder as in the complex plan of the Wolfsburg Cultural Center, or as reflected in Paul Rudolf's complaint to me once: Why does Aalto have to use three different light fixtures in one small room?

I think we can learn timely lessons about monumentality from Aalto's architecture. Architectural monumentality is used indiscriminately in our time and it wavers between dry purity and boring bombast. Mies's partisans have stressed the element of consistency in architectural monumentality at the expense of symbolic content and characteristics of scale. Le Corbusier's ubiquitous followers, not surprisingly, have not been able to emulate the heroic *tours de force* of an enigmatic genius at the end of his life; Le Corbusier's monumentality isn't for every architect or for everywhere, and explicit heroic rhetoric is not for our architecture at this moment. Aalto's monumentality is always appropriate in where and how it is used, and it is suggested through a tense balance, again between sets of contradictions. The auditorium at the Otaniemi Technical Institute combines collective scale *and* intimate scale, expressionistic forms *and* conventional forms, plain *and* fancy symbolism, and pure order interrupted by inconsistencies planned for the right places.

But Aalto's most endearing characteristic for me, as I struggle to complete this essay, is that he didn't write about architecture.

1   2

1 *Turun Sanomat* offices, Turku, Alvar Aalto. Stairwell
2 Enso-Gutzeit headquarters, Helsinki, Alvar Aalto

A Definition of Architecture as Shelter with Decoration on It, and Another Plea for a Symbolism of the Ordinary in Architecture
Robert Venturi

This essay was first published in **A+U,** January 1978, pp. 3–14.

One way to talk about architecture and analyze where you are in it is to define it. Every architect works with a definition in mind even if he or she doesn't know it, or if it is not explicit; every generation of architects has its own definitions. Our current definition is, architecture is shelter with symbols on it. Or, architecture is shelter with decoration on it.

For many architects this may be a shocking definition because definitions in the last seventy-five years have been put in spatial, technological, organic, or linguistic terms. Definitions of Modern architecture never included ornament, nor did they explicitly refer to shelter. Space and process were the essential qualities of architecture in Louis Kahn's definition, "architecture is the thoughtful making of spaces," and in descriptive phrases like Sigfried Giedion's "space-time and architecture," and Frank Lloyd Wright's "in the nature of materials"; space and form predominated in Le Corbusier's "architecture is the masterly, correct, and magnificent play of masses brought together in light." In his definition of a house as a machine for living in, technology and functionalism were the essential elements, although the implication of functionalism in this famous pronouncement is almost unique in Modern architecture despite the emphasis on functionalism in the general theory of that movement. And recently some theorists have attempted semiotic interpretations of architecture, applying in very literal terms some of the complex techniques of that verbal discipline to the perception of architecture. But ornament and symbolism—certainly applied ornament and the simple uses of association—have been ignored in architecture, or condemned. Ornament was equated with crime by Adolf Loos as long ago as 1906, and symbolism was

associated with discredited historical eclecticism; appliqué on shelter would have been considered superficial by theorists of the Modern movement and contrary to the industrial techniques integral to Modern architecture.

But we like emphasizing shelter in architecture, thereby including function in our definition; and we like admitting symbolic rhetoric in our definition which is not integral with shelter, thereby expanding the content of architecture beyond itself and freeing function to take care of itself.

To justify our definition of architecture and to clarify how we come to it, I shall use six comparisons—those between Rome and Las Vegas, Abstract Expressionism and Pop Art, Vitruvius and Gropius, Mies van der Rohe and McDonald's hamburger stands, Scarlatti and the Beatles, and plain and fancy styles of architecture. In the last three comparisons I shall try to justify a particular content for symbolism in architecture, that of the ordinary. For my arguments I shall use material from our book, *Learning from Las Vegas*, because I am elaborating here on a main theme in that book, and because I think hardly anyone has read that book or reads books in general anymore.

Rome and Las Vegas
As architects, we appreciate Rome *and* Las Vegas and we have learned from both sources. (I use Rome to stand for urban tradition—Medieval and Baroque—and Las Vegas to stand for urban sprawl in general.) It is in comparisons between the Roman piazza and the Vegas Strip— illustrating surprising similarities as well as obvious contrasts—that we learned about symbolism in architecture.

Our generation discovered Rome in the fifties. Enclosed exterior space and intimate urban scale were exciting revelations to those of us growing up among wide, ill-defined streets and vast parking lots in amorphous (although not yet hostile) American cities. As post-heroic Moderns reading Sigfried Giedion, we rediscovered history and acknowledged a traditional basis for architecture and urbanism. We had a particular sympathy for the spatial relationships, pedestrian scale, and urban quality of Italian towns exemplified in the piazza. We are now suffering from the results of that enthusiasm—witness the subsequent urban renewal piazzas that disrupt the social fabric and dry up the commercial and visual vitality of the centers of American cities. This is because, as architects of the fifties, we saw the piazza as pure space and we designed our piazzas as dry configurations of compositional elements—forms and textures, patterns and colors, rhythms, accents, and scale—balanced somehow to promote urbanity in space. Historical urban complexes we saw as abstract compositions like those of the Abstract Expressionist paintings of that decade: the symbolism of the buildings in the piazzas we hardly saw at all. We appreciated the rich evolutionary juxtapositions of historical styles—Baroque palazzo facing Romanesque duomo, for instance—but we limited our observations to the formal relationships of these styles. We ignored the symbolic content of the buildings because of our obsession with the composition of space. We forgot that forms were buildings, texture was sculptural relief, an accent was a statue (and a statue represented a person and ideals), articulation was a portal or decoration, rhythm was composed of pilasters, color and pattern were functions of walls, and that a focus was an obelisk—a sign commemorating an important event. We blotted out the explicit associations evoked by most of the architectural and sculptural elements of the piazza; the ornamentation on the facade of the palazzo symbolizing architectural and structural content and promoting dynastic virtues and civic values, and that of the cathedral, which is like a complex billboard with niches for saintly icons.

We ignored iconography in architecture when we stressed the functional and structural qualities of buildings in piazzas and idolized their spatial effects, but forgot their symbolic dimensions. We learned inspiring lessons about space in Rome, but the urbanity we were seeking would come from space and signs.[1] We had to go to Las Vegas to learn this lesson about Rome and to acknowledge symbolism in our definition of architecture. On the other hand, we were able to be easy and perceptive about Las Vegas in the sixties because we loved Rome in the fifties.

We had an exhilarating feeling of revelation in Las Vegas in the sixties, like that which we had in Rome in the previous decade. Our first reaction was that the Strip has a quality and a vitality—a significance—that Modern-designed urban landscapes don't have, and that, ironically, where Modern architecture had won out by supposedly bringing urbanity back to our cities, it didn't. When we analyzed our happy reaction and the peculiar quality and adhesion that exists in commercial urban sprawl, we found that their basis was symbolism. As we had learned from the spaces of Rome, we learned from the symbolism of Las Vegas. We soon learned that if you ignore signs as "visual pollution," you are lost. If you look for "spaces between buildings" in Las Vegas, you are lost. If you see the buildings of urban sprawl as forms making space, they are pathetic—mere pimples in an amorphous landscape. As architecture, urban sprawl is a

failure; as space, it is nothing. It is when you see the buildings as symbols in space, not forms in space, that the landscape takes on quality and meaning. And when you see no buildings at all, at night when virtually only the illuminated signs are visible, you see the Strip in its pure state.

This is not to say that the architecture I am describing is without formal content, but to emphasize the predominance of signs over buildings on the Strip and of symbolism over form in the buildings on the Strip as functions of the vast spaces they are seen in and the fast speeds they are seen at. We enumerated, in *Learning from Las Vegas*, the uses of mixed media in architecture, including bold representational kinds of architecture, to create impact and identity—indeed, to be perceived at all—from highways and over parking lots, day and night. In the landscape of the auto age a picture is worth a thousand forms.

In that book we concentrated on the techniques rather than the content of commercial vernacular architecture to help us learn how to design our own architecture. In learning from Las Vegas in this way we were not promoting manipulative giant corporatism or even acquiescing to it, as many of our critics—usually architects of the political left in Europe and those of the aesthetic right in the United States—would have it, any more than our Modern architectural grandfathers promoted exploitative free-market capitalism in learning from the industrial vernacular of their day, or than the same critics, if analyzing Versailles or il Gesú, would be advocating a return to absolutism or the Counter-Reformation. Separating technique from content is a traditional and still useful method of analysis and criticism of old or new art, high or low design.

The content of the symbolism of commercial sprawl is different from that of the traditional city, but the commercial messages of the Strip, although bolder to suit our coarser sensibilities and the more gross tempos of our time, are hardly more promotional than the messages on the palaces and cathedral in the piazza promoting civic and religious ideals and power, when you understand the iconography of these forms. Nor is the popular art of the Strip necessarily more promotional than the high design of the "masterly, correct, and magnificent play of masses" of the corporate headquarters, now that big business has taken over the "progressive" symbolism of orthodox Modern architecture. We ourselves often feel less uncomfortable with the crass commercial advertising on the roadside than we do with some of the subtle and tasteful persuasion inherent in the Modern formalist symbolism that pervades corporate architecture, including that of the industrial-military complex. We think that the sources of many of the visual problems of the roadside commercial environment are more economic, social, and cultural than aesthetic—stemming from the low economic status of some roadside communities, from the bad habits of Americans prone to littering and to "public squalor," and from the varying taste cultures of a multiethnic, heterogeneous society.

Abstract Expressionism and Pop Art
Pop Art in the sixties turned our sensibilities toward the commercial Strip as the painting of the decade before it confirmed our interpretation of the piazza. I have explained how we looked at the piazza in that decade in the same way that we looked at an Abstract Expressionist painting, and how this limited our vision of the urban landscape. The Pop artists opened up our eyes and our minds by showing us again the value of

representation in painting, and bringing us thereby to association as an element of architecture. They also showed us the value of familiar and conventional elements by juxtaposing them in new contexts in different scales to achieve new meanings perceived along with their old meanings. Definitions of architecture now included meaning via association as well as expression—a term of the fifties—via perception. And these artists held, we realized later, an ironic view in their love-hate relationship with their vulgar commercial subject matter, paralleling ours toward our ordinary commercial architecture; they made seeing Las Vegas easier, while being still a little uneasy. And now the photorealists of the seventies, whose subject matter is the urban landscape, paint Las Vegas, enhancing the ordinary and beautifying the spectacular.

Vitruvius and Gropius
My third comparison, in my attempt to justify architecture as the decoration of shelter, is between Vitruvius and Gropius. (I use the proper noun Gropius in this comparison to stand for orthodox Modern architecture in general and because of its alliteration.) You will recall the traditional Vitruvian definition of architecture in the words of Sir Henry Wooton: Architecture is firmness, commodity, and delight. The twentieth-century paraphrase of this definition might be: Architecture is structure, program, and expression. (Jean Labatut used to add: shake well before using.) Orthodox Modern architects, if not Walter Gropius then his followers, would significantly alter the Vitruvian juxtaposition of elements. Using the same words, they would have said: Structure and program *are* architecture. When you get structure and program right, expressive architecture will be the automatic result. You shouldn't try for beauty, if you

would, indeed, mention that word; architectural quality, the spatial and expressive quality of a building, comes out of the harmonious solution of structural and functional problems. Architecture became frozen process. Certainly the aesthetic element in a Vitruvian triad could not derive from appliqué ornament or from symbolism. Architecture could not represent beauty, it could only be.

It is obvious there is no ornament on Gropius's building of the mid-twenties for the Bauhaus in Dessau, but it is hard to believe its form is merely a result of process—of, as Gropius claimed, "our advance from the vagaries of mere architectural caprice to the dictates of structural logic."[2] This building is really a sensitive and effective reworking of an industrial architectural vocabulary of steel frame, glass walls, and flowing space, an adaptation of an existing industrial vernacular architecture of simple geometric forms. It is, indeed, a symbolic building, symbolic of industrial process and advanced technology, whose effect derives in part from the affective properties of its industrial forms. Gropius was doing something different from what he said. There is nothing wrong with this because architects' theories and work often don't correspond; the important thing is that the work be effective. But it is significant, I think, that although Gropius vehemently denied that the Bauhaus could "propagate any 'style,' system, dogma, formula, or vogue," and claimed "a 'Bauhaus Style' would have been a confession of failure and a return to that very stagnation and devitalizing inertia which I had called it into being to combat,"[3] he did what architects and artists inevitably do. They intuitively choose a formal vocabulary, an order, a system, a convention, and then adapt it (sometimes avowedly) to their own uses. The Modern

movement, whatever was said, picked an existing vocabulary of forms, as the Renaissance masters chose the Classical Roman orders, and as we are contemplating the contemporary commercial vernacular.

Of course there were other sources for the forms and symbols of Modern architecture of the heroic period, derived from fine art as well as vernacular art, Cubist painting being an obvious one. Le Corbusier, almost uniquely among the theorists of the Modern movement, admitted to his formalistic adaptations of Cubism and existing mechanical and industrial forms. He was frankly enamored of midwestern American grain elevators which he illustrated in *Towards a New Architecture* in the twenties, he painted Cubist compositions and liked steamships and automobiles. He also illustrated the early Christian basilica of S. Maria in Cosmedin in Rome, focusing on the severe, white, almost Cubist marble furniture in the sanctuary. It is significant that Le Corbusier's architecture of that period looked more like the midwestern grain elevators, steamships, and automobiles illustrated in his book than like the altar of S. Maria in Cosmedin. Why? Because S. Maria was symbolically wrong if formally right, whereas the other precedents were formally and symbolically appropriate. Le Corbusier admittedly employed a formal vocabulary that he adapted and used symbolically to a significant degree, taking existing forms and changing their context. Despite the revolutionary rhetoric of his words, association relying on past experience was part of his architecture.

The main trouble with rejecting a formal system in architecture is that the architects who do so in order to avoid the dangers of formalism, ironically, become more prone to formalism.

Late-Modern fundamentalist architects accepted the words of the artists of the heroic period but not the substance of their work. By attempting to exclude symbolism and decoration, and by emphasizing spatial and structural expression, they ended with an architecture of abstract expressionism: pure but limited, it was soon not enough. So they substituted articulation for decoration—articulation through the exaggeration of structural and functional elements: structure protrudes rhythmically, functions protrude sensitively, clerestories pulsate on the roof. Articulation provides visual richness for form stripped of decoration. In frequent cases, orgies of complex and contradictory articulations produce dramatic expression that becomes expressionism in architecture. Ironically, the exclusion of applied ornament distorts the whole building into *an* ornament. The result is fundamentally more irresponsible than an appliqué of ornament over unarticulated forms would be. We feel that ours is not an era for expressive form and architectural space, but for flat manifestations of symbolism in the landscape—not for the Gallerie des Machines, but for S. Maria in Cosmedin and for the frescoes that were originally applied all over it inside.

There are architects currently working who adopt forms eclectically rather than distort forms expressionistically, but these architects still shun ornamental appliqué. I refer to how the New York Five, sometimes known as the Whites, employ symbolism by quite literally adopting the forms of Le Corbusier's houses of the twenties, and those of De Stijl. Our argument with them is their choice of symbolism: are Cubist industrial forms interesting or relevant for an eclectic style now? Certainly the rather dry abstractions of the houses of the New York Five lack the tension

and complexity that was essential to the original houses. We enjoy the unintended irony, however, that these houses are little different in manner from the copies of Norman manor houses and eighteenth-century farmhouses which traditional architects were designing in the twenties and which Le Corbusier and his followers were reacting against at that time. The Italian Rationalists, like the New York Five, are adopting a particular historical style which is minus ornament, and in our context, full of irony; they are a proclaimed Communist-architectural group who are adopting the monumental forms of the Modern, as opposed to the historical-traditional branch of the Italian Fascist style of the twenties and thirties, with meager rationalization on their part for their rather de Chirico images.

Neither the expressionistic nor the eclectic approaches described above leaves much room for function. It seems that in the end pure functionalism in architecture has been deflected toward something more decorative where function is distorted for the sake of functionalist-structuralist styling or ignored as it is abstracted into pure symbolism. The definition of architecture as shelter with symbols on it presupposes an acceptance of the functional doctrine, not a rejection of it—an augmentation of it for the sake of maintaining it. Why not admit the impossibility of maintaining pure functionalism in architecture and the almost inevitable contradictions between functional and aesthetic requirements in the same building, and then let function and decoration go their own separate ways so that functional requirements need not be distorted for unadmitted decorative aims.

Mies van der Rohe and McDonald's hamburger stands

Our fourth comparison, between Mies van der Rohe and McDonald's hamburger stands, is to justify a particular kind of symbolism in architecture. We refer to Mies's work here as representative of the best in Modern architecture and to remind ourselves that Modern architecture went to the industrial vernacular for inspiration and for its forms. Mies's work, after he came to the United States, is an even more literal adaptation of an industrial vernacular than Gropius's or Le Corbusier's. His almost Classical orders, derived from the exposed steel I-beams of a certain kind of American factory, were applied, as is well known, with artful contortion, almost as pilasters, to symbolize industrial process and pure order and yet to conform to acceptable standards of fire protection for nonindustrial buildings.

A "factory" of Mies's is vernacular art enhanced as fine art; a McDonald's on the strip is folk art derived from fine art. The history of art reveals many evolutions between low art and high art, back and forth: third movement themes in the sonata form are scherzo folk tunes, plastic madonnas are Baroque survivals. The parabolic arches of a McDonald's pavilion—illuminated yellow plastic—produce a bold and picturesque image, an effective gestalt from the context of a car driving down the strip, but in the mind they symbolize advanced engineering and good eats.

I refer to the classic version of the pavilion with "structural" arches, rather than the tasteful version with mansard roof, current in our era of roadside beautification. But the iconographic evolution of the McDonald's arch is complex. In its original version it is perhaps derived from Le Corbusier's project, in the twenties, for the Palace of the Soviets, where the arch, in contrast to those of McDonald's, actually supports the roof by cables, and from Eero Saarinen's St. Louis arch, itself a symbol for the "gateway to the West." An original manifestation of the parabolic arch was Eugène Freyssinet's hangars at Orly—an almost pure engineering solution for spanning a great distance at a great height to economically house big dirigibles—whose form made a great impression on Modern architects. The final manifestation of the parabolic arch in these evolutions between high art and low art, form and symbol, and among engineering, architecture, and sculpture, is a commercial sign—the reincarnation of two parabolic arches as siamese twins and a letter of the alphabet—the Big M.

To say that a factory is beautiful was shocking fifty years ago. Since then the paintings of Sheeler and Leger, the covers of *Fortune* magazine, the whole repertory and literature of Modern architecture and sculpture have made industrial forms easy to like. But the shock value of this revelation was of tremendous importance at the time. The history of art contains many examples of shock treatment as an aid to the understanding of art. *Épater le bourgeoisie* is a constant theme in the thinking, theorizing, and practice of Modern painters of the nineteenth century. The introduction of pagan Classical orders in fifteenth-century Florence must have had an effect on late Medieval critics akin to the indignation aroused among our orthodox critics by the "crass materialism of our mass society" represented in the commercial vernacular architecture we are looking at now. This kind of outrage does not apply to the exploitative labor practices associated with the beautiful cast-iron fronts of early capitalist loft buildings nor to the harsh realities behind the crafted forms and symbols of primitive villages so admired by the

same critics today. And these latter-day Moderns fail to see the ironic parallel between their outrage over the commercial vernacular and that of their Beaux-Arts predecessors over the industrial vernacular as a source for fine art fifty years ago. There was shock value in the Romantic discovery of the natural landscape—of daffodils in fields as a fit subject for poetry, and of peasant architecture—in the Hameau off the allée at Versailles, as there was in the transposition of common speech in the prose and poetry of James Joyce and T.S. Eliot. Returning to the ordinary, looking at the existing again, enhancing the conventional, are old ways of making new art.

My second comparison illustrated the affinity of late Modern architecture to the Abstract Expressionism of the fifties. This fourth comparison connects with the 1850s which were the heyday of the Industrial Revolution. Although we refer to the Machine Aesthetic of the twenties, we tend to forget how much of the symbolism of Modern architecture is based on industrial forms, if not industrial process, and how very obsolete this basis is. Everyone else knows the Industrial Revolution is dead. Why don't the architects? Is it not time for architects to connect with some new revolution, perhaps the electronic one? The existing commercial Strip with moving lights and signs involving representation and symbolism and meaning, and elements far apart in space to accommodate cars moving and parked, is as relevant to us now as were the factories with their industrial processes and functional programs several generations ago. Of course this conclusion is made with hindsight; as artists we found we liked the Strip before we analyzed why it seemed right.

Scarlatti and the Beatles
A connoisseur of music will pride himself on the

catholicity of his taste. He will play for his friends, on the same evening, records of Scarlatti *and* the Beatles. Why will this person accept in his own living room, where you would expect him to be not at all tolerant of intrusions on his sensibilities, what he will not accept in the landscape? Why will he be outraged by the local commercial strip at the edge of town, support sign control in the belief that the way to limit bad architecture is to limit the size of signs, and confidently join the local design review board as an architectural connoisseur too? Why will he condemn pop architecture and accept pop music? That Scarlatti will live one thousand years and the Beatles only fifty years is beside the point, and he knows it; there is room for, and need for, a hierarchy of musical forms in our lives. Why not the same thing for architectural forms in our landscapes?[4]

The answer is that our connoisseur clings to outmoded ideas about architecture as a whole. One of these ideas is that there is one dominant and correct canon of taste in our culture and that any art where this canon has not been followed is deviant and inferior. Herbert Gans has effectively countered this idea as a sociologist in his work on the relativity of taste and by his enumeration of the multiple taste cultures in our society;[5] in most fields and media other than those of architecture the heterogeneous quality and ethnic diversity of American culture is accepted and is considered one of the strengths of our culture.

Other ideas which influence our connoisseur are promoted by Modern architects and they concern aesthetic unity: simple forms and pure order are the only good, and the architect (and later it would be the planner) will lead the community toward these goals. Gropius advocated "total design," but we are ending up with total control—total control through design review boards which promote high design, exclude popular architecture and in the process discourage quality in any architecture and stultify the diversity and hierarchy which have always been part of a balanced and vital community architecture.

Plain and fancy architecture

As there is room for high design and popular art in the architecture of our communities, there is the need for plain and fancy styles of architecture. The strip, for instance, is the place not only for spectacular symbols, but also for conventional symbols. Most architectural complexes include hierarchies of architectural symbolism. They include original and special elements and conventional and ordinary elements—what we call plain and fancy styles—that are applied with a sense of appropriateness. The palazzo in an Italian town sits among its *contorni*—the name for the vegetables arranged beautifully around the meat in the serving platter at an important meal as well as for the plain architecture at the foot of fancy architecture. I am not advocating hierarchies based on a social caste system, but I am saying that an art school, for instance, is not a cathedral, and that most architecture in a normal context should be plain. Most Modern architects have tended to lose a sense of appropriateness in their urban renewal piazzas and in the often strident college campuses and towns where Modern architecture dominates. This is a plea for a symbolism of the ordinary in the ornament applied to shelter.

We have written, in *Learning from Las Vegas*, of our propensity as architects for modest architecture based at first on necessity, on our experience as a little firm with small jobs and limited budgets, then on an intuition that our situation had a general significance, and finally on a conviction that ours is not an era for heroic or pure architectural statements. Rhetoric for our landscape, when it is appropriate, will come from a less formal and more symbolic medium than pure architecture—perhaps from combinations of signs and sculpture and moving lights which decorate and represent. The source for our fancy architecture is in the conventions of the commercial strip. Its prototype is not the spatial Baroque monument, but the Early Christian basilica, that plain barn smothered in frescoes, the decorated shed par excellence. Ours is also not an era for expensive buildings: our national budgets do not support the architectural glories of a Parthenon or a Chartres, our collective heart is not in architecture, our collective values direct us in other paths, sometimes social, often military, and our technology and our labor systems promote standard systems of conventional construction.

These are our reasons for advocating and for trying to design shelter with decoration on it: shelter as a manifestation of systems building, conventional in its form and ordinary in its symbolism, always plain and never fancy. But also shelter as a grid for decoration—ordinary in its symbolism if a plain style is appropriate (and it usually is) and heroic in its symbolism if (and only if) a fancy style is appropriate. Function and structure can now go their own ways without regard to rhetoric, and our glories can come perhaps from mass housing, universal and efficient as a structural shelter, but parochial and diverse in its ornamental and symbolic appliqué. This is a way to be sensitive to the practical needs and the expressive wants of the many different people in the world.

Learning the Wrong Lessons from the Beaux-Arts
Denise Scott Brown

This essay, untitled, was first published as part of a forum in **Oppositions 8,** Spring 1977–78, pp. 171–172. An expanded version, under the present title, was delivered at the Beaux-Arts Conference at the Architectural Association in London in May 1978.

The bizarre union of the Museum of Modern Art and the Beaux-Arts is spawning misinterpretations of architectural history as individual protagonists realign themselves to meet the new alliance. In the reshuffle, the Beaux-Arts itself is being reinterpreted to teach, I fear, the wrong lessons.

The Modern architectural establishment is picking up the Beaux-Arts for several wrong reasons: for its elitist programs ("history," "urbanism," and "pro bono publico," in the catalog preface sound like code words for upper-class architecture), for its good drawings, and to find some way of accepting, at last, the fifteen-year-old critique of the Modern movement without appearing to cave in; particularly without having to accept the call of Modern architecture's critics for social relevance, openness to the pluralist aesthetic, and understanding of the everyday environment. Beaux-Arts will enable Arthur Drexler, for instance, to "reexamine our architectural pieties," as he puts it, without having to heed Herbert Gans or learn from Las Vegas.

There are better reasons for·learning from the Beaux-Arts:

Professionalism
Beaux-Arts practitioners had enormous professional skill. This was partly owing to the rigorous training they received. Partly, it was engendered and supported by the confident and masterful world view inherited by the nineteenth-century rich men's sons who became architects. But mostly, Beaux-Arts expertise and skills were a heritage built up in Classical architecture over two hundred years of evolutionary, rather than revolutionary, change.

Programs
Despite the elitism of their school projects, Beaux-Arts architects evolved and handled new programs for new building types that resulted during the nineteenth century from the Industrial Revolution. Available Classical formulas and accepted planning processes were made to accommodate railroad stations, public libraries, art galleries, power stations, and even skyscrapers.

Techniques
Beaux-Arts architects unashamedly stressed the "Art of design." They were technically competent owing to their long and rigorous training, but they regarded knowledge of construction and detailing as unremarkable because they relied upon traditional and accepted ways of doing things. These ways were abandoned with the revolutionary changes of the Modern movement. Modern architects are much given to talking and thinking about technology, and the movement's early innovators, in that their training was traditional, were able to back their talk with technical and craft skills. Later generations, who faced the new materials and methods of the twentieth century without this training, tended, for ideological reasons, to overestimate the "imperatives of technology" in the construction industry. Particularly in America, where skills training was reduced when architectural education was elevated to graduate level, architects lost their technical skills and are still having trouble regaining them. Of course, Beaux-Arts architects drew very well too. This was part of their technical and professional competence as well as part of their art. But we should not see drawing as their only technical competence nor the only one we can learn from. We have yet to evolve tried-and-true techniques for using the conventional building methods of

our time as suavely as the Beaux-Arts architects used theirs.

Aesthetics
Part of Beaux-Arts technical competence lay in design. Beaux-Arts architects accepted well-defined aesthetic criteria for the composition of the formal elements of buildings. These criteria guided the design process and provided explicit standards for architectural criticism. No such shared standards exist now, or at least none of them have been explicated. The average school jury today flounders on undefined territory when it touches on aesthetics and, where aesthetic certainty exists in the profession, for example on design review boards, it supports a deadening architectural mediocrity. Our Modern means of aesthetic control, "total design," aesthetic zoning, and design review, are arguably more coercive than were the orders, massing, or axial planning. If we are looking for aesthetic unity, perhaps we should try to discover our own shared aesthetic values; but there is probably no possibility of a broad-based aesthetic consensus for us today. Perhaps we should not seek it, but rather try to enjoy our diversity.

Relation to the city, relation to history
These often are, but need not be, code words for ruling-class architecture set in plazas. We can learn other lessons from Beaux-Arts urbanism and historicism. For example, Burnham conceived of Chicago as a set of urban systems long before today's urban systems analysts. Beaux-Arts urbanists and architects dealt in multiple scales. Their urbanism suggests a view of the city as a plurality and an ordered complexity. Their familiarity and ease with history enabled them to accept the concept of multiplicity and to take a richer, more inclusive view of architecture and its possibilities than did the Moderns.

Because they considered themselves part of a continuous historical tradition, Beaux-Arts architects did not feel the need to return to first principles for every problem and could build on the experience of others.

Symbolism
Beaux-Arts architects and urban designers who used the architectural symbolism of the Classical tradition knew that its meaning would be shared by their clients and a large public. Modern architects deny the existence of symbolism in their work and hope that "the people" will eventually understand the new architecture. In the twenties, faced with Modern Art and the International Style, some Beaux-Arts architects adapted their decorative systems to Cubism. The resultant Art Deco architecture was the Beaux-Arts' reply to the Modern movement. Art Deco was the last gasp of the craft of architecture.

Education
Beaux-Arts education influenced world architectural education and still does. It gave us the studio system and juries, learning-by-doing and, through the charrette and the atmosphere around the Ecole, learning by camaraderie and high endeavor. Unfortunately, later versions of the system, particularly in America, seemed to pick up the Ecole's authoritarianism and miss its countervailing high spirits as well as its skills training. But Modern revisionists who decry the faults in the system risk chucking out the baby with the bath water. Studio education is a major contribution of the Beaux-Arts to us.

In sum, we should not yearn for Beaux-Arts programs or for the society that commissioned those programs, but should rather learn from what Beaux-Arts architects did very well. We should learn from their ability to work freely within an accepted formula or set of formulas, lessons about breadth and openness, order, suavity, skill and symbolism, that will be useful for a new, evolutionary architectural era.

MOMA is a Johnny-come-lately to the Beaux-Arts scene and is there for the wrong reasons. Even in the recent past MOMA was a pompier[1] of the Modern movement and an arch enemy of the Beaux-Arts. Those who continued or tried to recreate an interest in the Beaux-Arts had to contend with the architectural establishment that MOMA represents. A turnaround in thinking is assumed by Drexler when he states in the catalog preface that Modern architecture's "messianic fervor seems naive when it is not actually destructive," and that "Italian design in the sixties replaced moral imperatives with irony and humor." This change of heart was ardently fought by MOMA when it was first suggested by some social planners and a few architects; yet such a change had to come about before MOMA could accept the Beaux-Arts. MOMA still cannot accept the pluralism of the everyday landscape, or the message of Gans, or the question, "Who decides what is pro bono publico?" Therefore, I fear that current establishment interest in the Beaux-Arts will be a fad and an evasion—a continuation of Modern purism in a new guise. This would be unfortunate. A thoughtful reassessment of Beaux-Arts architecture could be a stimulus to new architectural sensibilities for our time, and an important contribution to a nondoctrinaire, humanist, late twentieth-century architecture.

Learning the Right Lessons from the Beaux-Arts
Robert Venturi

This was an illustrated lecture delivered at the conclusion of the Beaux-Arts Conference at the Architectural Association in London in May 1978. It was first published in **Architectural Design** magazine, London, vol. 49, no. 1, 1979, pp. 23–31.

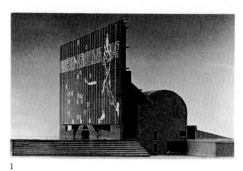

1

Is Robert Middleton a sadist? He scheduled for this conference a ten-course Edwardian banquet served by an Escoffier. I refer to the preceding lectures—to be followed by rice pudding for dessert—that is, this lecture on the work of Venturi and Rauch. Is Robin trying to prove Victor Hugo's thesis, eloquently described earlier by Neil Levine, concerning the imminent death of architecture, by juxtaposing the luscious architecture of the first decades of this century with some frugal examples of the last decades?

I shall talk as an architect, not as a theoretician, but as a Modern architect—not a Postmodern or neo-Beaux-Arts architect. Our work evolves from the recent past. In honoring our grandfathers on this occasion, I am not compelled to kill our fathers: I sometimes think my next text book should be called *Modern Architecture is Almost All Right*. So in a specific way we consider ourselves part of the Modern movement, evolving within it. But in a general way architects are always modern, modern with a small "m"; I think the architects of the Ecole des Beaux-Arts, in all its periods, considered themselves modern.

I am a Modern architect who was a student of Jean Labatut at Princeton, who himself went to the Ecole des Beaux-Arts and taught by its methods. Young architects here will hardly imagine how contemptible Princeton was to the outside world when I was there in the middle forties, what a reactionary backwater it was considered in that Bauhaus era dominated by the Harvard School of Design. But I am grateful to Labatut and Princeton for giving me things I couldn't get elsewhere then, things enumerated by Denise Scott Brown yesterday in her evaluation of Beaux-Arts education. That's where I learned I was part of a historical evolution, where I learned about aesthetic and critical

tolerance and the fragility of ideas; that today's rear guard can be tomorrow's avant-garde.

Before talking about our current work, I shall mention another teacher of mine at Princeton, Donald Drew Egbert, an art historian, who acknowledged the Ecole des Beaux-Arts in the late thirties. I shall read part of my introduction to his book on the history of the Grand Prix which he began in the forties but which is only about to be published posthumously, edited by David Van Zanten:

I took Egbert's course on the history of Modern architecture four times. I sat in on it as a freshman, was a projectionist as a sophomore, took it for credit as a junior, and taught it as a graduate student assistant. Other architecture students at Princeton over several decades were also drawn to it, became devotés, and were influenced by it.

Egbert saw Beaux-Arts architecture as a part of the complex of 19th- and early 20th-century civilization. His eyes were open to realities of that time that more doctrinaire historians, bent on proving points, could not see. For Egbert the influence of the Ecole des Beaux-Arts was an important part of the architectural history of the 19th and 20th centuries; this was not obvious 35 years ago. For Sigfried Giedion at that time the Beaux-Arts was what he called a transitory fact. Although history was not bunk for Giedion as it was for most Moderns in that period from the 40s through the 60s, it was subject to simplified and personal interpretation that allowed as constituent facts (this is again Giedion's phrase) only some of the historical antecedents of Modern architecture. Some Baroque architecture he recognized, as well as early industrial forms, but he excluded as transitory facts other antecedents, the main one being the architecture of the Ecole des Beaux-Arts.

2

Henri Labrouste he acknowledges in Space, Time and Architecture, *I recall, mostly for his use of cast-iron. Egbert's history of Modern architecture was inclusive, a complex evolution rather than a dramatic revelation made up of social and symbolic, as well as formal and technological, imperatives.*

Never doctrinaire, he was seldom in the mainstream. He focused on Beaux-Arts architecture at a time when Giedion's spatial technological Bauhaus view predominated in art history. His book called Social Radicalism in the Arts *countered another important trend in Modern architectural history, that pressed by Russell Hitchcock and Philip Johnson, whose influential work on the International Style had de-emphasised the radical social content of the Modern movement and set the stage for the dominance of formalism*

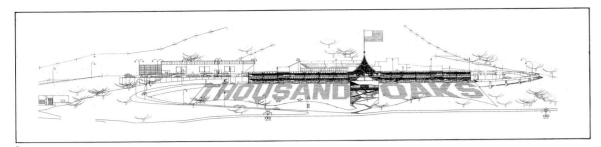

1 Model, billdingboard, National Football Hall of Fame
  project, 1967
2 Interior perspective of gallery
3 Proposal for town hall for Thousand Oaks, California,
  1969. Elevation
4 Site plan

3

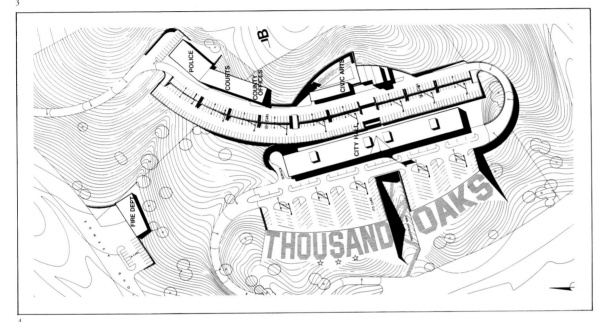

4

Here is our Football Hall of Fame project of eleven years ago, a later evolution of architecture as book, described by Neil Levine in his analysis of the Bibliothèque St. Geneviève—referring especially to its facade (fig. 1). We originally described this museum dedicated to the history of football as a "billdingboard." The inside, however, was to be a church more than a museum, containing a barrel-vaulted nave with side chapels paralleling the main facade. The billboard was to be electronically operated so that varying messages—pictorial, diagrammatic, and verbal—could be flashed on it. Its location, significantly, was not off a Place du Panthéon, but a vast parking lot, opposite a stadium in New Jersey. Its foreground is a reflecting pool and a *tapis vert* where you can have a picnic near your car. It has other symbolic elements: the entrance on the central axis of the *tapis vert* is shaped like a football and the outdoor stairs are rather Baroque.

71

in Modern architecture in America that still exists. Egbert studied history to search for truth, never to prove a point.

Another irony of Egbert's position today is that the Museum of Modern Art has now adopted the Ecole des Beaux-Arts. In the takeover the original protagonist whose unpopular stand was ignored for decades by the Modern architectural establishment has not been recognised, although two of the three historians who assisted in the exhibition, David Van Zanten and Neil Levine, were former students at Princeton. So it is significant perhaps that you have three Princetonians at this conference on the Beaux-Arts. Egbert's openness had a later gratifying effect on me. I have learned to expect, when I meet an author whose works have influenced me, or a former teacher who has meant much to me, that he will almost always be unable

to accept the direction my work has taken and will not see himself in it. This was not the case with Egbert, and I value very much a letter he wrote me as a former teacher soon before he died, in appreciation of work of mine. He also wrote in that letter: "of course the difference between an historian and an artist is that the historian has to try to be objective, although he can never succeed completely, whereas the good artist/architect has to be a man of utter conviction." I think Egbert himself combined those traits.

I said I was here as an architect so I shall get on with illustrating our work. My first examples will not be current, but I think they will respond to some of what has been said here in the last few days about the Ecole des Beaux-Arts and Classicism.

The barrel vault inside (fig. 2) is a vast movie screen on which are projected figures of football players—Baroque figures moving through their spatial apotheosis, more Tiepolo than "School of Athens." You might recall that in chapels are real relics—Knute Rockne's sweat shirt, for instance. We were trying for a building for the automobile era of vast spaces—hostile asphalt parking lots—of a moving point of view; a building which cannot depend on pure forms with architectural articulation on the outside, but rather on representation; on the building as sign.

Our competition entry of about ten years ago for a town hall for Thousand Oaks, California, is another example of architecture as a shelter with messages on it (figs. 3, 4). It is a building on a hill, to be "read" from a distance—from the Ventura Freeway several miles away. Close up it is a conventional building in the Mies van der Rohe style of exposed steel; from a distance what counts is a sign which evolves from a tower at the center of the long, low building. This sign is an American flag—the biggest in the world. Another sign is on the vast berm of the parking lot saying "Thousand Oaks" in flowers. Under the fourth, fifth, and sixth letters of "Thousand" are stars. I have noticed that the composition of this building is similar to that of the 1825 Grand Prix by Louis Duc for an Hôtel de Ville, now exhibited at the AA—that of a long narrow building with a tower in the center; in our tower there is some late Medieval tracery of Miesian steel sections representing the veins of an oak leaf.

Here is a building with a sign which dominates its architecture (figs. 5, 6). It is a small shopping center for a desert town whose mural depicts a green New England landscape which many people in this town are nostalgic for.

This six-foot-high book in our library at Oberlin College (fig. 7), covering an ugly mechanical detection device at the exit, I now see as a symbol of Victor Hugo's "Ceci tuera cela" as interpreted by Neil Levine earlier at this conference.

Here is a ghostly representation of Benjamin Franklin's house—a steel-frame construction painted pale lavender, built over the archaeological foundations of his house, and outlining the form of the house—since we were not able to accurately reconstruct the house itself in this memorial to Franklin (fig. 8). Might not this ghost also symbolize the death of architecture as predicted by Hugo?

And here are garlands, to please Peter Smithson,

on a wooden lattice-appliqué in the renovation of a jewelry shop with a low budget in Atlantic City (fig. 9).

I have been discussing projects which I think connect with some of the discussions in this conference on the symbolic bases of the architecture of the Ecole des Beaux-Arts. Now I would like to look at some of our buildings from

another viewpoint to illustrate that a lot of what we design has a Classical basis in form and symbol. The definition of Classical architecture on which I base this thesis includes the following elements: compositional unity and symmetry, big scale, and hierarchies of conventional elements—although combinations of these elements can be contradicted through Classical Mannerism.

5

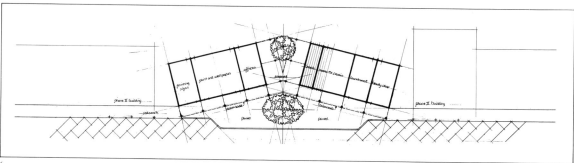

6

7

5 Merbisc Mart project, California City, California, 1970. Elevation
6 Plan
7 Six-foot high book in Allen Memorial Art Museum Library, Oberlin College, Ohio, 1973
8 Franklin Court, Philadelphia, Pennsylvania, 1972–1976

8

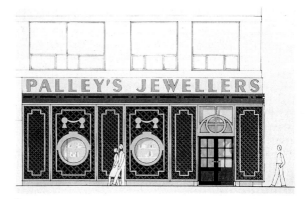

9

My mother's house in Chestnut Hill, built in 1964, is a broken pediment with some applied ornament which articulates the central axis of the composition and enhances the scale (figs. 10, 11, 12). It might seem funny that I thought of the rear pavilion at the Villa Maser (sans curved plan) when I designed the facade, and of the Porta Pia when I superimposed the mouldings at the entrance, but these forms and elements constituted daring ornamentation in the early sixties. This house has a central core containing fireplace, chimney, and stair, as well as entrance. This is not a Classical configuration, because Classical plans usually contain space at the center; but the core generates axial symmetry. The symmetry disintegrates however, at the edges, to accommodate particular requirements of the plan. We think setting up an order and then breaking it is in the Mannerist tradition of Classical architecture.

74

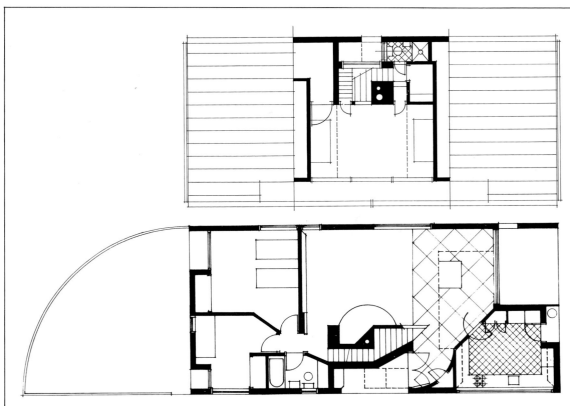

10

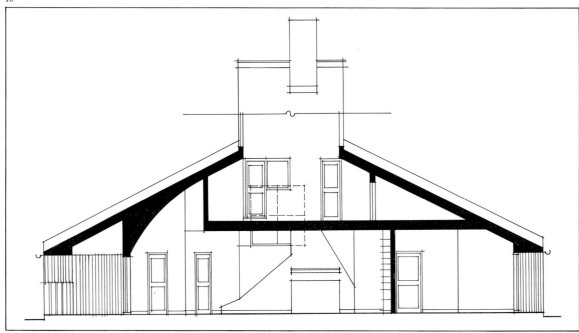

11

75

12

13

14

15

Guild House housing for the elderly in an urban site was constructed a little later (figs. 13, 14, 15). It too has a symmetrical plan with a central core, and its symmetry falls off at the ends a little. In elevation its six stories of virtually identical apartments are consistently stacked, but their ever-vertical rhythm and additive composition are contradicted by the series of balconies at the center which reads as a continuous shaft capped by the arched window of the common room on the top floor, which is exceptional in plan. On the ground floor in the center is the entrance to the building (with a column in the middle—there *is* Classical precedent for this). These central elements combine base, shaft, and cap—a giant order which plays against the minor order of the six stories. The white stripe of brick was daring in the early sixties; it suggests an attic story and creates a scale also beyond that of the individual story.

The Brant house in Greenwich, Connecticut, of the early seventies (figs. 16, 17, 18): again, symmetrical plans and elevations which diminish in consistency as they approach the edges, and again, a big scale for a relatively small building through combining different ceiling heights (reflected in the elevations and hierarchies of window sizes). Since this is an American country house, you enter via the garage and work your way to the center, which is a kitchen rather than a hall. This house has an overall pattern outside in green glazed brick—not very Classical here.

The Wike house project of 1969 for the country outside of Philadelphia (figs. 19, 20) combines Classical-Mannerist elements similar to those just described, including a curved facade generated from a point outside the plan which enhances the scale of the building and its centrality and unity.

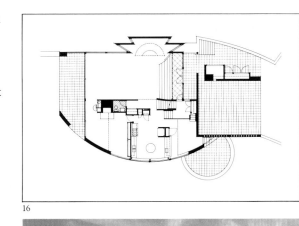
16

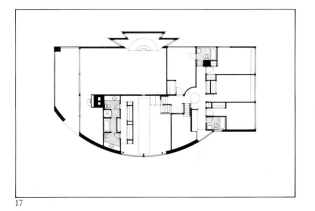
17

77

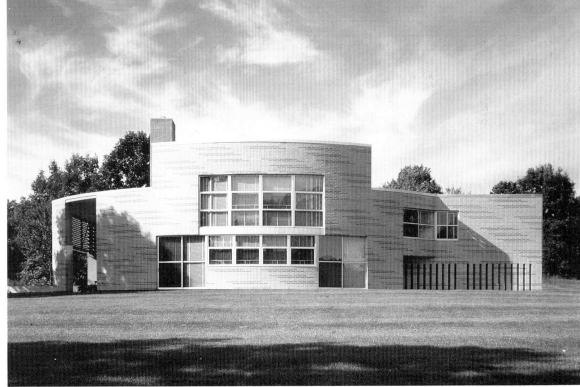
18

Fighting your way into this house is an adventure involving several right angles in your path while you skirt the central axis via the lower loggia and through the open stair which is also a tunnel—almost worthy of Lutyens. The four elevations are each different and reflect our enthusiasms for Vanbrugh—front and right side; Elizabethan manors—left side; and Bauhaus functionalism—the rear. We shook well before serving.

When we designed these two houses on the moor on Nantucket, it helped to think of the temples by the sea at Selinunte (fig. 21). They are pedimented temples, more Roman than Greek however, employing some architectural elements indigenous to the island of Nantucket. Besides being conventional, these houses are symmetrical with irregularities and big in scale beyond their size; the double-hung windows for instance, are bigger than you normally expect. We worked very hard to make these buildings look ordinary, if monumental. The house with the Palladian window is a little less ordinary than the other one.

I think of the more recent Tucker house also as both Classical and classic (figs. 22, 23, 24). Classical because of its central focus and essential symmetry and its monumentality considering its small size; classic because of the conventional quality of its form and its elements. To an American at least, it might look like a child's drawing of a house (figs. 25, 26, 27). It is shingled to meld into its wooded setting, and the living room is at the top to be in the treetops (fig. 28). The central core including fireplace, stairs, and storage replicates the silhouette of the house, and the walls inside are painted very light green to enhance the reflected light from the trees.

78

19

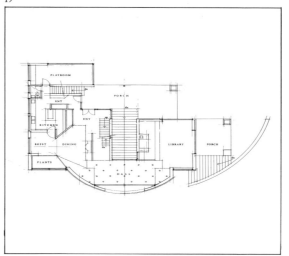
20

21

19 Wike house project, Devon, Pennsylvania, 1969. Model, front
20 Plan, ground floor
21 Trubeck and Wislocki houses, Nantucket, Massachusetts, 1970–1971

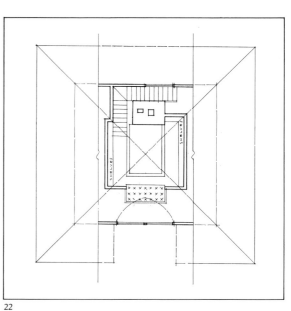
22

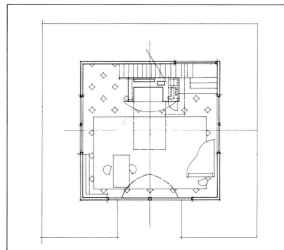
23

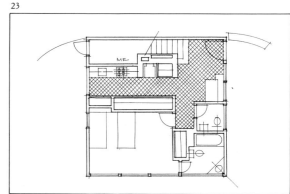
24

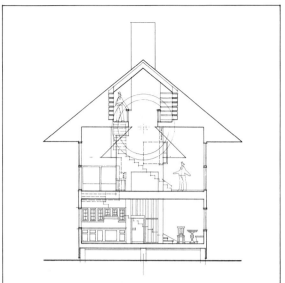

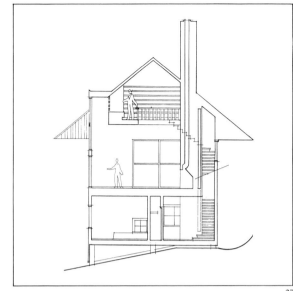

25

26

27

22 Tucker house, Katonah, New York, 1974. Plan, third floor
23 Plan, second floor
24 Plan, first floor
25 Elevation
26 Section
27 Section
28 Front view

28

The recent Brant ski house in Aspen, Colorado, is also a tower in the woods (figs. 29, 30, 31). Symbolically its elevation and setting on the side of a rocky mountain suggest a diminutive Arts and Crafts abode in a children's book, but its scale is terrible—I refer to Italian *terribilitá*. The inside is crammed with complex spaces like that of a yacht, but this is reflected outside on the symmetrical bulk of the house only in the irregular shapes, sizes, and placement of windows. The main room is the wooden groin-vaulted attic containing window niches for sitting and sleeping in.

The project for the D'Agostino house also combines axial and broken symmetry with a strong central focus and local symbolism (fig. 32). This house is in the Dutch country of upper New York State, and we were interested in making its architecture representational as well as expressive. You enter through the garage in this rural site in a cold climate, and the Classical axial plan, as always in our work, combines with Modern flowing space.

Another building done a long time ago: Fire Station No. 4 in Columbus, Indiana (fig. 33). While most of the buildings I have been describing have been Classical ducks, this is a Classical decorated shed. (You will remember the designation we made in *Learning from Las Vegas*: ducks are buildings whose whole form is sculptural and symbolic, and decorated sheds are those which are essentially plain shelter with applied decoration and symbolism.) This economical shed contains a distortedly symmetrical composition around a central axis in the form of a hose tower, and its glazed brick ornament juxtaposes ideal proportions upon the facade that the real functions inside the building would not permit. The sign looked big in 1964.

80

29

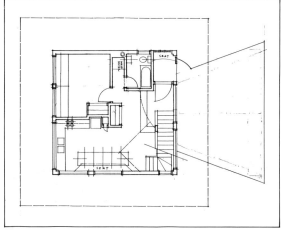

30

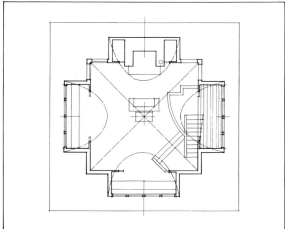

31

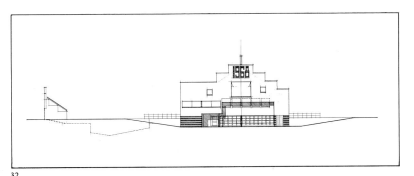

32

The Classical architecture of the Ecole des Beaux-Arts always employed a conventional vocabulary of elements; we do here too, although our elements are symbolically ordinary rather than monumental.

I came across the next illustration while going through our slide collection to prepare this lecture. It is the diagram illustrated in *Learning from Las Vegas*, published in 1972, of the duck and the decorated shed (fig. 34). Do you notice the pedimented facade of the AT&T Building? Elsewhere in that book we suggest a vast sign for a motel on a highway with the silhouette of a Chippendale highboy. Who would have guessed that our fantasy for a sign on a strip would end up years later as a corporate facade on Madison Avenue?

81

33

34

The addition to the Allen Memorial Art Museum at Oberlin College is a decorated shed added to a Classical building (fig. 35). The new building is independent of the old one in its form; that is, its form is symmetrical and doesn't inflect in its shape toward the old one. However, it does inflect in the location of its windows, which are not symmetrically placed and which imply a connection by their configuration. Harmony is achieved otherwise through combinations of elements old and new that are analogous or contrasting in their forms and symbolism. For instance, the symbolism of the shed as a whole is different from that of the villa; to an American it looks like an ordinary building of around 1940, but its overhang is analogous to that of the villa. The polychromy of the new wing is similar to that of the old, but the overall system of patterning is different from that of the bays of panels ornamenting the old building. The symbolism of the more recessed new wing is that of an ordinary, if generously scaled, loft building (this part of the building contains artists' studios), although its fenestration and overhang are consistent with that of the rest of the building.

The single "Ionic" column—referred to as an Ironic column in our office—is a sculptural incident at the rear of the building (fig. 36). I wish *Progressive Architecture* magazine with its erring sense of appropriateness had not put it on the cover, thereby misrepresenting its context and incidental function. This illustration shows the column in its obscure location.

In our sketch design for the Science Museum for downtown Charlotte, North Carolina (figs. 37, 38, 39, 40), we employ a black box; that is, a loft building without windows, to permit almost theatrical kinds of exhibition inside depending on

82

35

36

sophisticated artificial lighting effects. To make this kind of building not look like a supermarket is a matter of scale, ornament, and symbolism. There are exceptional shop windows in front along Main Street containing "living exhibitions," and a frieze above in the form of a moving electronic sign giving messages about ecological happenings in the world to passersby. In the center of this elevation on the roof is a big statue of a dinosaur, like the lion on the facade of Syon House. Around the corner from the Piranesian naturalistic entrance a sculptural landscape depicting the South Carolina terrain from inland

mountains to coastal marshes intrudes on this otherwise Miesian box.

Another decorated shed, with a duck on top Classically centered, but on a symmetrical facade: this is a jazz club, another low, square, black box, planned for Houston, Texas—a building to make an impact on a commercial strip. Our client wanted a big boat (figs. 41, 42). The exterior in a later development became a museum—a symbol of a museum whose Classical pediments and pilasters and capitals are picked out in neon, blinking alternately, and whose

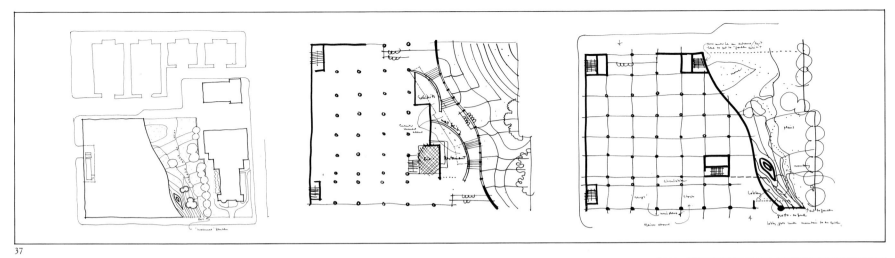

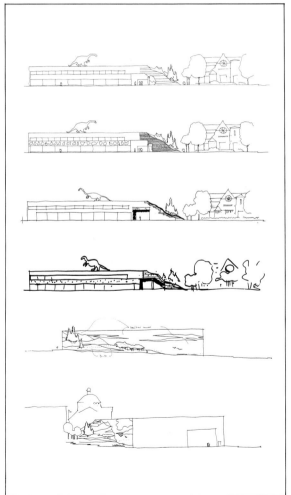

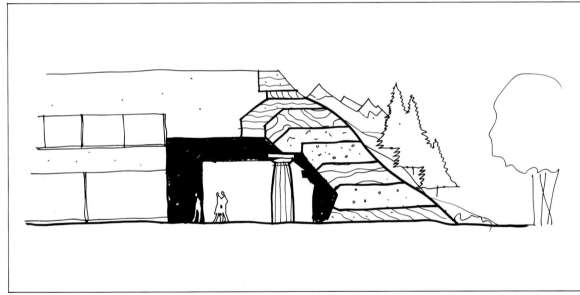

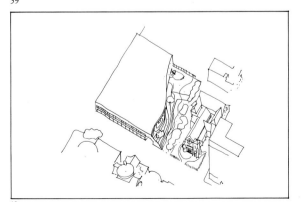

35 View of Allen Memorial Art Museum, Oberlin College, in 1977
36 Interior, Ellen Johnson Gallery of Modern Art, Allen Memorial Art Museum, Oberlin College
37 Science Museum project, Charlotte, North Carolina, 1977. Plans
38 Elevation studies
39 Entry
40 Aerial view

niches contain figures of Scott Joplin and Jelly Roll Morton instead of Raphael and Rembrandt (fig. 43). This building certainly will qualify as Classical, and it will be a good advertisement from the highway too. The room with the bar inside has a barrel vault, and the room where the musicians play is like an eighteenth-century court theater. The Rococo ornament on the balconies will be in neon, and the ceilings of both rooms will be vast screens containing changing rear slide projections of great paintings appropriate for a museum. But this will be better than a regular museum because the projections will be bigger and brighter than the original art, and you can smoke and drink and touch in here. The parking lot outside will contain an axial *tapis vert* and big urns to punctuate its expanse.

The ISI building is under construction now (fig. 44). It is a conventional office building loft, square in plan with flexible space inside and horizontal strip windows. The BCBA rhythm of the polychromatic glazed-brick pattern creates a central focus on the facade. This pattern is juxtaposed on the constant AAA rhythm of the structural bays and the conventional strip windows, so that you have here a closed *and* an open system of composition.

The Marlborough Blenheim Hotel and Casino: The challenges of this project were to preserve a distinguished old building, the Blenheim Hotel, on the boardwalk in Atlantic City, by William Price, circa 1906—or to preserve the most important part of it—and to design an addition many times the size of the original building while at the same time not overwhelming it in its new context (fig. 45). We made the vast new hotel two contiguous conventional slabs which, by the slight curve of their plans and some slight variations in their silhouette, become a

84

41

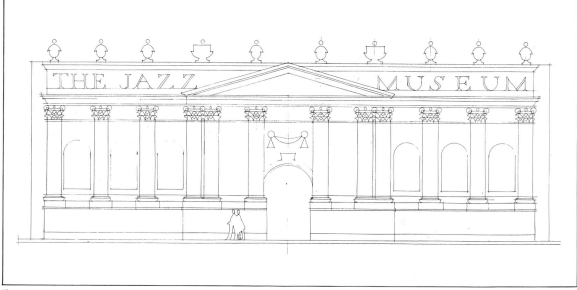

43

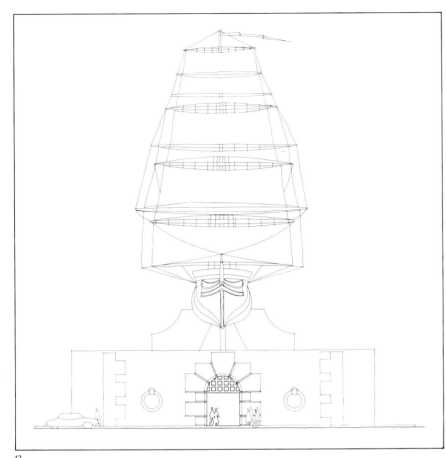

42

45

41 Nichol's Alley Jazz Club project, Scheme A, Houston,
   Texas, 1978. Section
42 Elevation
43 Jazz Club project, Scheme B, 1978
44 Institute for Scientific Information, Philadelphia,
   Pennsylvania, 1978
45 Marlborough Blenheim Hotel and Casino project, Atlantic
   City, New Jersey, 1977

44

background inflected toward the old building, enhancing its quality. The festoons radiating from the dome of the old building to the top of the new are like reflective beads which sparkle at night and further tie together the old and the new, the small and the big. The hanging gardens also tie together the hierarchical and axial composition and accommodate the people who don't want to mingle with the hoi polloi on the beach. Behind is a vast parking structure and the biggest gambling casino in the world. Unfortunately this project will not go ahead as we planned it.

Here is a recent project for a small branch bank in a community that likes "Colonial" architecture (fig. 46, 47). It is a decorated shed with big scale.

For the Brant house in Bermuda (figs. 48, 49, 50), we were requested by the clients and required by the community to design in the local eighteenth-century idiom with white stucco walls, dark green louvred shutters, stepped roofs for gathering rain water, and English Classical proportions and details of that period. All of these requirements seemed ecologically and symbolically sound for that place. Because of the irregular cliff site, this house is less formally unified than usual for us, but it still has a central pavilion from which larger wings generate. In the library are wooden Ionic pilasters and along the porch toward the sea are Tuscan Doric columns in wood that are stylized and simplified by being perfectly flat and visible only in silhouette—this to emphasize their symbolic function. The ramp-stair leading to the living room is made of alternating blocks of black and white marble as in Lutyens' Ednaston Hall. The axis of the wide stairway at the front door descending to the bedroom floor focuses on the surf below the cliff. If you look through a huge fan-light window you see the horizon of the sea beyond.

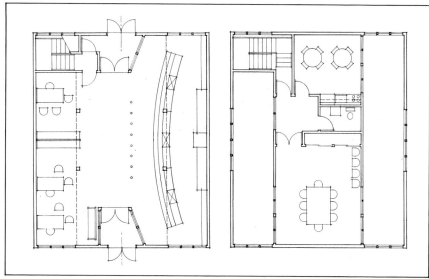

46

47

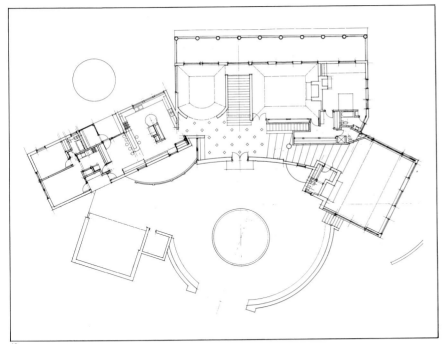

48

49

46 County Federal Savings project, Stratford, Connecticut, 1977. Plans
47 Elevations and section
48 Brant house, Tuckers Town, Bermuda, 1975. Plan
49 Elevations
50 View

50

Here is a house that won't be built because the client didn't like its design (figs. 51, 52). It is a decorated shed, a Classical shed—an economical Trianon in wood. Another little building with big scale—large elements including, literally, a giant order of pilasters. But all the Classical ornament is simplified, generalized, pictorialized, incorrect, and—it is our intention—witty. Why wit? Let me come back to that.

This outdoor mural for the side of a building is our suggestion for a small town in Pennsylvania where they wanted to enliven the side of a narrow street (fig. 53). It consists of porcelain-enamel panels with very bright colors set out from the wall and well lighted at night. The subject matter is a series of famous buildings in history. We think children would like it. I include it because it shows how we like to use ornament and symbolism without architectural content, or, when there is architectural subject matter, how we are free in our use of styles. I enjoy the mid-nineteenth-century painting by Thomas Cole called *The Architect's Dream,* and I think it is timely now: a return to Style, yes; a battle of styles, no. Yet it looks as if one is brewing. Many styles relating to many taste cultures is OK with us. We have learned this from Las Vegas and its Strip and from Herbert Gans, the sociologist. We can like Vivaldi *and* the Beatles and believe we need the same eclectic range of Pop and high art in our urban environments for the sake of variety and vitality. In a wide context, it's a question of is it vital, not is it great?

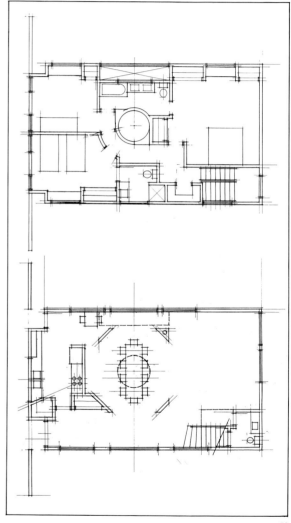

51 House project, Absecon, New Jersey, 1977. Elevations
52 Plans
53 Outdoor mural project, Scranton, Pennsylvania, 1976

88

SCALE 3/16" = 1'-0"

90

54 Eclectic House Series project, 1978. Doric
55 Basic Tuscan Doric
56 A garden party of styles

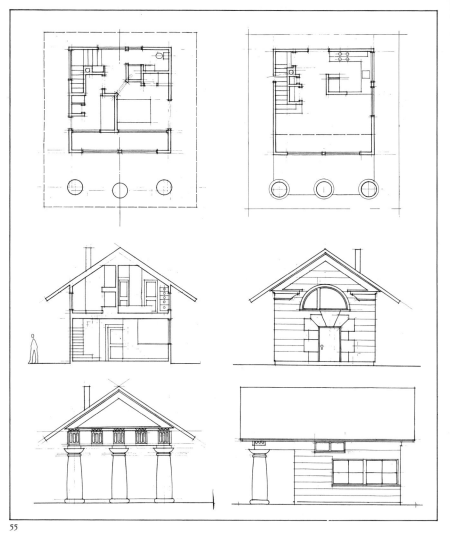

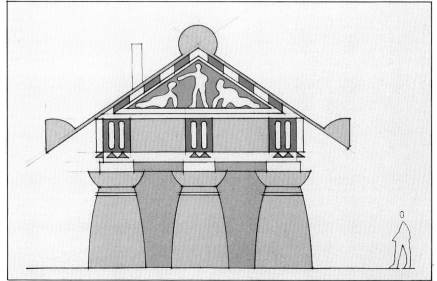

54

55

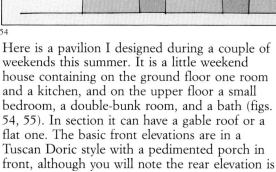

Here is a pavilion I designed during a couple of weekends this summer. It is a little weekend house containing on the ground floor one room and a kitchen, and on the upper floor a small bedroom, a double-bunk room, and a bath (figs. 54, 55). In section it can have a gable roof or a flat one. The basic front elevations are in a Tuscan Doric style with a pedimented porch in front, although you will note the rear elevation is Cinquecento.

The following illustrations will demonstrate the variety of styles the front of this little house can put on, and our adaptability and tolerance as architects.

And I don't mind designing garden pavilions. After all, they were, in the mid-eighteenth century, the basis of Romantic architecture and thereby the foundation of Modern architecture. Here is not a battle of the styles, but a garden party of the styles (fig. 56).

At a recent review of Princeton's School of Architecture there were examples of student designs which were archaeologically correct versions of nineteenth-century Classical architecture. A criticism was made that this architecture was inappropriate because its Classical expression did not conform to modern programs; I felt that the opposite was the case,

that the programs represented behind those facades were too directly connected with the Classical symbolism outside. The students had chosen, or were assigned, essentially institutional or civic programs promoting more or less monumental architecture. They did not include varieties of programs that satisfy the range of society's needs and that, in the end, might vitalize our architecture. We need housing and stores on the strip as well as opera houses and libraries on the plaza, even if a Classical style doesn't fit; but maybe it will fit.

My article called "A Definition of Architecture as Shelter with Decoration on It, and Another Plea for a Symbolism of the Ordinary in Architecture" proposes an architecture whose programmatic-structural functions are separated from its expressive-symbolic functions, allowing for contradictions between the two and for the combination of a systems approach on one hand and ornamental, representational rhetoric on the other. Since the article was written five years ago and has only recently been published (twice in foreign journals with the title wrong), I wrote a preface to bring it up to date—or rather to relate it to the current or incipient battle of the styles:

What I say in this article still holds, although I wrote it some years ago. Since then an architecture employing decoration has become acceptable. I refer to the Classical architecture derived from the Italian Rationalists; itself based on Neoclassical aspects of thirties architecture, and which in the wake of a recent exhibition on the Ecole des Beaux-Arts at the Museum of Modern Art has become manifest in the work of some avant-garde practitioners in the United States, and at some schools of architecture there. The proponents of this architecture call themselves Postmodernists, New Traditionalists, Radical Eclectics, Functional Eclectics, neo-Traditionalists; I am not sure what they are next month. But what is coming out of this Classicist movement for whatever Rationalist reasons, is Classical ducks, not classicized sheds; that is, buildings where the whole structure, back and front, inside and out, conforms more or less to a consistent Classical form, in a correct manner, in a universal style. What I propose in the article below, put in the context of this new movement, is decoration in architecture which is applied rather than integral, witty rather than correct, and selective rather than universal.

Applied: that is, to accommodate the complex and contradictory forms and structures, functions and spaces, contexts and symbols, that are realized from modern programs. The building can end up, therefore, Classical in front and Modern behind, or Classical outside and Modern inside.

Witty: How else can we use archaeological forms today without being lugubrious? Lutyens knew this years ago.

Selective: we can't be only Classical and accommodate the varied places our buildings are in, the varied needs and tastes of their users. The building can end up, therefore, Classical in front and Gothic behind, or Postmodern outside and Serbo-Croatian inside.

What I describe involves differences of attitude rather than style, and the attitude of the Postmodernists tends to be rigid; their rather vehement reactions to Modernism, their literal historicism, and correct Classicism are as rigid in the end as the puritanical antihistoricism and doctrinaire "total design" of the orthodox Modernists whom they accuse of rigidity and "total design"—that was Gropius's phrase. "Total design" is no worse than its other extreme, exclusive design; that is, limiting the range of building types to those with institutional, civic, and monumental programs, in order to make traditional function follow Classical form, and at the same time appeal to a narrow taste culture: libraries, yes; supermarkets, no! And there is little range in social planning too; pure Modern turned out to be too easy an answer, but Postmodern seems to be the same thing.

The last project I shall show is our plaza for the western end of Pennsylvania Avenue in Washington, D.C. You will see, of course, that it

runs contrary to the thesis I have been expounding. It is a Classical solution to a Classical program. But it is not too Classical.

Pennsylvania Avenue is an important street in Washington, used for presidential inaugural parades and to connect the Capitol and the White House. At least that was the original intention; although it is terminated by the great white dome at the eastern end of the axis, the western end now terminates in a formal and symbolic fizzle. This is because an early surveyor located the White House significantly off axis, and during the term of President Andrew Jackson, our first populist president, the Treasury Building was extended so it intruded into the axis. So much for the rational order of a Pierre L'Enfant in a pragmatic democracy. The Classical portico of this distinguished Greek Revival building by Robert Mills, because of its oblique angle in relation to the axis, is not big enough or forceful enough in size or scale to terminate the axis. Our job has been to give some identity to this western end of the axis and at the same time to make a square there accommodating the immediate neighborhood (figs. 57, 58, 59, 60).

One can say of L'Enfant's plan of Washington that it combined two orders, like those of a Baroque facade with columns—the giant order corresponding to the diagonal avenues terminated by important statues or buildings, and the minor order corresponding to the grid of streets. The diagonals relate to the monumental scale of the federal city, the rectangular pattern to the local scale of the neighborhoods. Where the two geometries intersect, circles and squares sometimes occur to mediate between the two scales.

As I have said, L'Enfant used the Baroque device

of terminating his axes with statues or buildings, but there is another method in the Baroque tradition, that of André Le Nôtre in the garden side of Versailles. He placed nothing central at the end of the principal axis. But he made the combination of open space and bare horizon positive by framing the vista with two sets of trees. We have proposed two pylons to do the same thing at the end of our axis—to frame the scene, to make positive the otherwise amorphous combination of too little portico in clumps of trees.

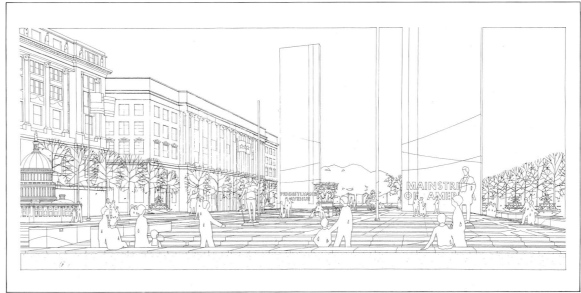

58

57

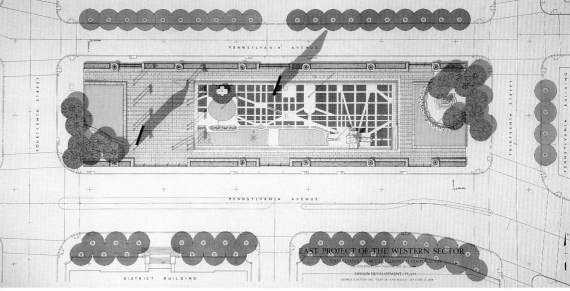

57 Western Plaza, Pennsylvania Avenue, Washington, D.C., 1977. The context
58 Perspective drawing
59 Site plan

59

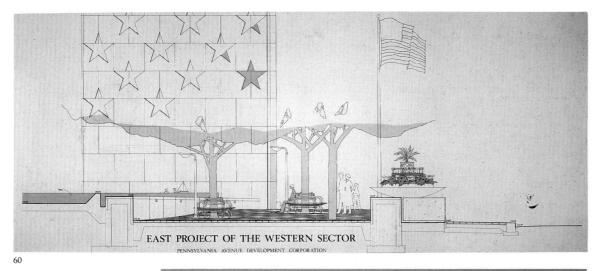

EAST PROJECT OF THE WESTERN SECTOR
PENNSYLVANIA AVENUE DEVELOPMENT CORPORATION

60

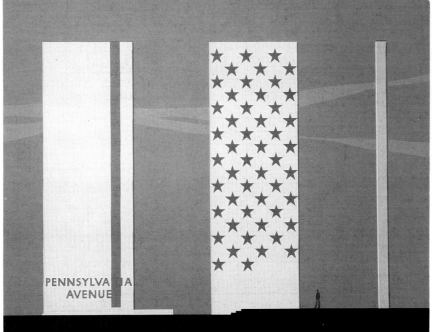

PENNSYLVANIA
AVENUE

61

The relative positions of the pylons appear to change as you get close to them and become aware that they are offset; they disintegrate as elements of a frame to accommodate to the local scale and spatial requirements of the plaza they are in. Although the pylons are relatively small (and economical) elements, twenty-five by eighty-five feet in elevation, you see them from up the avenue as bold white surfaces—they are of white marble—with the slight articulation of flush-inlaid black marble stripes near their inside edges to suggest mouldings. When you get even closer to the pylons you will see bas-relief ornament at eye level at the base in front and all over the back. Also, the pylons are very thin (three feet six inches) to contradict their Classical symbolism from the front, to articulate their scenographic frontality, and to dematerialize them from within the plaza (fig. 61). We hope to make the ornamentation polychromatic—red lettering on the front, blue stars on the back, and yellow sides painted on the white marble in the manner of some earlier Classical ornament in architecture.

The plaza itself orients to the local rectangular grid. Like most monumental architecture, it combines big scale with little scale, leaving out medium scale elements (fig. 62). Like some oriental rugs, it projects a bold order contained by borders—and then much rich detail to satisfy your interest when you get close. The plaza is raised three feet six inches above the surrounding streets and its outer border is a clipped hedge of that height; this elevation gives the plaza identity from the outer sidewalks and a sense of green softness. Otherwise the plaza is open and paved. The major portion of its surface is a parterre pattern, depicting L'Enfant's map of Washington with marble models of the Capitol and the White House, and with grass lawn on the "mall." Many

94

inscriptions are incised in the floor of the plaza at appropriate places on the map. Over the map, independent of its pattern, are placed pieces of sculpture—*objets trouvés* of historical outdoor sculpture of varying scales. The consistency of the design I have been describing is broken by exceptions to the order, including groups of trees off the Pennsylvania Avenue axis, flags, places to sit, urns with flowers in them, and other amenities and ornaments to enrich the functions and appearance of the whole and increase its scale.

We have tried to approach a difficult urban problem by starting with what's there, by striving for a maximum of effect through a minimum of means, and by mediating—in the tradition of Classical architecture—between the needs of the whole and of the part. In an earlier description of this project I wrote:

Our framed image is not so compelling as space articulated as infinity at the end of an axis in a French garden, nor is it strong on symbolic content, nor is it vivid as a form complementing the dome of the Capitol at the other end— although L'Enfant's executive mansion itself would not have had impact enough to counteract the Capitol dome. But our framed image does not make a bad picture, and it is picturesque in several ways. It is an asymmetrical composition, a Romantic scene of a Classical portico in a rural landscape, whose prettiness Mills in mid-century might have appreciated. It is reminiscent of the oblique view of the portico of San Giorgio across the lagoon framed by the two columns on the piazzetta of San Marco, and it is a symbol of American pragmatism perhaps, framed in a Baroque plan and developed not by the authority of a prince but through the vagaries of checks and balances.

60 Western Plaza. Section-perspective
61 Elevations of pylons
62 View of Capitol from Western Plaza

95

62

Il Proprio Vocabolario
Four Houses for *Gran Bazaar*
Robert Venturi

From an essay first published in **Gran Bazaar,**
January-February 1982, pp. 152–157.

96

In the ever-oscillating balance between form and symbol architecture today favors symbolism; architects are beginning to employ diverse vocabularies sensitive to the particular qualities of place and use, and to the particular taste cultures of the clients or users.

I bring this up as background for a comparison of four houses and one addition that our firm designed for one family within the decade of the seventies. The comparison is intended to describe the differences among these buildings and thereby to illuminate the development of eclectic symbolism in our architecture. The sites of the houses vary from New England to the Rocky Mountains to Bermuda and to New England again. Their uses include a family homestead, a ski lodge, a summer house, and a manor house. But the clients themselves changed over the decade too, not only in the makeup of their family—three of the five children arrived after the first house was built—but because the family adopted new roles for themselves and changed their tastes in significant ways.

House in Greenwich, Connecticut
Designed in 1971 and constructed in 1973, this house was for a very young couple who were New York cosmopolites, close friends of Andy Warhol, and inspired collectors of Pop Art and French Deco furniture of the twenties and thirties. The house was to contain these works of art in an easy way that did not emphasize their display. At the same time, some rooms were to contain fine examples of American antique furniture, assembled as the house went up. The site consisted of thirty acres of rolling green landscape and included an existing stable for the horses that were a developing interest of our clients.

The program of the house called for relatively

few but generous spaces—there is no separate dining room, no entrance hall, and the garage is near the entrance—reflecting an informal way of life dependent on a minimum of domestic help. The style of the house is Modern in that it has a flat roof, strip windows, aluminum sash, cantilever construction, and no overt historical symbolism. On the other hand, the flat roof is reminiscent of that of a Georgian country house, as is the near symmetry of the facade whose central focus is reinforced by ascending roof heights, a hierarchical window composition, and the flat curve in plan. Its stark setting on a manicured lawn resembles that of a Classical manor in the eighteenth century. On the other hand again, its quasi-Classical quality might refer to an anti-International Style Modernism like that of the Art Deco furniture within. An unusual feature of the exterior is the green glazed-brick walls with the dash-striped pattern. These make it the first building in the so-called Postmodern period with an all over and polychromatic decorative pattern. This element has been disregarded by current critics because the Modernists find ornament distasteful and the Postmodernists find this ornament anti-Classical. The use of the green makes the house striking symbolically—green is an unusual color for masonry architecture—but recessive formally, in the verdant context of the Connecticut landscape.

The interior contains decorative elements too—the alternate black and white marble risers and checkerboard floor pattern in the entry, and the pendant cove lighting and indirect natural lighting in the dining niche. These elements symbolize Art Deco styling.

1

2

1 House in Greenwich, Connecticut, 1970
2 Interior
3 Interior

Ski house in Vail, Colorado

Designed in 1974 and constructed in 1975 (William Ruoff, associate architect), this house can accommodate many guests in numerous small bedrooms and on the seats in the dormer-niches in the living room. It also accommodates a fine collection of American Mission furniture, mostly from the workshops of Gustave Stickley. Its immediate site is an aspen grove on the slope of a mountain in the Rockies, at the edge of town.

It is a small building with big scale. As a tower it displaces as few trees as possible and looks Romantic and playful. The living room is in the attic to be Romantic and to enjoy the best views. The materials and detailing are rustic in character, but abstract and precise. This tower with its big overhangs looks Nordic or Alpine, but it also reminds one of an Arts and Crafts grandfather clock.

6

4 Ski house, Vail, Colorado, 1975. Exterior
5 Interior
6 Section
7 House in Tuckers Town, Bermuda, 1975. Interior
8 Exterior

99

House in Tuckers Town, Bermuda

Designed in 1974 and constructed in 1975 (in association with Onions, Bouchard and McCulloch), this house is for summer vacations by the sea. It has a beautiful site on a barren cliff on a peninsula between the Atlantic Ocean and Castle Harbor Bay. Local restrictions required that it conform to the traditional style of architecture in Bermuda and employ stepped roofs for collecting water, white plaster walls and roofs to reflect the sun, and window shutters to modulate the light inside. We gladly accepted these limitations imposed by the historical style because they were environmentally practical as well as symbolically pleasing. This house also accommodates unusual furniture, this time a rare collection of eighteenth-century American and Bermudian pieces.

The house in Bermuda is different from the preceding houses in that its composition is not as highly centralized or axial, but rambling. Its complicated changes in level reflect its large size and irregular exposed site with different and stunning views. The entrance from the lane is grand in scale and formal with a kind of court d'honneur. In some parts the house is very grand, in other parts picturesque and cottage-like. It is different from the houses in Vail and Greenwich because of its site, its historical-cultural context, and the particular setting the clients wanted for their special antiques.

7

8

Addition to the Greenwich house

This project was commissioned in 1977–1978 because the family had changed in size with the arrival of triplets. The parents had diverted their collecting exclusively to American antique furniture and American primitive painting, and they had intensified their interest in horses to include breeding, polo, and racing, so they now had enormous new stables under construction. They had also changed in more subtle ways.

Specific requirements for the expanded houses were more bedrooms for family and guests, more service space, a proper dining room, a formal entrance hall with reception room, and a discrete garage remote from the house. A very big library was to be added for informal entertaining and for an extensive collection of books on horse breeding and equestrian sports.

We located the new entrance in the addition and at the rear of the present house so the new wing would dominate as you entered. To promote architectural formality, we created an entrance with a forecourt outside which corresponded to the central axis of the old house inside. A cross-axis penetrating the entrance hall formed a long gallery connecting the reception room at one end with the library at the other. The living room in the existing house became the new dining room, at a slightly lower level, on axis with the new front door. Kitchen and service in the existing house remained where they were. New bedrooms were on the second and partial third floors of the new wing.

The new wing of red brick was rather literally in the style of a late eighteenth-century manor, its chaste but rather grand form contrasting with that of the existing house. As a long and narrow element blocking out the old house from the entrance court, the new wing was almost literally a facade, a two-dimensional sign—in the end an expansive gesture.

We saw this addition as a challenging opportunity to create a building complex in the easy way the English modified and added to their country houses, over generations, in different architectural styles. I refer to those houses with Georgian fronts and Elizabethan behinds. Because the original house was frontal in layout, it was easy to place a red brick Georgian facade behind it and make it the main entrance. From the original front you would then see a Mannerist juxtaposition of a green brick form against a plane of even, red brick bays. This permitted, as I have said, an interior of some formality, but it

9 Proposed addition to House in Greenwich, 1978. Model
10 Front and rear elevations
11 Plan

9

100

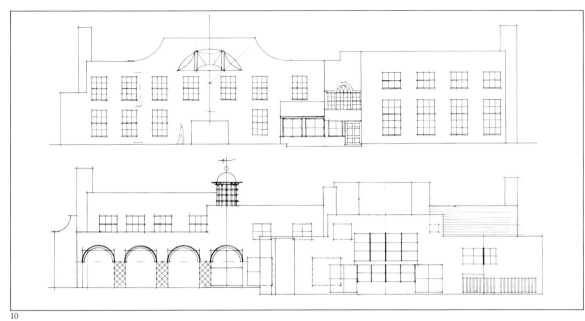

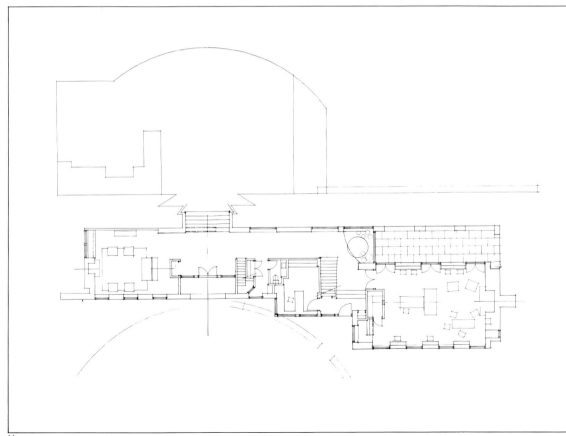

created as well a degree of idiosyncracy in plan which was quite in the vein of another English great-house tradition.

"Mount Vernon" house

Eventually our clients decided they did not want Mannerist complexity or aristocratic idiosyncracy. As they had also lost interest in the architectural symbolism that formed the basis of the original house, we suggested they build a new house altogether. At this time they purchased a neighboring estate containing other building sites and asked us to design a new house. It was to look like Mount Vernon and also to resemble some of the airy Classical houses McKim, Mead and White designed in the 1890s.

We were intrigued by the idea of designing a Mount Vernon in 1979, a building abounding in powerful symbolic content for Americans in general. For Americans, Mount Vernon is like the American flag. Perceived as patriotic symbol as much as building, it is an icon representing the home of the "father of our country." For our clients it symbolized a way of life. For us it would provide an opportunity to do for Mount Vernon what Jasper Johns did for the American flag—to represent it literally, but also to modify its context, its medium, and its scale, thereby making it familiar and strange at the same time and heightening our sensibilities toward it.

We produced a design that satisfied the programmatic requirements of the family for a way of life that is formal and rural at the same time. We also enjoyed balancing the differences between the original Mount Vernon and the new one. We did this by modifying scale within the building; for instance, the size of the lateral wings in the new Mount Vernon is bigger relative to that of the central pavilion than in the original Mount Vernon, and the scale of the windows in the lateral wings of the new house is bigger than that of the windows in the central pavilion because the wings of the new house contain important spaces for the present family to live in, rather than auxiliary spaces for the original slaves to work in. We also applied ornament explicitly in our Mount Vernon—no element is ornamental *and* structural: the characteristic piers on the back porch are two-dimensional boards; the keystones, rustication, and pediments are incised

linear pattern in consistently low relief; the false masonry done in wood is never made to fool the eye as in the original. Our ornament is flattened, simplified, and abstracted, to act as sign and to enhance the symbolic content of the whole. Yet our Mount Vernon is ambiguous as a whole; it is not (and cannot be) the real Mount Vernon, but it captures the essence of Mount Vernon through symbolism rather than imitation. It makes you see the old Mount Vernon *and* the new Mount Vernon at the same time; you see the old Mount Vernon with new eyes.

Some architects today have more literal leanings than we do. They don't want irony; they feel that Pop sensibility is out and "serious" historicism in. They "correct" Mount Vernon. We question whether architecture can be archeologically correct now, in the way it was on occasion in the nineteenth and early twentieth centuries. Are not

moments for apt *tours de force* of literal certainty very rare in our time? The almost literal revival of the International Style by the Whites in the sixties looked both flabby *and* lean when compared with the tense and witty compositions of Le Corbusier in the twenties. Might not a literal version of Mount Vernon today resemble a lugubrious funeral parlor in suburbia more than a conserving manifestation of a traditional ideal? Also, you never *are* archeologically correct, so why try?

We are grateful to our clients for the opportunity they gave us to work with such architecturally sensitive and interested patrons, and for the lessons we learned from them over the years about varying roles and tastes and how these evolve as people change over time.

12 Mount Vernon house project, Greenwich, Connecticut,
    1979. Front elevation
13 Plan
14 Side elevation
15 Rear elevation

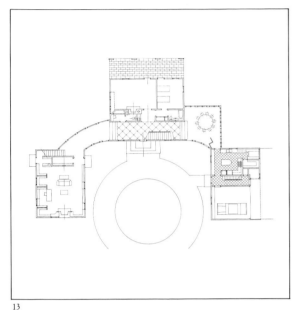

13

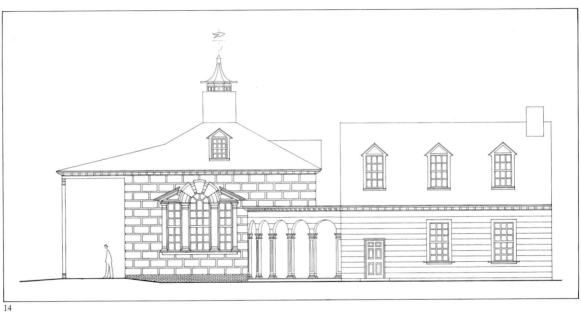

14

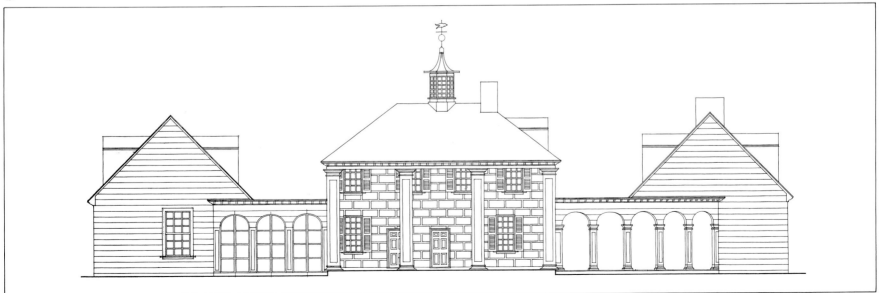

15

The RIBA Annual Discourse
Robert Venturi

This essay was first published by the Royal Institute of British Architects in **Transactions 1,** a record of papers presented to the RIBA for the Sessional Programme 1981–1982, pp. 47–56.

104

I would like to make this less of a discourse and more of a demonstration—less a discussion of architectural theory and more a presentation of work. This approach happens to correspond with what I want to say, which is that we architects are talking too much. Now is the time to do more and speak less, to concentrate on quality in practice rather than ideology in words.

I hope you won't think this too simple an idea, too obvious and unimportant to concern us here. For if that were so, why isn't it acknowledged by architects and critics? Why do we emphasize abstract theory over concrete works, fiery polemics over critical questions and the search for quality, publication over design, and slogans over subtleties? Why are we interested in being first rather than best, in naming styles rather than evolving them? Why are architects more interested in proclaiming new schools of architecture than in refining architectural proportions or seeking social and cultural relevance? And why do many architects project themselves as public personalities rather than artists at the service of their craft? Henry James said Walter Pater had "the most exquisite literary fortune: to have taken it all out, wholly, exclusively, with the pen (the style, the genius) and absolutely not at all with the person." He is, James said, "the mask without the face, and there isn't in his total superficies a tiny point of vantage for the newspaper to flap his wings on." Elsewhere James writes of the artist in triumph, of whom we see only "the back he turns to us as he bends over his work." [1]

I have done my share of talking and writing; indeed, some of my writing has had some influence on the content of current talking and on the tendency to talk. I write out of frustration. When my ideas about building exceed my opportunities to build, I get the ideas out in words rather than bricks and mortar. I wrote more when I was young than I do now because, luckily, we have more work now, although, as you will see, it is still relatively modest in scale and extent. Much architectural writing today is by young architects, probably for the same reason. But there is no justification for bad writing. When I read current architectural literature, I am often distressed by its pretension, confused by its obscurity, or bored by its banality. Yet when I look at everyday things I am not bored, and when I look at architectural history books I continue to learn.

I have also done my share of criticism and have discussed the significance of criticism as a creative tool for architects. What T.S. Eliot said of literature, I feel applies to architecture too: "Probably, indeed, the larger part of the labour of sifting, combining, constructing, expunging, correcting, testing: this frightful toil is as much critical as creative." [2] Writing architectural criticism is a useful activity, but it should serve as a means to enhance the quality of the art and not as an excuse for polemics and posturing. Today's polemical critics should get back to the main critical task, which is to evaluate quality—not to promote biases. As Edmund Wilson has said somewhere, "we must be able to tell the good from the bad, the first-rate from the second-rate. We shall not otherwise write . . . criticism at all."

Architects cannot escape Eliot's "frightful toil." It is their fate to sweat over details, not to pursue *mots justes*. They are known by their work, not their words. Sir Edwin Lutyens, an exemplar to many of us, wrote hardly anything but letters. Michelangelo wrote sonnets and Vanbrugh, plays. Palladio's Four Books on architecture have lived, but that is exceptional. Much architectural criticism today seems to have become a form of promotion and, to me, an excuse for not facing essential architectural issues of today.

In the rest of this talk I shall try to analyze some of these questions as I see them. But I shall analyze them through describing our work. Using our buildings, I shall proceed from the particular to the general and thereby present our theory as emanating from our architecture rather than vice versa. Lutyens wrote (in a letter) of Sir Herbert Baker: "God asked Adam to name the animals after He created them. Baker names his animals first and then starts to create round a name and words." [3] As architects, our theory, to a great extent, should derive from our practice.

Questions and issues that increasingly intrigue us and that are addressed in our work revolve around the following subjects:

Symbolism, diversity, and cultural relevance
In the ever oscillating balance between form and symbol in architecture, we now tilt toward symbol. But the symbolism being adopted—I refer particularly to that of the historicist Classical vocabulary of the Postmodernists—is in my opinion at once too pure and too consistent. It does not allow a diversity that is sensitive and adaptable to the plurality of taste cultures which our architecture must acknowledge if it is to be real and broad in its scope. [4] In promoting a rather literal version of the Latin Neoclassicism of the Italian Rationalists, Postmodernists, in the United States at least, go merely from Corbu to Ledoux; they impose a simplistic, esoteric symbolism upon our culture in 1982, as the introduction of the International Style did in the United States in 1932. Symbolism by its nature must be familiar. *Plus ça change . . .*

Representational symbolism

Representation, in our context, should involve depicting, rather than constructing, symbol and ornament in architecture. Renaissance architects, for instance, could essentially *do* Classical historicist architecture because of the general correspondence between ancient and contemporary technology and building types. We cannot construct Classical buildings, but we can *represent* them, via appliqué upon the substance of the building. This is what we have described elsewhere as the decorated shed; it also leads to the building as sign.

Appliqué ornament and overall pattern

Historical symbolism, achieved through representation, and applied rather than integral, is appropriate in architecture today; but so is pattern. More or less abstract and repetitive pattern can be an important aesthetic element in architecture now that articulation is outmoded as an aesthetic device. Repetitive pattern can accommodate the standardization that is typical of our industrial construction methods.

An aesthetic of richness and ambiguity over one of unity and clarity

Buildings whose structural and spatial systems are obfuscated by all-over appliqués of patterned and representational mosaics or frescoes serve as exemplars to us in our efforts to achieve richness of effect with today's methods and materials. We choose such exemplars over the beloved Classical archetypes, where simple, integral ornament articulates structure and space to achieve unity of effect.

The realities and diversities of architectural context and building program

Our architecture will be better by responding to all kinds of landscapes valid for today—the civic mall *and* the commercial strip. Paris is great because of the Place Pigalle as well as the Place de la Concorde. We might not like cars, but a large part of our population does, and depends on them. Our architecture too must accommodate all kinds of programs—town halls *and* supermarkets, Classical *or* Serbo-Croatian.

The relativity of taste and the multiplicity of taste cultures as described by Herbert Gans

This brings us full circle to the first question, and is the basis for our arguments for diversity and relevance of architectural symbol systems. The aesthetic pluralism of our society encourages an expansive scope for architecture at the same time that it discourages approaches that are esoteric, intolerant, and dogmatic. It encourages realism as well as idealism; it projects the architect as follower as well as leader.

These questions we approach, of course, in an American context, as practitioners within a specific and constraining set of cultures, which makes our responses not altogether applicable elsewhere.

1 Front door, Best Products Showroom, Oxford Valley, Pennsylvania, 1977

105

2

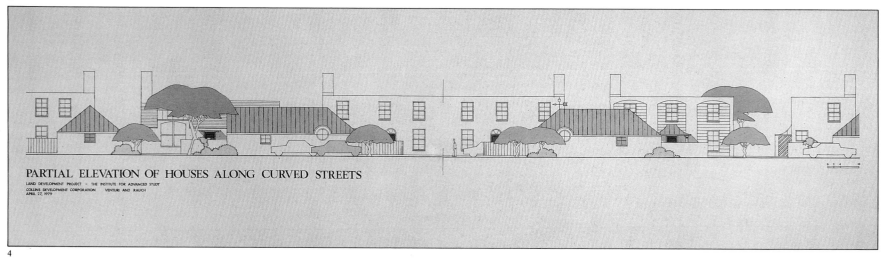

PARTIAL ELEVATION OF HOUSES ALONG CURVED STREETS

LAND DEVELOPMENT PROJECT · THE INSTITUTE FOR ADVANCED STUDY
COLLINS DEVELOPMENT CORPORATION   VENTURI AND RAUCH
APRIL 27, 1979

4

2 Dixwell Fire Station, New Haven, Connecticut, 1967
3 Best Products Showroom
4 Street elevation, Land Development project, Institute for
   Advanced Study, Princeton, New Jersey, 1978
5 Park Regency Housing, Houston, Texas, 1980

3

5

Diversity, Relevance and Representation in Historicism, or *Plus ça Change*...plus a Plea for Pattern all over Architecture with a Postscript on my Mother's House
Robert Venturi

The Walter Gropius Lecture, Graduate School of Design, Harvard University, 1982. This essay was first published in **Architectural Record,** June 1982, pp. 114–119.

When I was young, a sure way to distinguish great architects was through the consistency and originality of their work. Mies van der Rohe was known by his unmistakable vocabulary of finely detailed, glass and steel, veneered frames universally applied to high-rise buildings, university laboratories, or rich clients' houses. Le Corbusier was distinguished in his early years by *his* particular vocabulary of hovering Cubist planes and in his later years by monumental statuesque forms. In each of these periods he applied his more or less consistent vocabulary to all kinds of buildings, whether an art school in Cambridge or a house in Chandigarh. The same could be said of the work of Frank Lloyd Wright, Louis Kahn, or Alvar Aalto (although Aalto diverges from his peers in this respect in his tendency to work variations on conventional industrial elements and in his avoidance, therefore, of expressionistic originality). For these masters, varieties of style within their own oeuvres would have implied indecision and lack of commitment to a unified ideal, yet the work of each as a whole tended to look different from that of the others as each strove to assert the originality that was considered the sine qua non of artistic expression of Romantic and also of Modern artists. This was a time in architecture when form was emphasized over symbol and when universal industrial processes were considered essential determinants of form for all kinds of building everywhere, so that priority on the individual architect's original vocabulary was combined curiously with a rigid ideal of formal unity for architecture as a whole.

This should no longer be the case. Where the Modern masters' strength lay in consistency, ours should lie in diversity. But it still is the case. It shouldn't be because the Modern masters, and what they stood for, have been repudiated by

current architects—often with a vengeance, unfortunately—and we now look for inspiration to an architect like Sir Edwin Lutyens who, especially in his domestic architecture, worked in a variety of historical and decorative styles. The styles he chose were meaningful to his various clients and supported the roles they played as country squires, worldly capitalists, ambassadors to Washington, or viceroys in Delhi. I shall try to show that architects today should be distinguished by the rich variety of their work and the diversity of their architectural vocabularies, rather than by the unity of their work and the consistency and the originality of their vocabulary.

Some fifteen years ago in *Complexity and Contradiction in Architecture* and later in *Learning from Las Vegas,* we advocated architectural principles which were then considered polemical, but which are now accepted wisdom. We called for an architecture that promotes richness and ambiguity over unity and clarity, contradiction and redundancy over harmony and simplicity.

Our exemplar is the Byzantine interior of the Martorana Chapel (fig. 1) where, to achieve richness of effect, structural and spatial systems are obfuscated by an all-over appliqué of patterned and representational mosaics, frescoes, and Cosmati work. We choose this rather than another beloved archetype, the Pazzi Chapel (fig. 2), where simple integral ornament articulates structure and space to achieve unity of effect.

Such an architecture accommodates the intimations of local context over the dogma of universality. It provides pragmatic solutions to real problems rather than easy obedience to ideal forms—as Stanislas von Moos has put it, it solves

1

problems, but expresses them too. It encourages ornamental surface over articulated form, pattern over texture, and sometimes pattern over all. This architecture acknowledges again the fundamental issues of shelter as well as function. And finally, it employs symbol, as well as space and light, as the measure of its art—it derives meaning from its symbols as well as expression from its form. The symbols, depending on association by their very nature, promote elements and vocabularies that are familiar, ordinary, or conventional rather than original, outlandish, or avant-garde.

This approach expands the range of the vocabularies of architecture beyond the industrial vernacular and machine aesthetic of the International Style and the hi-tech of later Modernism, so that it can include local and commercial vernaculars and those of diverse historical styles. The freedom from consistency and the opportunity for diversity that result are important: inherent in them is sensitivity to place, time, and culture, and recognition of the multiplicity and relativity of tastes. Diversity is, indeed, an obligation if our architecture is not to be limited again by a single, high-culture vocabulary that is expected to "filter down" and

2

"unify" the environment. Such a vocabulary tends to degenerate in that process into prettified or extravagant travesties of the original vocabulary or into dry renditions of last year's avant-garde.

Plus ça change . . .
Although most of the principles cataloged above are by now a part of the accepted wisdom among architects and critics, today's architects, nevertheless, have achieved no more diversity or cultural relevance than their Modern forbears. It is this state of *plus ça change* that I shall deal with in this paper.

The trend toward symbolism today is not surprising as it is a reaction to the long period when symbol was banned as a manifestation of ornament or historicism; or went unacknowledged, as was the case with early Modern industrial symbolism; or was substituted for by expressionistic articulation of structure and form, as in the later years of the Modern movement. On the other hand, now that we again acknowledge symbolism in architecture, the problem becomes what to do with it. For me the answers so far have been too simple, too

dogmatic—yes, they have lacked complexity and contradiction.

Architects have traditionally used symbolism in architecture to enrich its content and to include other dimensions, some almost literary, which make architecture a not purely spatial medium. Symbolism expands the scope of architecture to include meaning as well as expression, and to promote explicit communication, denotative as well as connotative. (Unfortunately this has always meant that bad architecture can project pretentious symbolic ballyhoo as well as bombastic structural expressionism.)

Diversity
An essential reason for using symbolism today is that it can provide a diversity of architectural vocabularies appropriate for a plurality of tastes and sensitive to qualities of heritage and place. This use suits the need in our time to respond to both mass culture and pluralist expression. Today the world is at once smaller and more diverse, more interdependent yet more nationalistic; even small communities seriously maintain ethnic identities and carefully record local history. People are now more aware of the differences among themselves yet more tolerant of these differences.

It's a time in architecture too when the shifting balance between the universal and the unique favors the latter. The early Modern movement was named the International Style to proclaim, among other things, its universality. Our diversified approach to symbolism will distinguish our architecture from that of our recent predecessors whose buildings had to look like factories, or at least contain industrial references, and promote thereby a universal industrial order. But our approach to symbolism should

distinguish our architecture from that of other eras too. We are not able to use historicism, as did architects of the Renaissance, to institute a rebirth of a single architectural style; they were backed by a homogeneous culture that was broadly committed to a humanist heritage. Nor can we revive nineteenth-century revivalism and the battles of the styles for example, the battle between Perpendicular and Decorated Gothic advocated by the Oxford and Cambridge movements respectively, and promoted as the exclusive expression of the ecclesiastical dogmas of each. Our historicism should involve less a rivalry and more a medley of styles; like the free eclecticism of late eighteenth-century garden pavilions—Gothic *and/or* Greek—that evoked a variety of historical associations and Romantic moods, or like late nineteenth-century architecture where dexterous combinations of styles reflected the functions and contexts of individual buildings.

In recent architecture historicism has been the major manifestation of the new symbolism. But it is important to acknowledge other sources of symbolism, including high art and Pop—Scarlatti *and* the Beatles—if diversity is to be achieved. In the design of individual houses, our firm has adopted numerous local and vernacular vocabularies—more or less rustic or Classical. In our exhibition for the Smithsonian Institution we acknowledged the symbolic bases for American developer housing and studied the vernacular appliqués these houses accrete over time as they are renovated, expanded, and ornamented by their owners (fig. 3). In *Learning from Las Vegas* we analyzed commercial vernacular vocabularies of the highway environment and urban sprawl in a search for an appropriate symbolic architecture for our time (fig. 4). In the same book we discussed the machine aesthetic of the Modern

109

3

4

movement as a set of symbols rather than as a set of forms deriving from industrial processes of the modern world.

Another vehicle for symbolism in architecture is ornamental pattern. Ornamental pattern is different from historical, vernacular, or pop symbolism in that it can be freer and less consistent and can depend less on association. It could be extremely significant for architecture now and has enormous potential for development. I shall return to it later in this paper.

Relevance

Architecture can be many things, but it should be appropriate.[1] It should have cultural relevance. It is necessary to make this obvious point because today's architecture is frequently arbitrary in its symbolism. Architects who indulge their preferences for esoteric and exotic symbols tend to produce an architecture of whimsical pavilions and picturesque follies that makes insufficient reference to the diversities and subtleties of taste cultures at hand, or to the context of place which should give substance to form. But a sense of appropriateness should apply not only to a variety of cultural types, but also to a hierarchy of cultural values—not all buildings are equally important; not all buildings should be high art; most landscapes should include buildings plain and fancy.

In attempting to derive an architecture that is relevant for diversities of culture, taste, and place, I put the burden on the symbolic rather than the formal or technical aspects of architecture. This is because symbolic elements are more flexible and adaptable than formal and, especially, structural-technical elements. They are also less subject to limitations of use, cost, and physical

5

stability, and to the constraints of standardization. Building systems and their resultant forms should constitute the more universal qualities in our architecture and act as counterpoints to the unique qualities that will be symbolic. The construction method of our building in Iraq, for instance, (figs. 5, 6) is concrete frame with precast panels which is standard world-over; yet we designed some of the openings in the precast panels as pointed arches, to conform to the desire of our clients to symbolize national character and express cultural heritage in their architecture.

I have made a case for a separation between form and symbol in the article "A Definition of Architecture as Shelter with Decoration on It." My emphasis there was on contradiction as well as separation of form and function: allowing form and function to go their separate ways permits function to be truly functional—as it couldn't be, ironically, when Form followed Function, in the old Modern days, and had the obligation to look good as well as work well.

So the independence of form and function in the interest of more effective functionalism can distinguish our architecture from that of the Modern movement. But the independence of form and symbol in the service of cultural relevance can distinguish it also from traditional historicist architecture. Renaissance buildings for instance, were constructed more or less like the Roman buildings they emulated (although the Romans were more technically advanced in the use of concrete), while revivalist buildings of the last two centuries were also almost identical in the way they were constructed to the buildings they copied—Gothic, Classical, or Renaissance— give or take a few steel or cast-iron members imbedded in the masonry. And the vernacular

revivals of the turn of the century represented survivals more than revivals, in that "arts and crafts" as a building tradition continued to exist. Building technology hadn't changed much until recently. In most eras contemporary form and historical symbol could be integral for the whole building; it is only our age that has seen grand contradictions between structure and symbol, or form and symbol.

Modern technical forms and historical symbolic forms rarely harmonize now. Historical symbolism and ornamental pattern must almost inevitably become appliqué. Quoins on the corner of a facade *could* be structural in a Renaissance or Renaissance Revival facade even if they *were* applied; but not now, because we build differently. We see differently too. We don't *want* harmony between structure and symbol if it is forced or false. If we are at last "Postmodern" enough to accept structural and formal contradiction, we are still "Modern" enough to reject structural and formal "dishonesty." If we don't have to express structure, we don't want to falsify it. *Trompe l'oeil* in architecture is effective for us only so far as it doesn't work.

Representation

I have been discussing the what and the why of diversity and relevance in architectural symbolism —as it applies to historicist symbolism. I will now discuss the how of the subject which I will characterize as representation in architecture— representation in architecture achieved through depiction and appliqué.

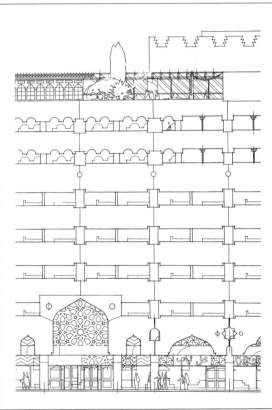

6

3 Symbolic sources for suburban house decorations
4 Las Vegas Strip
5 Building project, Khulafa Street, Baghdad, 1981. Model
6 Facade detail

The separation of wall and structure through the appliqué of panels on or within a frame is familiar to us in Modern architecture. When the independent walls or the modular panels were colored or textured (they were seldom patterned), they provided a quasi-ornamental effect otherwise rare in that architecture. But these nonstructural walls in Modern architecture were essentially spatial in function—the marble panels interspersed in the structural grid of the Barcelona Pavilion directed flowing space; the curving walls snaking through the bays of the Parliament in Chandigarh enclosed particular space while the modular panels complemented the structural grid in the same building. Instead, I have advocated the use of appliqué as sign, whose function is not basically spatial or structural, but communicative, via symbolism and ornament. It is this quality which distinguishes our appliqué from that of our recent predecessors. The most vivid historical precedent for our approach is again the interior of a Byzantine chapel where a fresco or mosaic appliqué communicates explicit messages—symbolic and representational—and is independent of the architecture in content and form. The content is religious, the form is pattern, and the configurations and rhythms have nothing to do with the spatial or structural elements they are applied to. The representation of a saint's head might be tilted forward on the curved surface of the ceiling vault while his feet might be amputated by an arched opening in the wall below.

In *Complexity and Contradiction in Architecture,* I analyzed spatial layering and "things within things" exemplified by the pierced multiple domes of Baroque churches and other kinds of architectural juxtaposition involving redundancy. These complex forms of appliqué I opposed to the complicated, Piranesian and Paxtonesque spatial configurations that late Modern architecture had substituted for symbolism and ornament. In *Learning from Las Vegas* we analyzed commercial roadside building as one model for a symbolic architecture, and illustrated our Football Hall of Fame Competition entry which we called a billdingboard. From these sign-appliqués we developed the idea of the decorated shed as a building type and as a vehicle for ornament in architecture.

In the progression of our ideas about appliqué, first as spatial layerings, then signboard, and then ornament, we came to appliqué as representation in architecture. Representation in this context involves the *depiction* as opposed to the *construction* of symbol and ornament. Manifestations of this approach to symbolism in architecture are essentially two-dimensional and pictorial. Examples of representation in historicist architecture could be Classical columns or hammerbeam trusses cut out as silhouettes which depict but don't reconstruct the originals, or Classical quoins which are incised on a facade and which brook no ambiguity as to their symbolic and decorative function (figs. 7, 8). Much of the early work of Gunnar Asplund and of some other early twentieth-century architects espoused a nonliteral historicism which was expressed through representational ornament. In other, less historical ornament, a flower pattern, for instance, may allude to conventional wallpaper flowers rather than to real flowers; the extra layer of meaning makes the symbolism richer.

Ornament in folk architecture is often representational high-art ornament simplified and rendered in two dimensions through painted patterns on flat surfaces, or through silhouettes.

7 Palazzo Rucellai, Florence
8 House near Wilmington, Delaware, 1978

8

The jigsaw carpentry of American front porches or the cutout boards of Alpine balustrades are examples. Economy and naiveté were probably the immediate reasons for this representational approach, but its aesthetic results were eloquent expressions of the essence of style. In our time, economy and industrial standardization on one hand and lack of craftsmanship on the other justify this simplified, repetitive, and depictive approach to ornament.

If we cannot construct historical architecture today or revive Revivalism, we can represent them through appliqué and sign. These techniques may seem simpleminded, but they can help us avoid the flaws of bad ambiguity and free us to create an architecture good for our time.

Plus *plus ça change*

I believe the source of the term Postmodern to be Princeton, where I first heard Jean Labatut use it to describe an architecture in the mid-forties. The term is widely and loosely used today to cover ever-divergent architectural trends. It includes, for example, the Italian Rationalist movement, although that movement is an entity in itself and has in fact influenced the American Postmodern movement, especially in its adoption of a Neoclassicist vocabulary.

My evaluation of Postmodernism will cover only the movement's approach to diversity, cultural relevance, and symbolism as I have been discussing them. My view will be limited by the bounds of my knowledge of current architecture and will be based more on the projects of Postmodernist architects than on their theoretical writings. I am in general agreement with the theoretical bases of Postmodernism; the concurrent architecture and its apparent implications are what concern me.

Postmodernism has, in my opinion, proclaimed in theory its independence from Modernism—from the singular vocabulary and the rigid ideology of that movement—and has substituted, in practice, a new vocabulary that is different from the old in its symbolism, but similar in its singularity, and as limited in its range, and as dogmatic in its principles as the old. The new movement does not provide the diverse symbolism and cultural relevance appropriate for our era. In this respect it is in no important way different from the previous movement. *Plus ça change . . .*

The Postmodernists have abandoned the universal industrial vocabulary of Modernism. As we said in *Learning from Las Vegas*, everyone but architects had come to know that the Industrial Revolution was dead and its continued glorification ironical. We pointed out that, although Le Corbusier's late-Modern *beton-brut* was symbolically anti-industrial, in the hands of his followers it had become expressionistically heroic and as irrelevant as the industrial vocabulary it replaced. However, the Postmodernists, in supplanting the Modernists, have substituted for the largely irrelevant universal vocabulary of heroic industrialism another largely irrelevant universal vocabulary—that of parvenu Classicism, with, in its American manifestation, a dash of Deco and a whiff of Ledoux. In substituting historical symbolism for Modern symbolism, they have promoted a kind of Neoclassicism, striving for a universalism which was appropriate at the turn of the eighteenth century to the aristocratic and republican patrons of Neoclassicism and to the essentially homogeneous preindustrial societies in which they lived, but which is inappropriate for postindustrial societies like ours which are complex and pluralist. In this context, the architectural jumps of the seventies from Le Corbusier to Ledoux, from Whites to pastels, were not such big leaps as they sound. The transition from the pure and simple Cubist forms of the International Style to the pure and simple Classical forms of Neoclassicism manifests architects' continuing formalist predilection for simplification. However, the White forms are now tinted in Mediterranean hues which pleases clients and makes projects and drawings more saleable.

Formal simplicity and symbolic consistency make architecture easy to identify, name, copy, learn, teach, promote, publicize, publish, draw, and exhibit. That this architecture is easy to name is obvious by its proliferation of names: Postmodernism, Rationalism, Radical Eclecticism, Free-style Classicism, the New Rules, etc. But doesn't the variety of its names belie the paucity of its content? Doesn't the ease and speed with which its authors name it expose its oversimplicity? The naming of movements and styles is the historian's, not the architect's responsibility. Architects should describe their work, not name it. Did Bernini know he was Baroque? That Postmodernism is easy to teach is obvious from its popularity among students and its acceptance in the architectural *academe* where archetypal simplification and easy universalities tend to be preferred to complexity and contradiction. That it is easy to promote is obvious because journalists love slogans. All this has obvious advantages and gives immediate satisfaction, but does it make for vigorous architecture that faces the complexities of reality?

Ledoux, in the context of the United States, is exotic as well as simplistic. I remember being startled at glimpsing out of the corner of my eye the Neoclassical city hall in the French Quarter of Montreal: it was truly a Neoclassical building. Having momentarily forgotten that I was in French Canada, I was subconsciously expecting a Greek Revival building typical of the United States—typical, indeed, of what I could have found immediately across the border in New York State. The differences between the pure, abstract, continental Ledouxian version of Classicism and the more literal, sometimes naive version of Doric that is Anglo-American, were, at this instant, subtle but telling.

If the symbolism of Postmodernism must be based on Classicism, why is it largely limited to Ledoux whose appropriateness on this continent, beyond Quebec, is questionable? The answer is because Ledoux is easy to take for former Modernists. He is one of the historical architects that Modern architects allowed themselves to admire and it is easy to move from liking him to doing him (douxing him and over-douxing him). He is also in vogue because of the influence within the Postmodern movement in this country of the Rationalist movement in Italy, with its distinctly Latin version of Neoclassicism. There are parallels here to the importation of the International Style to this continent in the thirties. Bauhaus architecture provided a similar strain of the exotic and irrelevant in the American context. What an irony that many of those who now discredit the rigid impositions of the International Style now follow in its footsteps. *Encore plus ça change.* In advocating versions of Classical symbolism such as Greek Revival, Palladian and Queen Anne, that are varied and natural to our place and time—connected, that is, to our heritage—and in employing them in our work, I am being realistic rather than chauvinistic, and rational more than Rationalist.

But why only Classical? In this paper I have discussed the rationale for embracing varieties of styles and employing appliqué and representation to achieve cultural relevance. In "A Definition of Architecture as Shelter with Decoration on It," I described a hypothetical building that sports a Serbo-Croatian front and a Mary Anne behind—its aesthetic contradiction justified by conflicting demands of form and function and accommodated by its configuration as a decorated shed. The more traditional interdependence of form and function and the more literal and "serious" identification of form and symbol in Postmodernism will not accommodate such functional contradictions. This tends to limit Postmodernism to a hierarchy of traditional building types and to institutional and civic buildings—the range of building types associated with Classicism—although, strangely to Americans, Neoclassical workers' housing seems to sit well with Communist mayors in Northern Italy.

But doesn't architecture encompass ordinary buildings too? I've seen a design for a catalog showroom in a highly literal Classical style. As a Postmodern building it was, to me, distinctly uncomfortable; as a decorated shed sporting Classical representation, it would have come off. Another recent design for a quarter in Paris is an exquisite collage of axes *à la* Le Nôtre (*au Nôtre?*). Hausmannian boulevards intersect delightful streets whose widths perfectly balance the heights of Classical facades, whose sky is punctuated by high-diving bi-wing planes seemingly piloted by World War I aces. The pedestrian density of this urban fabric would appeal to any antiquarian who strolls the streets of the eighteenth-century quarters of Paris or parts of Munich or Leningrad, but what about the reality of cars on the ground (over drawings of Messerschmitts in the air) in the late twentieth century, and the right of our cities to be civic and residential *and* commercial in their function, and of their symbolism to be nostalgic *and* real?

A plea for pattern all over

In this critique of Postmodernism I have emphasized historicism in architecture because it is the chief feature of that movement, and I have advocated an explicitly symbolic and representational historicism that is conveyed through appliqué. To put it another way, I have been concerned with ornament whose content is historical. But there is another type of ornament that has been acknowledged but little employed by Postmodernists, perhaps because of their lingering Modernist predilection for simplicity and the predominating influence of Italian Rationalism. This ornament consists of all over pattern. It is an ornamental direction of enormous range and potential. Pattern-ornament can be abstract, as in the decorative tile or brick surfaces of Moslem architecture—among the supremely beautiful and complex creations in the history of art. It can be representational, as in figured Byzantine mosaics or in the pretty floral wallpapers of Victorian interiors. It can be symbolically architectural, as in the facades of those Italian Romanesque churches (fig. 9) whose rows of bas-relief arcades crash into portal, rose window, or moulding, seeming discordant and lyrical at once.

Our additions to the Oberlin Art Museum, ISI Office Building, and Best Products Showroom, are decorated sheds where geometric and floral patterns are appliquéd using masonry and porcelainized panels. In the Best showroom loft, big flowers, bold *and pretty*, camouflage the inevitable banality of the architectural form and read as a sign across a vast parking lot and

speedy highway. Ornament that is pattern-all-over is currently the subject of painters of the Pattern and Decoration movement in New York. These painters have acknowledged an inevitable reaction against the Minimalism of late Modern aesthetics. As with the American Pop Art and Photorealist movements, the painters are ahead of the architects in their aesthetic sensibility. Architects too, I think, will have to recognize the impracticality of expressionist heroics, on the one hand, and of Minimalist indulgence on the other, and acknowledge the potential for richness in the decorated shed—and eventually in the decorated car, the decorated anything, all over our environment.

In this argument I have cast Modern architecture in a bad role, but I want to qualify my attitude toward the Modern movement and distinguish it from that of many of the Postmodernists. I have never intended to totally reject Modern architecture in words or work because I do, and I think our architecture should, in many important ways, evolve out of it, not revolt against it. Its masterpieces hold their own with those of any age. Forgetting the Rococo perhaps, the Modern was the first style since the Gothic to be based on an original symbolism (acknowledging its immediate derivation from the industrial vernacular of its time). Today we focus on its excesses and weaknesses at the end, to the exclusion of its successes and glory at the beginning. This makes some architects want to be revolutionary rather than evolutionary, anti-Modern rather than truly Postmodern.

One of the flaws of the Modern movement was its revolutionary zeal, its progressive rejection of the past. It is ironic that many critics of the rigidity and exclusiveness of Modernism who now fervently proclaim their liberation from its

9 Santa Maria della Piazza, Ancona

bondage display an equal, if opposite, revolutionary zeal; some of today's most intolerant Postmodern architects were "Whites" last year. It is too easy to hate our fathers in attempting to transcend them. In doing so we find refuge once again from a complex and contradictory world in simple formulas for our work and simple dogmas for our philosophy. Denise Scott Brown wrote in our preface to *Learning from Las Vegas*: "Since we have criticized Modern architecture, it is proper here to state our intense admiration of its early period when its founders, sensitive to their own times, proclaimed the right revolution. Our argument lies mainly with the irrelevant and distorted prolongation of that old revolution today." And now with that old revolution in a new guise.

A postscript on my mother's house
Although I am critical of much of the Classicism I see in Postmodern architecture, and because I am frequently dismissed as a Pop architect, I would like to make it plain that I consider myself an architect who adheres to the Classical tradition of Western architecture. I claim that my approach and the substance of my work are Classical, and have been from the beginning of my career. My mother's house in Chestnut Hill, Philadelphia (figs. 10, 11), the second building of my design to be built, is an explicitly Classical building in the substance of its plan and form and in the ornament of its elevations. This was unusual in 1964, the year of its completion.

But the house, though Classical, is not pure. Within the Classical aesthetic it conforms to a Mannerist tradition which admits contradiction within the ideal order and thereby enhances the ideal quality of that order through contrast with it. To perceive the ideal you must acknowledge the real. Contradiction in Classical architecture,

10

manifest in distortion and exception, occurs in the work of Palladio and many others who are my guides.

Some Classical and contradictory aspects of my mother's house are: the plan and the front and back elevations (figs. 12, 13, 14) are symmetrical about a central axis, but within the consistent perimeter of the plan the extremities vary to accommodate exceptions in plan; and within the consistent profile of the elevations, the extremities vary to conform to exceptions within. The configuration of windows is asymmetrical, if balanced, for the same reason. The central core of the house is a solid, not the void typical of a Palladian plan. The solid core consists of a fireplace, chimney, and stair, like that of a New England house of the seventeenth century. The central entrance reads on the front elevation as a void, rather big in scale like that of a porticoed

Palladian villa, but it is contradicted by the blank, set-back wall of the solid core which is itself distorted in plan to accommodate circulation around it. Symmetry in plan is therefore modified at the extremities via exceptions, and nearer the center via distortions.

The front and back elevations are Classically symmetrical with strong centralities. The front elevation is a Classical pediment. I derived this facade-as-pediment from the pavilion at the rear of Palladio's Villa Maser (fig. 15). A gable end as a front elevation was unusual in 1964. This gable is also a split pediment to reveal the central chimney block behind, to enhance the Mannerist effect of spatial layering, and to make of the facade thereby a kind of disengaged sign. The facade as disengaged pediment or abstracted sign (fig. 16) is also reinforced by the parapets of the front and back walls which make them seem

independent of the roof and sides of the house. In the rear elevation the central element is the big arched window, less than a semicircle in shape. As in Neoclassical facades, it promotes big scale and grand unity in a small pavilion.

Another unusual characteristic of this building for its time is its windows which look like windows. The sliding sash define holes in the wall in the traditional manner, rather than an absence of wall in the Modern manner. The horizontal cross muntin (a special element inserted within a standard Arcadia sash) depicts window through its association with traditional windows. This four-paned window with muntins—in manifestations large, small, sliding, awning, or double hung—is now a standard element of Postmodern architecture.

Perhaps the most unusual feature of these

11

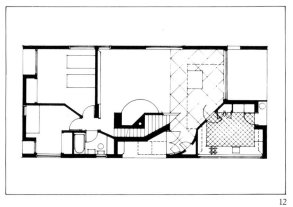

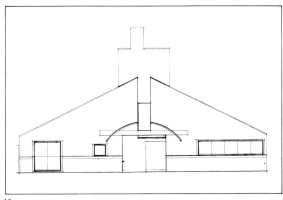

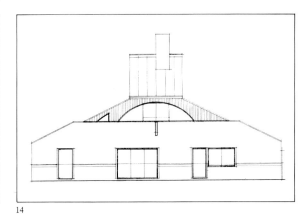

12   13

14

10 Vanna Venturi house, Philadelphia, Pennsylvania, 1962
11 Rear view
12 Plan, first floor
13 Front elevation
14 Rear elevation

elevations for 1964 was their applied decoration with its Classical character. There is a dado on the front and back elevations. It consists of a wood moulding placed a little high in terms of Classical precedent to enhance the scale of a small building. A shallow arch composed of the same moulding is applied above the entrance opening. The arch is juxtaposed on the concrete lintel that sits flush with the stucco wall. Arch and lintel together further enhance the scale of the already relatively big central opening. This use of ornamental redundancy and Classical association completes the Classical composition of the whole. The abstract linear quality of the Classical ornament applied to the smooth plaster walls, together with the disengagement of the walls at the parapets, makes the facades look almost like drawings and enhances their quality as representations of Classical architecture.

There are important elements of this design which are not Classical, for example the industrial sash and the strip window of the kitchen. But these act as counterpoint; they form part of the Classical-Mannerist element of contradiction within the whole and they establish this architecture as evolving Modern as well as reviving Classical. I did not explain this house as explicitly Classical in *Complexity and Contradiction in Architecture* because in the sixties I was more interested in describing its Mannerist than its Classical qualities. I did, however, make analogies with historical Classical architecture in my description of the building, and this has since become a Postmodernist literary device.

The Classicism that is essential to my mother's house is typical of most of the buildings I have designed. These buildings are more often Castle Howard[2]-as-built, with the ultimate asymmetry of

15

its north front, than Castle Howard-as-designed, with its unbroken symmetry; but they are Castle Howard nonetheless

In the end I am speaking of a historicist symbolism that seeks the essence of a style—or a place, or a tradition. I hope that my mother's house achieves an essence of Classicism in its context; for achieving essence is our ultimate aim in using symbolism in architecture—but that is the subject of another paper.

Some have said my mother's house looks like a child's drawing of a house (fig. 17)—representing the fundamental elements of shelter—gable roof, chimney, door, and windows. I like to think this is so, that it achieves another essence, that of the genre that is house and is elemental.

16

118

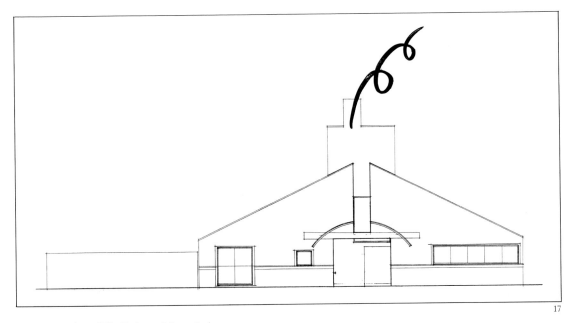

17

15 Rear pavilion, Villa Barbaro, Maser, Italy
16 Vanna Venturi house, rear view showing parapet
17 Front elevation with graffiti

Captions
1 Dates listed in all captions are of the approximate initiation of the projects.

"Leading from the Rear": Reply to Martin Pawley
1 See *Journal of the American Institute of Planners,* January 1970, p. 73.

Learning from Pop
1 John Kenneth Galbraith: "To my new friends in the affluent society—greetings," *Life,* March 27, 1970.

Plain and Fancy Architecture by Cass Gilbert at Oberlin and the Addition to the Museum by Venturi and Rauch
1 Kenneth Severens has kindly shown me two of Cass Gilbert's letters written in 1905 and 1911 where that architect discusses his reasons for the use of Romanesque at Oberlin. In addition, I am indebted to Mr. Severens for his encouragement in the writing of this article and for his enrichments to the arguments during several conversations.

A Definition of Architecture as Shelter with Decoration on It, and Another Plea for a Symbolism of the Ordinary in Architecture
1 The urbanity came, of course, from space and signs *and* an urban way inside and outside the buildings on the Italian piazza. This is the main reason why the piazzas of the sixties in America can't work. I discussed this in *Complexity and Contradiction in Architecture.* It is interesting, however, that there are American piazzas of the same period, without civic pretensions—those of the shopping centers surrounded by parking lots—which tend to work as commercial and social centers.
2 Walter Gropius, *The New Architecture and the Bauhaus,* Cambridge: MIT Press, 1965, p. 44.
3 Ibid. p. 92.
4 Our connoisseur might say that the strip architecture is not as good as the Beatles, but probably the high design architecture in his community is not up to Scarlatti.
5 Herbert J. Gans, *Popular Culture and High Culture: An Analysis and Evaluation of Taste,* New York, Basic Books, 1974.

Learning the Wrong Lessons from the Beaux-Arts
1 Pompier was a term used by Beaux-Arts architects to describe the most rigid of their members. What we call Beaux-Arts, they called pompier. [An index of architectural change: In 1984, "Beaux-Arts" is likely to be a term of approbation and is rarely used pejoratively to signify "too rigid." *DSB*]

RIBA Annual Discourse
1 I am indebted for these quotations to Denis Donoghue in his article "Hide and Seek" in *New York Review of Books,* 14 May, 1981, p. 40.
2 *T.S. Eliot: Selected Essays,* 1917–1932, New York: Harcourt, Brace and Co., 1932, p. 18.
3 Mary Lutyens: *Edwin Lutyens by his Daughter,* London: John Murray, 1980.
4 I am grateful for these ideas on cultural relevance and aesthetic pluralism to Denise Scott Brown. I am grateful to her too for editing this article.

Diversity, Relevance and Representation in Historicism, or Plus ça Change...*plus a Plea for Pattern all over Architecture with a Postscript on my Mother's House*
1 I am indebted to Denise Scott Brown for ideas in two essays, "A Worm's Eye View of Recent Architectural History" in *Architectural Record,* February 1984, and "Architectural Taste in a Pluralistic Society," in Harvard *Architectural Review,* Spring 1980.
2 Castle Howard was designed by Sir John Vanbrugh and Nicholas Hawksmoor in 1702–1732 and is in Yorkshire, England.

Figure Credits

The Campidoglio: A Case Study
Figs. 1, 3, 5, reprinted from *The Achitectural Review*

A Billdingboard Involving Movies, Relics, and Space
Fig. 2, photographed by Rollin R. La France
Figs. 4, 5, 8, 9, photographed by George Pohl

Learning from Lutyens: Reply to Alison and Peter Smithson
Figs. 1, 2, 3, reprinted from *RIBA Journal*

Learning from Pop
Figs. 1, 3, 16, photographed by Denise Scott Brown
Figs. 2, 5, 7, 8, 9, 10, 11, "Learning from Levittown" studio
Fig. 4, courtesy of Caesars Palace Hotel, Las Vegas
Fig. 6, courtesy of City Planning Commission, Philadelphia, PA
Figs. 12, 13, 14, 15, "Learning from Las Vegas" Studio
Fig. 17, photographed by Steven Izenour

Some Houses of Ill-Repute
Fig. 4, photographed by George Pohl
Figs. 18, 19, photographed by Steven Izenour

Complexity and Contradiction in the Work of Furness
Fig. 1, reprinted from *Pennsylvania Academy of the Fine Arts Newsletter*

Plain and Fancy Architecture by Cass Gilbert at Oberlin and the Addition to the Museum by Venturi and Rauch
Figs. 2, 7, 14, reprinted from *Allen Memorial Art Museum Bulletin*
Figs. 18, 19, 20, 22, 23, 24, 25, photographed by Tom Bernard

Learning the Right Lessons from the Beaux-Arts
Figs. 7, 44, 45, 50, 57, 62, photographed by Tom Bernard
Fig. 8, photographed by Mark Cohn
Fig. 12, photographed by Rollin R. La France
Fig. 13, photographed by Steven Izenour
Fig. 18, photographed by Cervin Robinson
Fig. 19, photographed by Stephen Hill
Fig. 28, photographed by Tom Crane
Fig. 33, photographed by David Hirsch

Il Propio Vocabolario, Four Houses for Gran Bazaar
Figs. 1, 2, 3, photographed by Cervin Robinson
Figs. 4, 5, photographed by Steven Izenour
Figs. 7, 8, 9, photographed by Tom Bernard

The RIBA Annual Discourse
Figs. 1, 3, photographed by Tom Bernard
Fig. 2, photographed by Steven Izenour

Diversity, Relevance and Representation in Historicism, or Plus ça Change... *plus a Plea for Pattern all over Architecture with a Postscript on my Mother's House*
Figs. 1, 15, photographed by Charles Brickbauer
Figs. 3, 5, photographed by Tom Bernard
Fig. 4, photographed by Steven Izenour and Tom Bernard
Fig. 10, photographed by Rollin R. La France
Figs. 11, 16, photographed by George Pohl

Robert Venturi and Denise Scott Brown are partners in the firm of
Venturi, Rauch and Scott Brown.

Robert Venturi, FAIA, was educated at Princeton University. He has
taught at the University of Pennsylvania and Yale University, was the
Architect in Residence at the American Academy in Rome, and has
lectured widely in Europe and America. He has been the recipient of many
design awards, including the Arnold W. Brunner Memorial Prize in
Architecture, the AIA Medal for *Complexity and Contradiction in
Architecture*, and the Hazlett Memorial Award for Excellence in the Arts.

Denise Scott Brown, ARIBA, was educated at the Architectural
Association in London and the University of Pennsylvania. She has taught
at Yale University and the universities of Pennsylvania and California, and
has lectured widely in Europe and America. She holds honorary doctorate
degrees from Oberlin College and the New Jersey Institute of Technology
and has received many awards for design. Her design and writing are
acclaimed for bringing particular attention to the relation between
architecture, planning and social conditions.

Bibliography

Writings about and References to Venturi, Rauch and Scott Brown

1960
"From Repainting to Redesign." *Architectural Forum*, January 1960, pp. 122–130.

"NYU—Duke House." *Interiors*, March 1960, pp. 120–125.

1961
"New Talent USA—Architecture." *Art in America*, vol. 49, no. 1 (1961), p. 63.

Rowan, Jan C. "Wanting to Be: The Philadelphia School." *Progressive Architecture*, April 1961, pp. 131–163.

1963
"FDR Memorial Competition: Discussion." *Casabella*, November 1963, pp. 12–13.

"High Style for a Campus Eatery." *Progressive Architecture*, December 1963, pp. 132–136.

1964
"Americans to Watch in 1964: Architecture—Robert Venturi." *Pageant*, February 1964, p. 72.

Moore, Charles. "Houses: The Architect Speaks to Man's Needs." *Progressive Architecture*, May 1964, pp. 124ff.

1965
Architectural League of New York: Architecture and the Arts Awards. Honorable Mention, 1965.

"Complexities and Contradictions." *Progressive Architecture*, May 1965, pp. 168–174.

Love, Nancy. "The Architectural Rat Race." *Greater Philadelphia Magazine*, December 1965, pp. 55ff.

Osborn, Michelle (with Romaldo Giurgola). "A Personal Kind of House." *The Philadelphia Evening Bulletin*, October 15, 1965, p. 55.

"Paths of Younger Architects." *The Philadelphia Inquirer Magazine*, March 3, 1965.

Van Trump, James D., ed. "The House Made with Hands: Recent Houses Designed by Pennsylvania Architects." *Charrette—Pennsylvania Journal of Architecture*, November 1965, pp. 10–15.

"Robert Venturi." *Arts and Architecture*, April 1965, p. 22.

"Venturi's Philadelphia Fountain Exemplifies Vernacular Urban Scale." *South Carolina AIA Review of Architecture*, 1965, pp. 29–31.

1966
"Are Young Architects Designing Prototypes of Your Future Models?" *American Builder*, October 1966, pp. 60–71.

"Dynamic Design with Angular Planes." *House and Garden Building Guide*, Spring/Summer 1966, pp. 132–135.

McCoy, Esther. "Young Architects: The Small Office." *Arts and Architecture*, February/March 1966, p. 28.

Scully, Vincent. "America's Architectural Nightmare: The Motorized Megalopolis." *Holiday*, March 1966, pp. 94–95, 142–143.

Stern, Robert A.M. *40 under 40*. New York: Architectural League of New York, 1966.

Stern, Robert A.M. "Review of *l'Architecture d'Aujourd'hui* Issue on USA '65." *Progressive Architecture*, May 1966, pp. 256, 266.

"Venturi House–'Mannerist.'" *Architectural Review*, February 1966, p. 49.

1967
Blake, Peter. *Architectural Forum*, June 1967, pp. 56–57. (Review of *Complexity and Contradiction in Architecture*; discussion, July 1967, p. 16.)

Colquhoun, Alan. "Robert Venturi." *Architectural Design*, August 1967, p. 362.

"Fourteenth Annual Design Awards." *Progressive Architecture*, January 1967, pp. 144–154.

Journal of the American Institute of Architects, June 1967, p. 94. (Review of *Complexity and Contradiction in Architecture*.)

"Maison R. Venturi." *l'Architecture d'Aujourd'hui*, January 1967, p. 26.

Miller, N. *Journal of the Society of Architectural Historians*, December 1967, pp. 381–389. (Review of *Complexity and Contradiction in Architecture*.)

"New-Old Guild House Apartments." *Progressive Architecture*, May 1967, pp. 133–137.

"New Schools for New Towns." *Design Fete IV*. Houston: School of Architecture, Rice University, 1967.

Pile, J.F. *Interiors*, July 1967, p. 24. (Review of *Complexity and Contradiction in Architecture*.)

Ramsgard, Birgitte. "Om Kompleksitet i Arkitektinen (Complexity and Contradiction)." *Arkitekten*, 1967, pp. 608–609.

Rykwert, J. *Domus*, August 1967, p. 23. (Review of *Complexity and Contradiction in Architecture*.)

Scott Brown, Denise. *Team 10, Perspecta 10 and the Present State of Architectural Theory*. American Institute of Planners, January 1967, pp. 42–50.

"The Permissiveness of Supermannerism." *Progressive Architecture*, October 1967, pp. 169–173.

"Three Projects." *Perspecta 11*, 1967, pp. 103–111.

Wellemeyer, Marilyn. "An Inspired Renaissance in Indiana." *Life*, November 17, 1967, pp. 74–84.

Whiffen, M. *Journal of the Society of Architectural Historians*, October 1967, pp. 198–199. (Review of *Complexity and Contradiction in Architecture*.)

"Young American Architects." *Zodiac 17*, 1967, pp. 138–151.

1968
Bottero, Maria. "Passanto e presente nell'architettura 'pop' Americana," *Communita*, December 1968.

"L'Architecture en tant qu'espace, l'architecture en tant que symbole," *l'Architecture d'Aujourd'hui*, September 1968, pp. 36–37.

"Less is Bore." *Toshi-Jukatu: A Monthly Journal of Urban Housing*, June 1968, pp. 42–46ff.

Lobell, John. "Both-And: A New Architectural Concept." *Arts*, February 1968, pp. 12–13.

McCoy, Esther. "Buildings in the United States," *Lotus*, vol. 4 (1967/1968), pp. 15–123.

Norberg-Schulz, Christian. "Less or More?" *Architectural Review*, April 1968, pp. 257–258.

Osborn, Michelle. "Dilemma in a Time of Change." *The Philadelphia Evening Bulletin*, April 26, 1968.

"Pop Architecture." *Architecture Canada*, October 1968. (Entire issue.)

Record of Submissions and Awards, Competition for Middle Income Housing at Brighton Beach. Brooklyn (N.Y.): HDA, City of New York, 1968.

"Two New Buildings by Venturi and Rauch." *Progressive Architecture*, November 1968, pp. 116–123.

1969
Berson, Lenora. "South Street Insurrection." *Philadelphia Magazine*, September 1969, pp. 87–91ff.

"Education and Extension." *Annual Report, 1969--1970*. Toronto: Art Gallery of Ontario.

Huxtable, Ada Louise. "The Case for Chaos," *The New York Times*, January 26, 1969, section 2, p. 32.

Jencks, Charles. "Points of View," *Architectural Design*, December 1969, p. 644.

Jenson, Robert. "Resort Hotels: Symbols and Associations in Their Design." *Architectural Record*, December 1969, pp. 119–123.

Love, Nancy. "The Deflatable Fair." *Philadelphia Magazine*, April 1969, pp. 137–140.

Richard, Paul. "Learning from Las Vegas." *The Washington Post*, January 19, 1969, pp. K1, K8.

Richard, Paul. "Learning from Las Vegas." *Today's Family Digest*, November 1969, pp. 12–17.

Scully, Vincent. "A Search for Principle between Two Wars." *Journal of the Royal Institute of British Architects*, June 1969, pp. 240–247.

Scully, Vincent. *American Architecture and Urbanism*. New York: Frederick A. Praeger, Inc., 1969.

Stern, Robert A.M. *New Directions in American Architecture.* New York: George Braziller, 1969.

Watson, Donald. "LLV, LLV:? VVV." *Novum Organum 5* (Yale School of Art and Architecture), 1969.

Wolfe, Tom. "Electrographic Architecture." *Architectural Design*, July 1969, pp. 380–382.

1970
"A Question of Values." *American Heritage*, August 1970, p. 119.

"Academic Village: State University College, Purchase, New York; Social Science and Humanities Building." *Architectural Forum*, November 1970, pp. 38–39.

Annual Report 1970 of the Director of University Development. New Haven: Yale University, 1970, pp. 19–23.

Berkeley, Ellen Perry. "Mathematics at Yale." *Architectural Forum*, July/August 1970, pp. 62–67.

Berson, Lenora. "Dreams for a New South Street are Spun at Theatre Meetings." *Center City Philadelphia*, February 1970.

"Choosing a Non-Monument." *Architectural Forum*, June 1970, p. 22.

"Competition-Winning Building to Provide Yale Mathematicians with New Quarters." *Journal of the American Institute of Architects*, July 1970, p. 8.

"Co-op City Controversy." *Progressive Architecture*, April 1970, p. 9.

"Co-op City: Learning to Like It" (letters to the editor). *Progressive Architecture*, February 1970.

Davis, Douglas. "Architect of Joy." *Newsweek*, November 2, 1970, pp. 103–106.

Eberhard, John P. "American Architecture and Urbanism." *Journal of the American Institute of Architects*, August 1970, pp. 64–66.

Huxtable, Ada Louise. "Heroics are Out, Ordinary is In." *The New York Times*, January 18, 1970, section 2, p. 27.

Huxtable, Ada Louise. *Will They Ever Finish Bruckner Boulevard*. New York: Macmillan Company, 1970.

"In Defense of the Strip." *Journal of the American Institute of Architects*, December 1970, p. 64.

Jacobs, Jay. "A Commitment to Excellence." *The Art Gallery*, December 1970, pp. 17–32.

Kurtz, Stephen A. "Toward an Urban Vernacular." *Progressive Architecture*, July 1970, pp. 100–105.

"Mathematics at Yale: Readers' Response." *Architectural Forum*, October 1970, pp. 64–66.

"Ordinary as Artform." *Progressive Architecture*, April 1970, pp. 106–109.

Osborn, Michelle. "The Ugly American Architect." *Philadelphia Magazine*, April 1970, pp. 52–56.

Pawley, Martin. "Leading from the Rear." *Architectural Design*, January 1970, p. 45.

Reif, Rita. "A Family Who Built a 'Real Dumb House' in a 'Banal Environment.'" *The New York Times*, August 17, 1970, p. 22L.

"Saint Francis de Sales Church." *Liturgical Arts*, August 1970, pp. 124–126.

Schulze, Franz. "Chaos as Architecture." *Art in America*, July/August 1970, pp. 88-96.

"Seventeenth Annual Progressive Architecture Design Awards." *Progressive Architecture*, January 1970, pp. 76–135.

Sica, Paolo. *L'immagine della citta da Sparta a Las Vegas*. Bari: Laterza, 1970.

Smith, C. Ray. "Electric Demolition, A Milestone in Church Art: St. Francis de Sales, Philadelphia." *Progressive Architecture*, September 1970, pp. 92–95.

"Your Point of View." *Progressive Architecture*, November 1970.

"Zoning Rebuilds the Theatre." *Progressive Architecture*, December 1970, pp. 76ff.

1971
"A House on Long Beach Island." *International Asbestos Cement Review*, April 1971, pp. 6–8.

Architecture for the Arts: The State University of New York College at Purchase. New York: The Museum of Modern Art, 1971.

Cliff, Ursula. "Are the Venturis Putting Us On?" *Design and Environment*, Summer 1971, pp. 52–59ff.

Davis, Douglas. "New Architecture: Building for Man." *Newsweek*, April 19, 1971, pp. 78–90.

Eisenman, Peter, et al. "The City as an Artifact." *Casabella*, vol. 35, no. 359/360 (December 1971).

Glueck, Grace. "Don't Knock Sprawl." *The New York Times*, October 10, 1971, p. 16D.

Goldberger, Paul. "Less is More–Mies van der Rohe. Less is a Bore–Robert Venturi." *The New York Times Magazine*, October 19, 1971, pp. 34–37ff.

Goodman, Robert. *After the Planners*. New York: Simon & Schuster, 1971.

Huxtable, Ada Louise. "Celebrating 'Dumb, Ordinary' Architecture." *The New York Times*, October 1, 1971, p. 43.

Huxtable, Ada Louise. "Plastic Flowers are Almost All Right." *The New York Times*, October 10, 1971, p. 22D.

Jensen, Robert. "Images for a New Cal City." *Architectural Record*, June 1971, pp. 117–120.

Kauffman, Herbert H. "A Sophisticated Setting for Two Suburban G.P.'s." *Medical Economics*, December 6, 1971, pp. 88-90.

Kay, June Holtz. "Champions of Messy Vitality." *The Boston Sunday Globe*, October 24, 1971, p. 25A.

McLaughlin, Patsy. "Ms. Scott Brown Keeps Her Own Taste to Herself." *The Pennsylvania Gazette*, December 1971, p. 38.

Nelson, Nels. "Bonkers over Billboards–and Very Cereus." *The Philadelphia Daily News*, September 24, 1971, p. 3F.

Osborn, Michelle. "The Crosstown is Dead. Long Live the Crosstown." *Architectural Forum*, October 1971, pp. 38–42.

Papachristou, Tician, and James Stewart Polshek. "Venturi: Style, not Substance." *The New York Times*, November 14, 1971, p. 24D.

"Robert Venturi." *Architecture and Urbanism* (Japan), October 1971.

"Robert Venturi." *Kenchiku Bunka*, March 1971, pp. 84–94.

Scully, Vincent. "The Work of Venturi and Rauch, Architects and Planners." Whitney Museum of American Art, September 1971.

"Venturi and Rauch." *l'Architecture d'Aujourd'hui*, December 1971/January 1972, pp. 84–104.

"Venturi and Rauch Projects Shown in New York." *Architectural Record*, November 1971, p. 37.

Vrchota, Janet. "Bye, Bye Bauhaus." *Print*, September/October 1971, pp. 66–67.

"Yale Mathematics Building." *Architectural Design*, February 1971, p. 115.

1972

"Aprendiendo de Todas Las Cosas." *Arte Y Comento* (Bilbao), November 20, 1972.

Abelardo, Oquerdo. "Arquitectura Pop." *El Comercio* (Lima), April 16, 1972.

Blasi, Cesare and Gabriella. "Venturi." *Casabella*, no. 364 (April 1972), pp. 15–19.

Miguel, Pere Ferrero. "Brown, D.S., y Venturi, R.; 'Aprendiendo de Todas Las Cosas.'" *ABC* (Madrid), April 26, 1972.

Corrigan, Peter. "Reflection on a New American Architecture: The Venturis." *Architecture in Australia*, February 1972, pp. 55–66.

Cuadernos de Arquitectura (Barcelona), January 1972. (Review of *Aprendiendo*.)

Davis, Douglas. "From Forum to Strip." *Newsweek*, October 1972, p. 38.

Donohoe, Victoria. "Buildings: Good and Bad." *The Philadelphia Inquirer*, June 30, 1972, p. 18.

Drew, Philip. *Third Generation: The Changing Meaning of Architecture*. New York: Praeger Publishers, 1972. (Published in German as *Die Dritte Generation: Architektur zwishen Produkt und Prozess*. Stuttgart: Verlag Gerd Hatje, 1972.)

Flanagan, Barbara. "Venturi and Venturi, Architectural Anti-Heroes." *34th Street Magazine*, April 13, 1972, pp. 1, 4.

Friedman, Mildred S., ed. "Urban Redevelopment: 19th Century Vision, 20th Century Version." *Design Quarterly*, no. 85 (1972).

Groat, Linda. "Interview: Denise Scott Brown." *Networks 1*, California Institute of the Arts, 1972, pp. 49–55.

Hoffman, Donald. "Monuments and the Strip." *The Kansas City Star*, December 10, 1972, p. 1D.

Holmes, Ann. "Art Circles." *Houston Chronicle*, May 7, 1972.

Huxtable, Ada Louise. "Architecture in '71: Lively Confusion." *The New York Times*, January 4, 1972, p. 26L.

Jackson, J.B. "An Architect Learns from Las Vegas." *The Harvard Independent*, November 30, 1972.

Jellinek, Roger. "In Praise (!) of Las Vegas." *The New York Times*, December 29, 1972, p. 23L.

"Learning from Las Vegas by Robert Venturi, Denise Scott Brown and Steven Izenour." *The New Republic*, December 2, 1972.

Maldonado, Thomas. *Design, Nature and Revolution, Toward a Critical Ecology*, trans. Mario Domandi. New York: Harper & Row, 1972. (Originally published as *La Speranza progettuale, ambiente e societa*, Nuovo Politecnico 35. Turin: Einaudi, 1970.)

Marvel, Bill. "Can McDonald's, Chartres Find Happiness?" *The Miami Herald*, February 20, 1972, pp. 49K–50K.

Marvel, Bill. "Do You Like the Arches? Sure, Easy, I Love Them!" *The National Observer*, February 12, 1972, pp. 1, 24.

McQuade, Walter. "Giving Them What They Want: The Venturi Influence." *Life*, April 14, 1972, p. 17.

Plous, Phyllis. "The Architecture of Venturi and Rauch." *Artweek* (Santa Barbara, Calif.), November 1972, p. 3.

"Renovation of St. Francis de Sales, Philadelphia, 1968." *Architectural Design*, June 1972, p. 379.

Robinson, Lydia. "Learning from Las Vegas." *The Harvard Crimson*, December 4, 1972, p. 2.

Schwartz, Marty. "Radical-Radical Confrontation: I.V. Is Almost All Right." *UCSB Daily News*, November 16, 1972, p. 5.

Sealander, John. "Appreciating the Architectural UGLY." *The Highlander* (University of California, Riverside), November 30, 1972.

Gerardo Delgado, Jose Ramon Sierra. "Unas notas sobre, 'Aprendiendo de todas las cosas,' de Robert Venturi." *El Correo de Andalusia*, May 2, 1972.

"Un diseno per al consumisme." *Serra D'Or*, Oriul Bohigas, February 1972, p. 18.

Vandevanter, Peter. "Unorthodox Architect." *Princeton Alumni Weekly*, December 12, 1972, p. 15.

Vandevanter, Peter. "Venturi: Controversial Philadelphia Architect." *The Daily Princetonian*, February 26, 1972, pp. 5ff.

Vermel, Ann. *On the Scene*. January 1972, pp. 1–2.

Waroff, Deborah. "The Venturies–American Selection." *Building Design*, no. 113, August 4, 1972, pp. 12–13.

Wines, James. "The Case for the Big Duck: Another View." *Architectural Forum*, April 1972, pp. 60–61, 72.

1973
"Award of Merit." *House and Home*, May 1973, pp. 116–117.

"Best Houses of 1973." *American Home*, September 1973, p. 52.

Blanton, John. "Learning from Las Vegas." *Journal of the American Institute of Architects*, February 1973, pp. 56ff.

Carney, Francis. "The Summa Popologica of Robert ('Call Me Vegas') Venturi," *Journal of the Royal Institute of British Architects*, May 1973, pp. 242–244.

Cook, John W. and Klotz, Heinrich. *Conversations with Architects*. New York: Praeger Publishers, Inc., 1973. (Interview with Robert Venturi and Denise Scott Brown is reprinted as "Ugly is Beautiful: The Main Street School of Architecture," *The Atlantic Monthly*, May 1973, pp. 33–43.)

"En Passant Par Las Vegas." *Architecture, Mouvement, Continuite*, September 1973, pp. 28–34.

Fowler, Sigrid H. "Learning from Las Vegas." *Journal of Popular Culture*, vol. 7, no. 2 (1973), pp. 425–433.

French, Philip. "The World's Most Celebrated Oasis." *The Times* (London), February 26, 1973.

Glixon, Neil. "Is This Art?" *Scholastic Voice*, November 29, 1973, pp. 2–8.

Hack, Gary. "Venturi View of the Strip Leads to Las Vagueness." *Landscape Architecture*, July 1973, pp. 376–378.

Holland, Laurence B. "Rear-guard Rebellion." *The Yale Review*, Spring 1973, pp. 456–461.

Huxtable, Ada Louise. "In Love with Times Square." *The New York Review of Books*, October 18, 1973, pp. 45–48.

Kemper, Alfred M., Sam Mori, and Jacqueline Thompson. *Drawings by American Architects*. New York: John Wiley and Sons, 1973.

Kurtz, Stephen A. *Wasteland: Building the American Dream*. New York: Praeger Publishers, 1973.

132

Levine, Stuart G. "Architectural Populism." *American Studies*, Spring 1973, pp. 135–136.

McCoy, Esther. "Learning from Las Vegas." *Historic Preservation*, January/March 1973, pp. 44–46.

Matsushita, Kazuyuki. "Learning from Las Vegas." *Architecture and Urbanism* (Japan), April 1973, p. 116.

Merkel, Jayne. "Las Vegas as Architecture." *The Cincinnati Enquirer*, December 16, 1973, p. 6G.

Moore, Charles. "Learning from Adam's House." *Architectural Record*, August 1973, p. 43.

Neil, J. Meredith. "Las Vegas on My Mind." *Journal of Popular Culture*, vol. 7, no. 2 (1973), pp. 379–386.

Neuman, David J. "Learning from Las Vegas." *Journal of Popular Culture*, Spring 1973, p. 873.

O'Gorman, James F. *The Architecture of Frank Furness*. Philadelphia: The Falcon Press, 1973.

Pawley, Martin. "Miraculous Expanding Tits versus Lacquered Nipples." *Architectural Design*, February 1973, p. 80.

Silver, Nathan. "Learning from Las Vegas." *The New York Times*, Book Section, April 29, 1973, pp. 5–6.

"Some Decorated Sheds or Towards an Old Architecture," *Progressive Architecture*, May 1973, pp. 86–89.

Stern, Robert. "Stompin' at the Savoye." *Architectural Forum*, May 1973, pp. 46–48.

"Strip Building." *Times Literary Supplement*, April 6, 1973, p. 366.

von Moos, Stanislaus. "Learning from Las Vegas/Venturi et al." *Neue Zuricher Zeitung*, September 1973.

Wolf, Gary. "Review of *Learning from Las Vegas*." *Journal of the Society of Architectural Historians*, October 1973, pp. 258–260.

Wright, L. "Robert Venturi and Anti-Architecture." *Architectural Review*, April 1973, pp. 262–264.

1974
"A Pair of Seaside Summer Cottages." *Second Home*, Spring-Summer 1974, pp. 68–71.

Allen, Gerald. "Venturi and Rauch's Humanities Building for the Purchase Campus of the State University of New York." *Architectural Record*, October 1974, pp. 120–124.

Batt, Margaret. "Historical Foundation Picks Strand Planners." *The Galveston Daily News*, November 24, 1974, p. 1.

Beardsley, Monroe. "Learning from Las Vegas." *The Journal of Aesthetics and Art Criticism*, Winter 1974, pp. 245–246.

Cambell, Robert. "Yales Sums Up State of the Arts." *The Boston Globe*, December 22, 1974, p. 26A.

Ciucci, Giorgio. "Walt Disney World." *Architecture, Mouvement, Continuite*, December 1974, pp. 42–51.

Cohen, Stuart. "Physical Context/Cultural Context: Including It All." *Oppositions 2*, January 4, 1974, pp. 1–40.

DeSeta, Cesare. "Robert Venturi, dissacratore e provocatore." *Casabella*, no. 394 (October 1974), pp. 2–5.

Eisenman, Peter. "Real and English: The Destruction of the Box. I." *Oppositions 4*, October 1974, p. 7.

Faghih, Nasrine. "Semiologie du signe sans message." *Architecture, Mouvement, Continuite*, December 1974, pp. 35–40.

Farney, Dennis. "The School of 'Messy Vitality.'" *The Wall Street Journal*, January 4, 1974, p. 20.

Ferebee, Ann, ed. "Women in Design." *Design & Environment*, vol. 5, no. 1 (Spring 1974).

Fitch, James Marston. "Single Point Perspective." *Architectural Forum*, March 1974, p. 89.

Garau, Piero. "Robert Venturi: architetto della strada." *Americana*, May/June 1974, pp. 37–40.

Hall, Peter. "*Learning from Las Vegas*." *Regional Studies*, vol. 8, no. 1 (1974), pp. 98–99.

Hine, Thomas. "City Planners Often Forget That People Must Live There." *The Philadelphia Inquirer*, May 6, 1974, p. 11E.

Hine, Thomas. "Franklin Shrine to Center on Abstract 'Ghost' House," *The Philadelphia Inquirer*, July 19, 1974, pp. 1D, 3D.

Hine, Thomas. "Learning from Levittown's Suburban Sprawl." *The Philadelphia Inquirer*, February 17, 1974, Section H, I.

Holmes, Ann. "The Pop Artist Who Isn't Kidding Plans to Give Vitality to the Strand." *Houston Chronicle*, November 24, 1974, part A, section 4.

Kay, Jane Holtz. "Learning from Las Vegas." *The Nation*, January 12, 1974.

Koetter, Fred. "On Robert Venturi, Denise Scott Brown and Steven Izenour's *Learning from Las Vegas*." *Oppositions 3*, May 1974, pp. 98–104.

Kramer, Paul R. "Wir lernen vom Rom und Las Vegas." *Werk, Architektur und Kunst*, February 1974, pp. 202–212.

Kuhns, William. "*Learning from Las Vegas*." *New Orleans Review*, Fall 1974, p. 394.

Moore, Charles W. and Nicholas Pyle, eds. *The Yale Mathematics Building Competition*. New Haven and London: Yale University Press, 1974.

Navone, Paola and Bruno Orlandoni, *Architettura "radicale*." Milan: Casabella, 1974.

"Nears Final Design." *The Hartford Times*, June 1974.

Raynor, Vivien. "Women in Professions, Architecture." *VIVA*, May 1974, pp. 30–31.

Redini, Maria Caterina, and Carla Saggioro. "Il tema della decorazione architettonica nell'America degli anni '60 attraverso *Perspecta, The Yale Architectural Journal*." *Rassegna dell'Istituto di architettura e urbanistica* (University of Rome), August/December 1974, pp. 99–125.

Schmertz, Mildred F. "Vincent Scully versus Charles Moore." *Architectural Record*, December 1974, p. 45.

Schulze, Franz. "Toward an 'Impure' Architecture." *Dialogue*, vol. 7, no. 3 (1974), pp. 54–63.

Scully, Vincent. *The Shingle Style Today*. New York: Braziller, 1974.

Sky, Alison. "On Iconology." *On Site 5/6 on Energy*, 1974.

Sorkin, Michael. "Robert Venturi and the Function of Architecture at the Present Time." *Architectural Association Quarterly*, vol. 6, no. 2 (1974), pp. 31–35.

Tafuri, Manfredo. "L'Architecture dans le boudoir: The Language of Criticism and the Criticism of Language," *Oppositions 3*, May 1974, pp. 37–62.

Treu, Piera Gentile, *Della complessita in architettura: Problemi di composizione urbana nella teorica di Robert Venturi*. Pauda: Tipografia "La Garangola," 1974.

"21st Awards Program: A Year of Issues." *Progressive Architecture*, January 1974, pp. 52–89.

"Venturi." *Architecture Plus*, March/April 1974, p. 80.

"Venturi and Rauch 1970–74." *Architecture and Urbanism* (Japan), November 1974.

Zobl, Engelbert. "Architektur USA–East II: Robert Venturi–John Rauch." *Architektur Aktuell—Fach Journal*, April 1974, pp. 17–18.

1975
Berliner, Donna Israel and David C. "Thirty-six Women with Real Power Who Can Help You." *Cosmopolitan*, April 1975, pp. 195–196.

Goldberger, Paul. "Tract House, Celebrated." *The New York Times Magazine*, September 14, 1975, pp. 68–69, 74.

Hine, Thomas. "East Poplar's Curious 'Victory.'" *The Philadelphia Inquirer*, June 29, 1975.

Hine, Thomas. "Pretzel-Land Welcomes the World." *The Philadelphia Inquirer*, *Today Magazine*, April 13, 1975, pp. 35–42.

Huxtable, Ada Louise. "Modern Architecture in Question." *The New York Review of Books*, November 27, 1975, pp. 6–10.

Isozaki, Arata. *Dissection of Architecture*. Tokyo: Fine Arts Publishing Co., 1975. (In Japanese.)

Polak, Maralyn Lois. "Architect for Pop Culture." *The Philadelphia Inquirer, Today Magazine*, June 8, 1975, p. 8.

"Robert Venturi." *Current Biography*, July 1975.

Rykwert, Joseph. "Ornament is No Crime." *Studio*, September 1975, pp. 95–97.

Tucker, Carll. "Specifications." Unpublished poem dedicated to Robert Venturi.

von Moos, Stanislaus. "Las Vegas, et cetera." and "Lachen, um, nicht zu weinen," *Archithese 13*, 1975, pp. 5–32.

1976
"America: An Exhibition by Venturi and Rauch." *Domus*, December 1976, pp. 46–47.

Beck, Haig. "Elitist!" *Architectural Design*, November 1976, pp. 662–666.

Beck, Haig. "Letter from London." *Architectural Design*, February 1976, p. 121.

Burroughs, Betty. "Speakers Express Views on Museums of the Future." *Wilmington Evening Journal*, November 5, 1976, p. 23.

Carpenter, Edward K. "Salute to the National Park Service–Exhibits at Franklin Court." *Design & Environment*, Fall 1976, pp. 32–33.

Coombs, Robert. "Philadelphia's Phantom School." *Progressive Architecture*, April 1976, pp. 58–63.

D'Amato, Claudio. "La Crisis del International Style y el espacio post-Kahniano: Estados Unidos en busca de so identidad." *Summarios*, undated, pp. 3–13.

Dixon, John. "Show Us the Way." *Progressive Architecture*, June 1976.

Domenech, Lluis. "Stern Star Estrella: La Obra de Robert A.M. Stern." *Arquitecturas*, September 1976, pp. 12–14.

Dunster, David. "The Same Coin." *Architectural Design*, November 1976, pp. 659–661.

"Entretien avec Robert Venturi et Denise Scott Brown." *Architecture Mouvement Continuite*, June 1976, pp. 95–102.

"First Photos of Allen Art Building's New Addition." *Oberlin Alumni Magazine*, September/October 1976, pp. 13–15.

Forgey, Benjamin. "Keeping the Cities' Insight." *The Washington Star*, February 29, 1976, pp. 1, 24C.

41st International Eucharistic Congress, *Exhibition of Liturgical Arts*, 1976, pp. 63-64.

"Franklin Court." *Progressive Architecture*, April 1976, pp. 69–70.

Futagawa, Yukio, ed. *Global Architecture 39: Venturi and Rauch*. Tokyo: A.D.A. EDITA, 1976.

Geddes, Jean. "Is Your House Crawling with Urban Symbolism?" *Forecast*, May 1976, pp. 40–41.

Goldberger, Paul. "How to Love the Strip: 'Symbols in the American City.'" *ARTnews*, September 1976, pp. 50, 54.

Hess, Thomas B. "White Slave Traffic." *New York*, April 5, 1976, pp. 62–63.

Hine, Thomas. "Shrine for Now, a Park Forever." *Philadelphia Inquirer*, April 18, 1976, pp. 1, 8B.

Hoelterhoff, Manuela. "A Little of Everything at the Whitney." *The Wall Street Journal*, June 9, 1976.

Hoffman, Donald. "Art Talk." *The Kansas City Star*, February 8, 1976, p. 3D.

Hughes, Robert. "Overdressing for the Occasion." *Time*, April 5, 1976, pp. 42, 47.

Huxtable, Ada Louise. "The Fall and Rise of Main Street." *The New York Times Magazine*, May 30, 1976, pp. 12–14.

Huxtable, Ada Louise. "The Gospel According to Giedion and Gropius is under Attack." *The New York Times*, June 27, 1976, section 2, pp. 1, 29.

Huxtable, Ada Louise. "The Pop World of the Strip and the Sprawl." *The New York Times*, March 21, 1976, p. 28D.

Kaye, Ellen. "New Kind of Ugly." *Philadelphia Inquirer, Today Magazine*, September 12, 1976, pp. 30–31.

Kleihues, Josef Paul, ed. *Dortmunder Architekturausstellung 1976*. Dortmund (West Germany): Dortmunder Architekturhefte No. 3, 1976.

Knight, Carleton, III. "Park Service Opens Franklin Court." *Preservation News*, August 1976, pp. 1, 6.

Kramer, Hilton. "A Monumental Muddle of American Sculpture." *The New York Times*, March 28, 1976, pp. 1, 34D.

Kron, Joan. "Photo Finishes." *New York*, March 22, 1976, pp. 56–57.

Lebensztejn, Jean-Claude. "Hyperealisme, Kitsch et 'Venturi.'" *Critique*, February 1976, pp. 99–135.

Lipstadt, Helene R. "Interview with R. Venturi and D. Scott Brown." *Architecture, Mouvement, Continuite,* 1976.

Marsh, Peter. "Venturi Strip." *Building Design*, July 9, 1976, p. 8.

Marvel, Bill. "On Reading the American Cityscape." *National Observer*, April 19, 1976.

Miller, Robert L. "New Haven's Dixwell Fire Station by Venturi and Rauch." *Architectural Record*, June 1976, pp. 111–116.

Morton, David. "Venturi and Rauch, Brant House, Greenwich, Conn." *Progressive Architecture*, August 1976, pp. 50–53.

"Off the Skyline and into the Museum." *Newsday*, April 14, 1976, pp. 4A–5A.

Orth, Maureen, with Lucy Howard. "Schlock is Beautiful." *Newsweek*, March 8, 1976, p. 56.

Papademetriou, Peter. "News Report: Report from Galveston." *Progressive Architecture*, December 1976, pp. 26–27.

Pfister, Harold. "Exhibitions." *The Decorative Arts Newsletter* (Society of Architectural Historians), Summer 1976, pp. 3–5.

"Philadelphia Architects Give Ten Annual Awards." *Building and Realty Record*, p. 1.

Pinon, Helio. "Actitudes Teorices en la Reciente Arquitectura de Barcelona." *Arquitectura*, May/July 1976, pp. 27–32.

Quinn, Jim. "Dumb is Beautiful." *Philadelphia Magazine*, October 1976, pp. 156ff.

Quinn, Jim. "Learning from Our Living Rooms." *Philadelphia Magazine*, October 1976, pp. 160–163, 165–168, 170, 172–175.

Quinn, Michael C. and Paul H. Tucker. "Dixwell Fire Station." *Drawings for Modern Public Architecture in New Haven*. New Haven: Yale University Art Gallery, 1976, pp. 19–24.

Reichlin, Bruno and Martin Steinman, eds. *Archithese 19*, pp. 3–11.

Richard, Paul. "Rooms with a View on Life." *The Washington Post*, April 13, 1976, pp. 1B–2B.

Robinson, Cervin. "Brant Conflict." *The Architectural Review*, June 1976, pp. 360–364.

Rosenblatt, Roger. "The Pure Soldier." *The New Republic*, March 27, 1976, p. 32.

Russell, Beverly. "Real Life: It's Beautiful." *House and Garden*, August 1976, pp. 79ff.

Ryan, Barbara Haddad. "Gaudy Reality of American Landscape Shines in Renwick Show." *Denver Post*, May 9, 1976.

Shore, Benjamin. "'Symbols of American City' a Monument to Bad Taste?" *St. Louis Globe Democrat*, April 8, 1976.

"Signs of Life." *Signs of the Times*, November 1976, pp. 38–39.

"Signs of Life: Symbols in The American City–Le Paysage Urbain Americain." *Creations et Recherches Esthetiques Européenes*, November 1976, pp. 46–49.

Smyth, Janet. "Living: Sign Language." *House and Garden*, May 1976, p. 8.

Stein, Benjamin. "The Art Forms of Everyday Life." *The Wall Street Journal*, April 22, 1976.

Stephens, Suzanne. "Franklin Court." *Progressive Architecture*, April 1976, pp. 69–70.

Stephens, Suzanne. "Signs and Symbols as Show Stoppers." *Progressive Architecture*, May 1976, p. 37.

"Symbols." *The New Yorker*, March 15, 1976, pp. 27–29.

Tafuri, Manfredo. "Order and Disorder, The Dialectic of Modern Architecture." *A + U*, October 1976, pp. 97–120.

Von Eckhardt, Wolf. "Signs of an Urban Vernacular." *The Washington Post*, February 28, 1976, pp. 1, 3C.

von Moos, S. "Americana: Zwei Ausstellungen in Washington." *Neue Zurcher Zeitung*, July 17–18, 1976.

Vrchota, Janet. "Preservation." *Design & Environment*, Fall 1976, pp. 30–31.

Wallach, Amei. "Levittown, You're Really OK." *Newsday's Magazine for Long Island*, November 14, 1976, pp. 8–11, 32–33.

Winn, Stephen. "Acceptance of the American Character Found in a Drive Down 1st Ave. South." *Washington Highline Times* (Seattle, Wash.), July 14, 1976.

1977

"Allen Art Building New Wing Dedication." *Oberlin Alumni Magazine*, March/April 1977, pp. 9–14.

"Amerika, Pop und Volkstumlichkeit in der Architektur." *Werk-Architehese*, November/December 1977, pp. 79–87.

Apraxine, Pierre. *Architecture I*. Catalog for exhibition at Leo Castelli, New York, N.Y., 1977.

Berti, Vincenzo. "6 Architture Recenti di Venturi & Rauch." *Parametro*, pp. 28–35.

Campbell, Robert. "Architecture's Gurus of the Garish." *The Boston Sunday Globe*, October 23, 1977.

Cohen, Stuart. "A summing up." *Progressive Architecture*, October 1977, pp. 50–54.

Congress for Creative America. *The Congress Transcripts: Discourse from the Congress for Creative America*, George Gelles ed. Philadelphia: Greater Philadelphia Cultural Alliance, 1977.

Cullinan, Helen. "Allen Museum's Wing Adds Dimensions in Modern Dress." *Cleveland Plain Dealer*, January 9, 1977, section 5, p. 20.

Dixon, John Morris, ed. "Venturi and Rauch." *Progressive Architecture*, October 1977, pp. 49–69.

Dunster, David. "After the Fall." *Progressive Architecture*, December 1977, pp. 85–88.

"Elusive Outcome." *Progressive Architecture*, May 1977, p. 92.

Filler, Martin. "Seeing the Forest for the Trees." *Progressive Architecture*, October 1977, pp. 56–59.

Fox, Martin and Edward K. Carpenter. *Print Casebooks 2, Second Annual Edition: The Best in Exhibition Design*. Washington (D.C.): R.C. Publications, Inc., 1977.

Gallagher, Hugh. "Allen Museum Completes Expansion." *Tempo*, January 7, 1977, pp. 1, 3.

Gebhard, David and Deborah Nevins. *200 Years of American Architectural Drawing*. New York: Whitney Library of Design, 1977.

Goldberger, Paul. "Architectural Drawings Raised to an Art." *The New York Times*, December 12, 1977.

Goldberger, Paul. "Design Notebook." *The New York Times*, September 22, 1977, p. 12C.

Goldberger, Paul. ". . . In Its Satisfying New Theater." *The New York Times*, October 19, 1977, p. 31.

Hine, Thomas. "Architectural Honor Awards Won for Two Buildings Here." *Philadelphia Inquirer*, May 13, 1977, p. 3B.

Hine, Thomas. "It's Not Easy to Put Modern Addition on Traditional Building." *Philadelphia Inquirer*, April 10, 1977, p. 13G.

Huxtable, Ada Louise. "Architectural Drawings as Art Gallery Art." *The New York Times*, October 23, 1977.

Huxtable, Ada Louise. "The Fine Points of Drawings." *The New York Times*, September 25, 1977, pp. 33, 36D.

Huxtable, Ada Louise. "The Latest Style is 'Jeweler's Mechanical.'" *The New York Times*, December 25, 1977, pp. 1, 27.

Huxtable, Ada Louise. "The Venturi 'Anti-Style' of Architecture." *The New York Times*, January 30, 1977, pp. 27, 36D.

Huxtable, Ada Louise. "What's Happening in American Architecture: Counterrevolution." *America Illustrated*, August 1977, pp. 10–12.

International Congress of Women Architects, Iran, 1976. *Report of the Proceedings: The Crisis of Identity in Architecture*. Tehran (Iran): Ministry of Housing and Urban Development, 1977.

Jencks, Charles. "Venturi et al Are Almost All Right." *Architectural Design*, vol. 47, no. 7–8 (1977), pp. 468–469.

Johnson, Malcolm L. "New Space to Open Up Stage Company Season." *The Hartford Courant* (Hartford, Conn.), April 10, 1977, p. 1F.

Killian, Tom. "Views." *Progressive Architecture*, June 1977, p. 10.

Klotz, Heinrich. "Das Pathos des Funktionalismus." *Werk-Archithese*, March 1977, pp. 3–4, 22.

Kron, Joan. "Hello Atlantic City." *The New York Times*, April 14, 1977, section 3, p. 3.

"A Man and His Home." *Industrial Design*, July/August 1977, p. 29.

"Mobili parlanti per il 'Bicentennial.'" *Modo*, June 1977, p. 5.

Morton, David. "Mission accomplished." *Progressive Architecture*, October 1977, pp. 60–63.

"Non la Riconstruzione ma l'Idea." *Domus*, March 1977, p. 53.

Raggi, Franco. "Bob Venturi: il piacere della contraddizione." *Modo*, July/August 1977, pp. 28–31.

Roth, Alfred. "Some Thoughts on Venturi and Marxism." *Werk-Archithese*, May 1977.

Ruckman, Andy. "Big Donors a Museum Make." *Oberlin News Tribune*, January 13, 1977, pp. 1, 6–7.

Skude, Flemming. "USA–Valgfriheden som Kulturel Kataljsator." *Lousiana Revu*, June/August 1977, pp. 6–7. (In Danish; summary in English.)

Smith, C. Ray. *Supermannerism: New Attitudes in Post-Modern Architecture*. New York: E.P. Dutton, 1977.

Stephens, Suzanne. "Casino qua non." *Progressive Architecture*, October 1977, pp. 67–69.

Stern, Robert A.M., guest ed. "America Now: Drawing towards a More Modern Architecture." *Architectural Design*, June 1977.

Stern, Robert A.M. *New Directions in American Architecture* (revised edition). New York: George Braziller, 1977.

Stern, Robert A.M. "Something Borrowed, Something New." *Horizon*, December 1977, pp. 50–56.

Tafuri, Manfredo, "Ordine e disordine," *Casabella*, January 1977, pp. 36–40.

Torre, Susana, ed. *Women in American Architecture: A Historic and Contemporary Perspective*. New York: Whitney Library of Design, 1977.

"Venturi & Rauch: Pour Franklin Court, un acte poetique." *Architecture Interieure*, December 1977/January 1978, pp. 72–73.

"Views." *Progressive Architecture*, December 1977, p. 8.

von Moos, Stanislaus, ed., "Venturi and Rauch: 25 Public Buldings." *Werk-Archithese*, July/August 1977, pp. 2–64. (In French and German.)

von Ranson, Brooks. "A Theatre is Born." *Connecticut*, October 1977, p. 30.

Wines, James. "Il Linguaggio eretico della disarchitettura." *Modo*, November 1977, pp. 37–42.

Wood, James M. "Art Museum at Oberlin Shocks the Eye, Wins the Heart." *The Cleveland Plain Dealer*, February 13, 1977, pp. 1, 4.

1978
Architecture & Media. Catalog for exhibition, Herbert F. Johnson Museum of Art, Cornell University, Ithaca, N.Y., September 20–November 5, 1978.

"Architecture: Does Everything Have to Go?." *Philadelphia Magazine*, June 1978, pp. 107–110, 112, 114–115.

"Architecture: Service, Craft, Art." Catalog for exhibition, Rosa Esman Gallery, April 13–May 13, 1978.

"Backstage along the Strand." *Progressive Architecture*, November 1978, pp. 72–77.

Boudon, Philippe. *Richelieu, ville nouvelle*. Paris: BORDAS, 1978.

Bradley, Jane. "Borough Picks Consultant for Downtown." *The Princeton Packet*, November 22, 1978.

Donohoe, Victoria. "Can a Rebel be at Home in the Establishment?" *The Philadelphia Inquirer*, May 9, 1978, pp. 1C, 4C.

Donohoe, Victoria. "Saving Marlborough Blenheim: A Chance to Blend Old and New." *The Philadelphia Inquirer*, February 5, 1978, p. 16K.

Donohoe, Victoria. "A Teacher Who Fills the House." *The Philadelphia Inquirer*, March 6, 1978, pp. 1D–3D.

Dunster, David, ed. "Venturi and Rauch." *Architectural Monographs 1*. London: Academy Editions, 1978.

Edwards, Ellen. "Architects Arrive to Tackle Washington Avenue Project." *The Miami Herald*, August 11, 1978, p. 4D.

Emery, Marc, ed. *l'Architecture d'Aujourd'hui*, no. 197 (June 1978), issue devoted to firm.

"Forceful Gesture on a Wooded Hillside." *AIA Journal*, Mid-May 1978, pp. 102–105.

Forgey, Benjamin. "The Continuing Battles of Pennsylvania Avenue: An Artist, Wounded, Withdraws." *The Washington Star*, April 11, 1978, p. D2.

Glueck, Grace. "Art People: A Tale of Two Pylons." *The New York Times*, April 7, 1978.

Goldberger, Paul. "Architecture: Venturi and Rauch." *Architectural Digest*, January/February 1978, pp. 100–107.

Goldberger, Paul. "Corporate Architecture: A Study in Banality." *Saturday Review*, January 21, 1978, pp. 36–38.

Goldberger, Paul. "Design Notebook." *The New York Times*, April 13, 1978, p. C10.

Goldberger, Paul. "Siblings by the Seaside." *The New York Times Magazine*, May 21, 1978, pp. 73, 84.

Goldberger, Paul. "Westway Architects Selected by State." *The New York Times*, February 24, 1978, p. 16.

Goodman, M. Louis. "Venturi and Rauch, Architects and Planners." Architecture: Service, Craft, Art, 1978. (Exhibition Catalogue)

Heyer, Paul. *Architects on Architecture* (revised edition). New York: Walker and Company, 1978, p. 412.

Hine, Thomas. "Basco Gives the High Sign." *The Philadelphia Inquirer*, November 6, 1978, pp. 1B, 3B.

"Hotel-Casino in Atlantic City, N.J." *Werk-Archithese*, May/June 1978, pp. 53–54.

Huxtable, Ada Louise. "Architecture for a Fast-Food Culture." *The New York Times Magazine*, February 12, 1978, pp. 23–36.

"In progress." *Progressive Architecture*, December 1978, p. 36.

Indelman, Alta. "After the climax of a Major Era–Venturi-ism?" *Crit 4: The Architectural Student Journal*, Fall 1978, pp. 11–15.

Johnson, Richard. "Top Pop Thinker on Westway." *The New York Post*, July 20, 1978.

Knight, Christopher. "History/Art." *Journal*, October 1978, pp. 27–29.

Kutner, Janet. "Venturi designs by emotion." *The Dallas Morning News*, May 24, 1978, p. 20A.

"Learning from Versailles." *Horizon*, August 1978, p. 51.

"Less is a Bore." *Newsweek*, November 6, 1978, pp. 84–85.

Lewin, Susan Grant. "Eclectic." *House Beautiful*, August 1978, pp. 58–61.

Levy, Alan G. "Robert Venturi, FAIA." *Bulletin* (Philadelphia Chapter, Institute of Architects), March/April 1978, p. 18.

Lippincott, H. Mather, Jr. "John K. Rauch, FAIA." *Bulletin* (Philadelphia Chapter, Institute of Architects), March/April 1978, p. 14.

Lobell, John. "Kahn and Venturi: An Architecture of Being-in-Context." *Artform*, February 1978, pp. 46–52.

Luschin, Hanno. "Robert Venturi & Geometric Form." Unpublished.

"Maison Dans Le Delaware, Etats-Unis." *l'Architecture d'Aujourd'hui*, December 1978, pp. 96–99.

"Make Your Voice Heard on Plans for Downtown." *The Princeton Packet*, November 29, 1978, p. 4A.

Maxwell, Robert. "The Venturi Effect." *Architectural Monographs 1.* London: Academy Editions, 1978.

Nakamura, Toshio, ed. "Recent Works by Venturi and Rauch." *Architecture and Urbanism*, January 1978. (Entire issue.)

"The New Westway Math." *The New York Times*. March 4, 1978, p. 20.

"Our Museum." *Oberlin News-Tribune*, January 5, 1978, p. 4.

Palley, Robin. "Guess What's Coming Next!" *The Philadelphia Inquirer, Today Magazine*, January 1, 1978, p. 14.

Pinnell, Patrick. "On Venturi I: Drawing as Polemic." *Skyline*, December 1978, p. 5.

Pommer, Richard. "Philip Johnson and History." *Artform*, October 1978, pp. 26–29.

Quinn, Jim. "Does Everything Have to Go?" *Philadelphia Magazine*, June 1978, pp. 107–112.

Richard, Paul. "New Design for a 'National Square.'" *The Washington Post*, May 24, 1978, p. C13.

Scholl, Jaye. "Princeton Hires Firm to Guide Growth." *Trenton Times*, November 17, 1978, p. B1.

Snow, Richard F. "The Marlborough-Blenheim: A Last Look?" *Americana*, March/April 1978, p. 70.

Stern, Douglas L. "Mixed Feelings Greet Return Appearance." *Landscape Architecture*, May 1978, pp. 239–40.

Stern, Robert A.M. "Something Borrowed, Something New." *Horizons USA*, 1978, pp. 46–55. (Reprinted from *Horizon*, December 1977.)

Stern. Robert A.M. "Venturi and Rauch: Learning to Love Them." *Architectural Monographs 1*. London: Academy Editions, 1978.

Thomas, George F. "Architectural Preservation." *Arts Exchange*, March/April 1978, pp. 6–7.

"Unity of Old and New." *Bauen & Wohnen*, July/August 1978, pp. 289–291.

"Universitatsclub, State College, USA." *Baumeister*, December 1978, p. 1106.

"Venturi & Rauch." *Architectural Design*, vol. 48, no. 1 (1978), pp. 38–40.

Von Eckhardt, Wolf. "Focus for the Avenue." *The Washington Post*, May 27, 1978, pp. B1, B6.

Wiley, Doris B. "Shared Careers." *The Sunday Bulletin*, April 23, 1978, section 5, p. 1.

Wood, James, ed. *Trends in Contemporary Architecture*. Catalog for exhibition, The New Gallery of Contemporary Art, Cleveland, Ohio, 1978.

"World Famous Architect: Robert Venturi." *Nikkei Architecture*, October 2, 1978, pp. 100–101.

1979

Barucki, Tadeusz. "What Next." *Architektura*, May/June 1979, pp. 37–41.

Bowles, Jerry. "Building in the Vernacular." *The Philadelphia Inquirer, Today Magazine*, September 23, 1979, pp. 12–15, 18, 34.

Buildings for Best Products, New York: The Museum of Modern Art, 1979.

Clark, Roger H. and Michael Pause, and 20 students of the School of Design. *Analysis of Precedent* (School of Design, North Carolina State University, Raleigh), vol. 28 (1979), p. 9-211 *passim*.

"Conbribucion a la Teoria; Relacion con otras teorias Americanas." *Arquitecturas*, nos. 30–31 (September/December 1979), pp. 49–50.

Costa, J.M. "Una Nueva vision de la ciudad." *El Pais*, April 11, 1979.

Esposto, Francesca. "L'Opera di Robert Venturi." Unpublished thesis, Facolta di Architettura Firenza.

The Federal City in Transition, Catalog for exhibition, The Barbara Fiedler Gallery, 1979.

Goldberger, Paul. "Architecture: Designs for Catalogue Emporiums." *The New York Times*, December 13, 1979, p. C17.

Goldberger, Paul. "Nantucket Gropes for Architectural Future." *The New York Times*, August 20, 1979.

Goldberger, Paul. "Ten Buildings with a Style of Their Own." *Portfolio*, June/July 1979, pp. 32–39.

Graham, Dan. "Art in Relation to Architecture–Architecture in Relation to Art." *Artforum*, February 1979, pp. 22–29.

Hine, Thomas. "Philadelphia: Venturi City." *The Philadelphia Inquirer, Today Magazine*, September 23, 1979, pp. 35–39.

Hine, Thomas. "The Rowhouse: A Home of Many Facets." *The Philadelphia Inquirer*, July 29, 1979, section H, pp. 1–2.

Hughes, Robert. "Doing Their Own Thing." *Time*, January 8, 1979, pp. 52–59. (Reprinted in Italian as "Mr. Architetto Ad Una Svolta," *Casa Vogue*, June 1979, pp. 168–177.)

Jodidio, Philip and Michel Ragon. "Eloge du laid et de L'Ordinaire." *Connaissance des Arts*, October 1979, pp. 86–93.

Kallmeyer, Lothar. "Funktionalismus und Widerspruch." *Problemfeld Architektur*, March 1979, pp. 113–122.

Klotz, Heinrich. "Zuruck zur Fassade!" *Problemfeld Architektur*, March 1979, pp. 129–133.

"Kunstgewerbemuseum Zurich: Venturi and Rauch." *Schweiz*, November 1979, pp. 57–58.

"Les Signes Urbains ou Le Nouveau Symbolisme." *Affichage*, July 1979, pp. 13–19.

Madden, Richard L. "2,997 Win Degrees in 278th Yale Ceremony." *The New York Times*, May 22, 1979, p. 2.

McNally, Geoffrey. "Best Launches Flower Showroom Near Philadelphia." *Catalog Showroom Business*, December 1979, pp. 47–48.

"Monumental Main Street." *Progressive Architecture*, May 1979, pp. 110–113.

"Ornament ist Kein Verbrechen." *Feuilleton*, November 19, 1979, p. 10.

Pinnell, Patrick L. "On Venturi II: Allegory and Kitsch." *Skyline*, January 1979, p. 5.

"Projet D'Habitation Rurale." *l'Architecture d'Aujourd'hui*, December 1979, pp. 51–53.

Quinn, Jim. "Computer Chic Enters the Building Scene Courtesy of Venturi and Rauch." *Philadelphia Magazine*, January 1979, pp. 91, 152–153.

Quinn, Jim. "Jim Thorpe is Alive and Well and Blooming in Pennsylvania." *Philadelphia Magazine*, November 1979, pp. 178–183, 282–288, 290.

Roose, Harry and Thomas Schregenberger. "Weniger Ist Langweilig." *Tages Anzeiger*, October 1979, pp. 6–7.

Rubino, Luciano. "Contro Ogni Inutile Eroismo." In *Le Spose del Vento*. Verona (Italy): Bertani Editore, 1979, pp. 219–225.

Schulze, Franz. "On Campus Architecture." *Portfolio*, August/September 1979, pp. 34–39.

Schulze, Franz. "Plain and Fancy out on the Prairie." *ARTnews*, April 1979, pp. 42–45.

"Siege social de l'Institute for Scientific Information, Philadelphia." *l'Architecture d'Aujourd'hui*, October 1979, pp. 74–75.

Slesin, Suzanne. "Two New Furniture Showrooms: Venturi and Saladino." *The New York Times*, December 13, 1979, pp. C1, C10.

Thomas, George E. "A Punchcard with its own Music." *The Bulletin*, August 26, 1979, p. D9.

Thomas, George E. "Enter, Grand–Consider the Door." *The Bulletin*, November 4, 1979.

"Venturi, Rauch and Scott Brown." *Summarios*, May 1979. (Entire issue.)

Viladas, Pilar. "Rich with Eclecticism." *Interiors*, November 1979, pp. 76–77.

von Moos, Stanislaus, ed. "Venturi and Rauch." *Architektur im Alltag Amerikas*. Catalog for exhibition, Kunstgewerbemuseum Zurich, 1979.

1980
"Alles Geht Wieder! Postmodernismus." *Schoner Wohnen*, December 12, 1980, pp. 95, 104, 106, 108, 110.

"Architecture contemporaine." *Encyclopaedia Universalis*, 1980, pp. 202–209. (In French.)

Belluzzi, Amedeo. "Ripetizione e differenza dell'architettura di Robert Venturi." *Parametro*, January/February 1980, pp. 34–39.

Brown, Lance Jay, ed. *Grants Recognition Program, The National Endowment for the Arts*, vol. 1 (August 1980), pp. 26–27, 76–77, 120–121.

Camesano, Phyllis. "Post Modern Architecture–Is It for You?" *Building Manual*, Winter 1980, pp. 54–55, 166–167.

"Centre D'Exposition Knoll." *l'Architecture d'Aujourd'hui*, September 1980, pp. xi–xx, 56–57.

Cohen, Edie Lee. "Complexity and Contradiction." *Interior Design*, March 1980, pp. 226–231.

Constantine, Eleni M. "The Sophisticated Shed." *Architectural Record*, May 1980, pp. 97–100.

Cook, Eugenia. "Atlantic City." *Trenton Times*, September 28, 1980, pp. 12–17.

Coote, James. "Eight for the Eighties." *Texas Architect*, July/August 1980, pp. 67–78.

Crowell, S. Fiske, Jr. "Denise Scott Brown." In *Contemporary Architects*. New York: St. Martin's Press, 1980, pp. 731-733.

Doubilet, Susan. "Trend-setting architects still dazzle with designs." *The Globe and Mail*, February 7, 1980, p. T7.

"Ein Team Lernt von Las Vegas." *Art*, July 1980, pp. 18–27.

Emanuel, Muriel, ed. *Contemporary Architects*. New York: St. Martin's Press, 1980.

Filler, Martin. "Learning from Venturi." *Art in America*, April 1980, pp. 95–101.

Forgey, Benjamin. "The Plaza that Might Have Been." *Washington Star*, December 28, 1980, pp. D11–D13.

"Forum Discussion." *The Harvard Architecture Review*, vol. 1 (Spring 1980), p. 190.

Friedman, Arnold. "Postmodernism." *Interior Design*, March 1980, pp. 232–235.

Futagawa, Yukio, ed. *Global Architecture---GA Document*, special issue 1970–1980, pp. 6, 122–123, 220–221.

Garfield, Eugene. "New Year, New Building." *Current Comments*, January 7, 1980, pp. 5–8.

Georges, Rip and Jim Heimann. *California Crazy*. San Francisco: Chronicle Books, 1980.

Giurgola, Romaldo. "Robert Venturi." In *Contemporary Architects*. New York: St. Martin's Press, 1980, pp. 848–850.

Goldberger, Paul. "A Leisurely Look at Our Roadside Architecture." *The New York Times*, February 21, 1980, p. C10.

Goldberger, Paul. "Western Plaza in Washington Gets a Somewhat Flat Reception." *The New York Times*, December 18, 1980, p. 18.

Gordon, Robert K. "Venturi Firm to Plan Butler Building." *The Daily Princetonian*, May 21, 1980, pp. 1, 9.

"Gute Nachbarn." *Der Spiegel Magazine*, March 23, 1980, pp. 248–254. (In German.)

Hernandez, Antonio. "Fragen in Sachen Venturi and Rauch." *Archithese*, March 1980, pp. 75–76.

Hine, Thomas. "Hard Bargain–Chinatown Getting New Homes, But, Oh, The Price." *The Philadelphia Inquirer*, April 24, 1980, p. 3B.

Hine, Thomas. "Philadelphia Influence in Architecture on Decline." *The Philadelphia Inquirer*, September 8, 1980, pp. 1M–2M.

Hine, Thomas. "A Yearning for the Old Ways Finds Expression in New Ruins." *The Philadelphia Inquirer*, March 16, 1980, p. L1.

Holschneider, Johannes. "Lernen von Venturi." *Architektur & Wohnen*, April 1980, pp. 164–170.

Hoyt, Charles K. "Interiors: Knoll Center by Robert Venturi." *Architectural Record*, March 1980, pp. 97–102.

Huxtable, Ada Louise. "Atlantic City–Analyzing an Urban Phenomenon." *The New York Times*, September 21, 1980, p. D29.

Huxtable, Ada Louise. "Totalitarian Tools of Seduction." *The New York Times*, December 23, 1980, pp. 1, 31–32.

Huxtable, Ada Louise. "The Troubled State of Modern Architecture." *The New York Review of Books*, May 1980, pp. 22–29.

Kender, Dorothy, ed. "New Art Museum at Oberlin College." *Building Stone Magazine*, September/October 1980, pp. 46–47.

Klotz, Heinrich, ed. "Robert Venturi." *Jahrbuch Fur Architektur, Neues Bauen*, 1980/1981, pp. 90–94. (Herausgeber: Deutsches Architekturmuseum, Frankfurt am Main.)

Kron, Joan. "The Almost-Perfect Life of Denise Scott Brown." *Savvy*, December 1980, pp. 28–35.

"Le Contraddizioni dell'architettura secondo Venturi." *Casa Vogue*, June 1980, p. 209.

Lippert, Kevin. "Influential Post-Modernist." *Princeton Alumni Weekly*, November 3, 1980, p. 20.

A Look at Architecture. Columbus (Ind.): Visitors' Center, 1980.

MacNair, Andrew. "Venturi and the Classic Modern Tradition." *Skyline*, March 1980, pp. 4–5.

McGuigan, Cathleen. "The Architect." *TWA Ambassador*, September 1980, pp. 77–80.

Miller, Robert L. "Designs for Living." *TWA Ambassador*, April 1980, pp. 39–41.

Miller, R. Leonard. "Evaluation: Admiring Glance at a Celebrity." *AIA Journal*, February 1980, pp. 38–41.

Morton, David. "Miami Beach." *Progressive Architecture*, August 1980, pp. 64–65.

"Museum fur Kunsthandwerk in Frankfurt." *Baumeister*, August 1980, pp. 766–775.

National Trust for Historic Preservation, *Old & New Architecture: Design Relationship*. Washington (D.C.): The Preservation Press, 1980, pp. 82, 92, 103, 180.

Pinon, Helio. "Modernitat y Avantguarda." *Arquitecturas No. 32/33*. March/April 1980, pp. 5–11.

"Post-Modernists: Out of the Glass Box." *Forbes* (Arabic edition), 1980, pp. 19–22.

"Princeton Notebook." *Princeton Alumni Weekly*, October 20, 1980, pp. 12–13.

"Projet d'amenagement de la Western Plaza, Washington." *l'Architecture d'Aujourd'hui*, February 1980, pp. 17–20.

Radice, Barbara. "Il Ritorno Delle Colonne." *Casa Vogue*, November 1980, pp. 222–226.

Reese, Teresa. "Rude Graphics, or Learning from Las Vegas." *Print*, September/October 1980, pp. 42–51, 92, 94.

Rixse, James. "Blueprints Sketch Butler College Social Center." *The Daily Princetonian*, pp. 1, 8.

Rubin, Jerome and Cynthia Rubin. *Mission Furniture*. San Francisco: Chronicle Books, 1980.

Russell, Beverly. "The Editor's Word: Winners." *Interiors*, January 1980, p. 79.

Sachs, Sid. "Art and Architecture in Philadelphia." *The New Art Examiner*, October 1980.

Samuels, Cynthia A. "Robert Venturi's Architectural Theory: The Philosophical Source." Unpublished manuscript, 1980.

Schwartz, Frederic. "Design for the City." *CRIT 8, The Architectural Student Journal*, Fall 1980, pp. 12–13.

Strauss, Robert. "Atlantic City: Rich Tradition of Hoke." *Philadelphia Daily News*, September 10, 1980, pp. 27, 32.

"The New York Showroom." *Progressive Architecture*, July 1980, pp. 74–76.

"Tucker House." *Architectural Design*, May/June 1980, pp. 30–32.

"Venturi, Rauch and Scott Brown." *Progressive Architecture*, January 1980, pp. 104–105.

Viladas, Pilar. "Economy that Works." *Interiors*, November 1980, p. 71.

Vogel, Carol. "Architecture: Robert Venturi." *Architectural Digest*, October 1980, pp. 88–95.

Von Eckardt, Wolf. "Bare & Square." *The Washington Post*, December 20, 1980, pp. D1, D5.

von Moos. Stanislaus. "Architektur als Bilderbogen." *Jahrbuch Fur Architektur, Neues Bauen*, 1980/1981, pp. 95–112. (Herausgeber: Deutsches Architekturmuseum, Frankfurt am Main.)

1981
Allen, Gerald and Richard Oliver. "Robert Venturi, John Rauch & Denise Scott Brown." *Architectural Drawing: The Art and the Process*. New York: Whitney Library of Design, 1981, pp. 142–147.

Berg, Steve. "A Glittering New Life Proposed to Hennepin Ave." *Minneapolis Tribune*, April 19, 1981, pp. 4–6, 8–11.

"Budget Lighting has the Attributes of Quality." *Architectural Record*, February 1981, pp. 108–111.

"Buildings in the News." *Architectural Record*, December 1981, p. 41.

Busch, Akiko. "The Decorated Surface." *Metropolis*, December 1981, pp. 14–17.

Camesano, Phyllis. "Handcrafted Houses." *Building Manual*, Summer 1981, pp. 94–98. (Brant House, Vail, Colorado)

Campbell, Robert. "Ritz University Place Contextual Triumphs." *Boston Sunday Glove,* Nov. 15, 1981, pp. B1, B4. (Reference to Robert Venturi; Guild House)

Dean, Andrea O. "Eero Saarinen In Perspective." *AIA Journal*, November 1981, pp. 36–51. (Saarinen's work and influence on prominent architects of today such as Venturi)

Forgey, Benjamin. "Magnets for People: Planning the Parks Along Pennsylvania Avenue." *The Washington Post,* December 19, 1981. (Reference to Western Plaza)

Freeman, Robert. "Venturi." *Attenzione*, February 1981, pp. 30–35.

Futagawa, Yukio, ed. "Modern Houses." *Global Architecture Book 3*. Tokyo: A.D.A. EDITA, 1981.

Galletta, Bruno. "Knoll International, New York." *L'Industria Delle Construzioni*, January 1981, pp. 70–72. (In Italian.)

Gandee, Charles K. "Record Houses 1981–Private House, Bermuda." *Architectural Record*, Mid-May 1981, pp. 57–61. (Also in Japanese, *Nikkei Architecture*, 1981, Nos. 9–14, pp. 9–93.).

Gilbert, Lynn and Gaylen Moore. *Particular Passions*. New York: Clarkson N. Potter, 1981.

Goldberger, Paul. "Collecting on a Grand Scale." *Home Design, The New York Times Magazine*, 1981, part 2, pp. 49–105 *passim*.

Graham, Dan. "Not Post-Modernism: History as Against Historicism, European Archetypal Vernacular in Relation to American Commercial Vernacular, and the City as Opposed to the Individual Building." *Artforum*, December 1981, pp. 50–58.

Graham, Dan. "Signs." *Artforum*, April 1981, pp. 38–43.

"A Grander Vista for Inauguration Crowds." *U.S. News & World Report*, January 19, 1981, pp. 48, 49.

Gregotti, Vittorio. Introductory remarks to Robert Venturi's lecture, Italy. Unpublished, July 8, 1981. (In Italian)

Hoffman, Donald. "Styles Reflect Flexibility and Temper of the Era." *The Kansas City Star,* November 29, 1981, p. 16F. (Denise Scott Brown)

"Intangibles." *Fetish*, Spring 1981, p. 12.

"Interiors Events: Second Annual Interiors Awards." *Interiors*, April 1981, pp. 44–46.

Johnson, Eugene J. "United States of America." *International Handbook of Contemporary Developments in Architecture*. Westport and London, 1981.

Klotz, Heinrich. "Die Wiedereinfuhring der Saule." *Jahrbuch fur Architektur*, 1981–1982. Vieweg, Deutsches Architekturmuseum, Frankfurt am Main, and Braunschweig/Wiesbaden, 1981.

Kron, Joan. "My Son, the Architect: Houses for Parents." *The New York Times*, November, 12, 1981, pp. C1, C6.

Kulterman, Udo. "Space, Time and the New Architecture." *A+U*, February 1981, pp. 14–15, 22.

"La Caserma Dei Pompieri." *Interni*, April 1981, pp. 44, 45.

Langdon, Philip. "Architects Who Mock Modernism." *The Buffalo News*, pp. F1, F3.

"L'Architettura E'Anche Una Canzone." *Modo*, November 1981, pp. 19–22.

Leccese, Michael, ed. "America's Main Street." *Preservation News*, January 1981, pp. 1, 11.

"Maison Brant-Johnson, Vail Colorado." *l'Architecture d'Aujourd'hui*, February 1981, pp. 46–48.

"Miami Beach Art Deco Hotel Razed Under Cover of Night." *AIA Journal*, June 1981, pp. 18–20.

Morris, Michele. "Beached in Bermuda." *Diversion*, December 1981, pp. 219–222.

Muntanola, Josep. *Poetica y arquitectura*. Barcelona: Editorial Anagrams, 1981.

Nakamura, Toshio, ed. "Venturi, Rauch and Scott Brown." *A+U* (Japan), December 1981.

Norberg-Schultz, Christian. "Arkitektur som billede." *Huset som billede*, September/October 1981, pp. 55–56.

Oliver, Richard and Gerald Allen. "Robert Venturi, John Rauch and Denise Scott Brown." *Architectural Drawing: The Art and the Process*. New York: Whitney Library of Design, 1981, pp. 142–147.

Pain, Richard J.K. "Venturi Vandalised." *Architectural Review*, January 1981.

Papadakis, Andreas C., ed. "Current Projects." *Architectural Design*, December 1981, pp. 86–129 *passim*.

"Park Regency Cites Architect." *The Houston Post*, August 29–30, 1981, pp. 1DD, 5DD.

"Park Regency Chosen for Exhibit." *The Houston Post,* October 3–4, 1981, pp. 11DD.

Pelli, Cesar, ed. "Robert Venturi." *Yale School of Architecture Seminar Papers*, 1981, vol. 1, pp. 187–241.

Pirovano, Carlo, ed. "Venturi, Rauch and Scott Brown." *Domus*. Milan: Gruppo Editoriale Electa, 1981.

Poggi, Christine. "The Relationship of Modernist Thought to the Theories and Architecture of Venturi, Rauch and Scott Brown." Unpublished paper, June 4, 1981.

"Private House, Bermuda." *Nikkei Architecture*, 1981, Nos. 9–14, pp. 90–93. (In Japanese; English translation, *Architectural Record*, Mid-May 1981, pp. 57–61.)

Sachs, Randi T. "Large Success from a Small Budget." *Administrative Management*, March 1981, pp. 26–29, 68.

Safdie, Moshe. "Private Jokes in Public Places." *The Atlantic Monthly*, December 1981, pp. 62–68.

Sanderson, W., ed. *International Handbook of Contemporary Developments in Architecture*. Westport and London: 1981.

Sidener, Jack. "Franklin would appreciate Franklin Court." *The Philadelphia Inquirer*, September 20, 1981.

Speaking a New Classicism: American Architecture Now, 1981, pp. 54–58. (House based on Mount Vernon, and Knoll Showroom included in exhibition catalog published by Smith College Museum of Art, Northampton, Mass.)

Stephens, Suzanne. "Women in Architecture." *House & Garden*, March 1981, pp. 146, 147, 149, 196, 197.

"Symbols for the Young." *Building Design*, July 10, 1981, p. 2.

Thorndike, Joseph Jr., ed. *Three Centuries of Notable American Architects*. New York: American Heritage Publishing Co., Inc., 1981.

"Venturi, Rauch and Scott Brown." *Progressive Architecture*, January 1981, p. 98.

Viladas, Pilar. "Life after Mies." *Interiors*, January 1981, p. 64.

Vogel, Carol. "Architettura: Robert Venturi." *Italian Architectural Digest*, June 1981, pp. 102–109, 155. (In Italian; translation of article in *Architectural Digest*, October, 1980, pp. 88–95.)

Werner, Frank. *Die vergeudete Moderne*. Deutsche Verlags-Ansalt: Stuttgart, 1981, pp. 19–211 *passim*.

Wolfe, Tom. *From Bauhaus to Our House*. New York: Farrar Straus Giroux, 1981. (Reprinted in part in *Harper's*, July 1981, pp. 40–59.)

1982

Abercrombie, Stanley. "Architecture's Brave New World?" *Interior Design*, April 1982, pp. 210–211.

"America Redresses its Main Street." *Engineering News Record*, June 24, 1982, pp. 24–25, 28.

Architettura Nei Paesi Islamici, Seconda mostra internazionale di architettura. Venice: La Biennale di Venezia, 1982.

"Art in Public Places: The One-Percent Solution." *Houston Arts*, Second Quarter 1982, p. 5.

Bach, Penny Balkin. "The Process." *Form and Function: Proposals for Public Art for Philadelphia*. Catalog for exhibition, PAFA and Fairmount Park Commission, Philadelphia, Pa., 1982.

Bodine, Sarah. "Machinemade." *Metropolis*, June 1982.

Borja, Manuel J. "Venturi & Co., The Concept of Decorated Shed." Unpublished manuscript, 1982.

Bregman, Lillian. "Architectural Digest." *Philadelphia Magazine*, October 1982, pp. 186, 193.

Bruegman, Robert. "Two Post-Modernist Visions of Urban Design." *Landscape*, vol. 26, no. 2 (1982), pp. 31–37.

Campbell, Robert. "Architect Venturi Speaks at Harvard." *The Boston Globe*, April 16, 1982, p. 16.

"Completion of residential colleges scheduled for September 1983." *Campaign Bulletin* (Princeton University), vol. 1, no. 3 (April 1982), pp. 4–5.

Cortes, Juan Antonio. "Unidad Frente A Tipo." *Arquitecturas*, January/June 1982, pp. 22–24.

"The Contemporary Coffee Pot (and Tea Service) as Fine Art." *Architectural Record*, Mid-February 1982, p. 35.

Dean, Andrea O. "Women in Architecture: Individual Profiles and a Discussion of Issues." *AIA Journal*, January 1982, pp. 42–51.

DeWolf, Rose. "They Share Plans But Not Credit." *Philadelphia Daily News,* August 24, 1982, p. 31. (Profile of Venturi & Scott Brown)

Duka, John. "Contradiction and Complexity Create a Home." *The New York Times*, October 28, 1982, pp. C1, C6.

"Ecole de Philadelphie: Steven Izenour, Paul Muller, Marc Schimmenti, Frederic Schwartz, John Reddick." *La modernite ou l'espirit du temps, Biennale de Paris, section architecture 1982.* (Brief descriptions of projects by above VRSB architects; in French)

Eisenman, Peter. "Interview: Robert Venturi." *Skyline*, pp. 12–15.

Filler, Martin. "The Art of VRSB." *House & Garden*, October 1982, pp. 8, 13.

Filler, Martin. "History Reinvented: Adam and His Heirs." *Art in America*, Summer 1982, pp. 87–97.

Forgey, Benjamin. "Duck Soup: Confusion at the Corner." *Washington Post*, May 15, 1982, pp. C1, C4.

Friedman, Mildred S., ed. "Hennepin Avenue." *Design Quarterly*, no. 117 (1982).

Gandee, Charles K. "The Coxe Studio Block Island, RI." *Architectural Record*, Mid-May 1982, pp. 54–55.

Germany, Lisa. "The Comeback of the Column." *Texas Monthly*, August 1982, pp. 152, 154–158.

Gimenez, Carmen and Juan Munoz, ed. *Correspondences, 5 Architects, 5 Sculptors*. Catalog for exhibition, Palacio de las Alhajas, Madrid, Spain, October–November 1982.

Goldberger, Paul. "Architecture That is Bred to the Sea." *The New York Times Magazine*, August 22, 1982, pp. 62–64.

Goldberger, Paul. "Robert Venturi–In Love with the Art of Building." *The New York Times*, September 19, 1982, pp. H27–H28.

Hine, Thomas. "Learning from Atlantic City." *AIA Journal*, November 1982, pp. 44–47.

Hine, Thomas. "Today's Atlantic City, where character is as much at stake as cash." *Philadelphia Inquirer*, pp. 1D, 4D.

Jencks, Charles. "Venturi, Rauch and Scott Brown." *Architectural Design*, January/February 1982, pp. 68–71.

Kimmelman, Michael. "Sitting Pretty." *Horizon*, September 1982, pp. 16–24.

"La Doppia Riflessione." *Gran Bazaar*, November 1982, pp. 150–155.

Maxwell, Robert. "Venturi, Rauch and Scott Brown at Protetch." *Skyline*, November 1982, p. 15.

Moschini, Francesco. "Ironic Order." *Domus*, August 1982, pp. 44–58.

"The New Vernacular." *Building Manual*, Winter 1982, pp. 53–55.

Papadakis, Andreas C., ed. "Free-Style Classicism: The Wider Tradition." *Architectural Design*, January/February 1982, pp. 14–102 *passim*.

Papademetriou, Peter C. "Go West John Nash." *Progressive Architecture*, February 1982, p. 22.

Rave, Ligia and David Slovic. "Venturi, Rauch and Scott Brown's Realist Approach." *Skyline*, February 1982, p. 6.

"Robert Venturi Delivers the 1982 Walter Gropius Lecture." *HGSD News*, Summer 1982, p. 7.

Romano, Carlin. "Finally, a Memorial to Penn." *The Philadelphia Inquirer*, October 29, 1982, p. 1C.

Schmertz, Mildred F. "Learning from Denise: The Role in Architecture of DSB." *Architectural Record*, July 1982, pp. 102–107.

Stephens, Suzanne. "The Historicist Vision: The Shingle Style Genre." *Skyline*, pp. 18–19.

"Venturi, Rauch and Scott Brown." *Gran Bazaar*, February 1982, p. 43.

"Venturi, Rauch and Scott Brown." *Progressive Architecture*, January 1982, pp. 186–189.

Viladas, Pilar. "Deco Rating." *Progressive Architecture*, November 1982, pp. 90–95.

Viladas, Pilar. "Wall papers at Protetch." *Progressive Architecture*, November 1982, p. 35.

Werner, Frank. "8 Einsichten an 16 Beispielen." *Bauwelt*, January 8, 1982, pp. 22–23.

Wines, James. "Setting the Record Straight." *Express*, Fall 1982, pp. 12, 13.

Yanchewski, Joan. "Robert Venturi and Virginia Woolf: An Androgynous View of Art." *Threshold* (School of Architecture, University of Illinois at Chicago). Chicago: Rizzoli, 1982.

Yee, Roger, ed. "Where INA/CIGNA Investment Goes Public." *Corporate Design*, November/December 1982, pp. 52–57.

1983

Aldegheri, Claudio and Maurizio Sabini, eds. *Immagini del Post-Moderno*. Venice: Edizioni Cluva, 1983.

At Home with Architecture: Contemporary Views of the House. Exhibition catalog, Mandeville Art Gallery, University of California, San Diego, February 10–March 20, 1983.

Barron, James. "Princeton Head Tells Graduates to Serve Society." *The New York Times*, June 8, 1983, p. B4.

Bassin, Joan. "Venturi, Laguna Gloria Begin Honeymoon." *Austin-American Statesman*, May 1, 1983, p. 35.

Boles, Daralice D. "What Does Wu Mean?" *Progressive Architecture*, October 1983, p. 38.

Bowen, William. "The Difficulty Unity of Inclusion." *Princeton Alumni Weekly*, October 5, 1983, pp. 14–16.

Brickhouse, Robert. "Championing the Ugly and Ordinary in Architecture." *The Daily Progress*, April 17, 1983, pp. F1, F3.

Busch, Akiko. "By Design." *Metropolis*, September 1983, p. 25.

Chimacoff, Alan and Alan Plattus. "Learning from Venturi." *Architectural Record*, September 1983–II.

DeLong, David G. "Historic Preservation: A Movement in Search of Professional Standards." *Interior Design*, October 1983, p. 189.

Dietsch, Deborah. "A Degree of Design Innovation on Campus." *Interiors*, December 1983, p. 32.

Forgey, Benjamin. "Ornament Expressed: Showing Off the Inventive, the Grand and the Absurd." *The Washington Post*, July 9, 1983, pp. C1, C5.

Forgey, Benjamin. "Tarnished Brilliance: Western Plaza: No Wonder It's 'Not Quite Right.'" *The Washington Post*, June 18, 1983, pp. C1, C4.

Gandee, Charles K. "At Home: Venturi, Scott Brown House." *Architectural Record*, September 1983–I, pp. 108-113.

Giovannini, Joseph. "Architectural Imitation: Is it Plagiarism?" *The New York Times*, March 17, 1983, pp. C1, C6.

Giovannini, Joseph. "Design Notebook: Tea Services with the Touch of an Architect." *The New York Times*, November 17, 1983.

Giovannini, Joseph. "Designs for Today's Kitchen: A Place to Work and Live." *The New York Times*, pp. C1, C6.

Giovannini, Joseph. "Embellishing 80's Interiors: The Return of Decoration." *The New York Times*, May 12, 1983, pp. C1, C8.

Giovannini, Joseph. "Regional Styles Enter the Architectural Mainstream." *The New York Times*, September 22, 1983, pp. C1, C6.

Goldberger, Paul. "Small Building, Big Gestures." *The New York Times*, June 19, 1983, pp. 35–36.

"Gordon Wu Hall Dedicated at Reunions." *Campaign Bulletin*, Princeton University, Summer 1983, p. 8.

Guenther, Robert. "Newer Than New?" *The New York Times*, August 1, 1983.

Gutman, Robert. "Venturi's Masterclass." *The Architects' Journal*, September 7, 1983, pp. 36–39.

Hargreaves, George. "Post Modernism Looks Beyond Itself." *Landscape Architecture*, July/August 1983, pp. 60–65.

"HQ Cited as 'Ornamental' Architecture." *Vision*, August 1983, p. 3.

Hine, Thomas. "The Art Deco Duel of the Buildings." *The Philadelphia Inquirer*, February 13, 1983.

Hine, Thomas. "Awards Reflect a Rare Period of Pluralism." *The Philadelphia Inquirer*." May 8, 1983, p. 14H.

Hine, Thomas. "New Princeton Building Links Past to Future." *The Philadelphia Inquirer*, October 30, 1983, p. 20–I.

Hine, Thomas. "Welcome Park's Exposed Look Overshadows Its Tribute to Penn." *The Philadelphia Inquirer*, January 14, 1983, pp. 1D, 8D.

"In Architecture, Too, Anything Goes." *U.S. News & World Report*, August 1, 1983, p. 58.

Jencks, Charles, ed. *Abstract Representation*. New York: St. Martin's Press, 1983.

Kaliski, John. "Diagrams of Ritual and Experience: Learning from The Park Regency." *Cite*, Spring 1983, pp. 8–13.

Kramer, Teresa. "Office Design Affects Productivity." *The Best of Business*, Spring 1983, p. 57.

"Learning from Minneapolis." *Planning*, March 1983, p. 4.

Lewin, Susan Grant. "An Old Tradition Reborn." *House Beautiful*, May 1983, pp. 112–117.

"Life at the Top." *Vogue*, August 1983, p. 283.

Linker, Kate. "Reviews: Venturi, Rauch and Scott Brown." *Artforum*, January 1983, pp. 78–79.

Morozzi, Cristina. "L'Anima a Colori." *Modo*, October 1983, pp. 55–58.

Munoz, Maria Teresa. "Sobre el Realismo en Arquitectura." *Arquitecturas*, March 1983, pp. 15–18.

Neisser, Judith. "Architecture's 'Stand-Up Comic.'" *United*, October 1983, pp. 90–94.

"The 1983 Hazlett Memorial Awards Exhibition for the Visual Arts." Exhibition catalog, Southern Alleghenies Museum of Art, 1983.

"1983 Honor Award." *RI-AIA Newsletter*, No. 179, May/June 1983, pp. 5–6.

Olsen, Florence. "Romantic Victorian: An Old, New Look." *Houston Home & Garden*, July 1983, pp. 30–34.

"Park Design Regency-Inspired." *The Houston Post*, September 5–6, 1981, p. 7DD.

Perkins, Bradford. "Review of *Form & Purpose*, by Moshe Safdie." *Architectural Record*, January 1983, pp. 77–79.

"Philadelphia Architect Wins Life-Work Award." *The Philadelphia Inquirer*, July 19, 1983.

Plumb, Barbara. "Living: Discoveries." *Vogue*, November 1983, p. 336.

Portoghesi, Paolo. "Com'e vera quest'illusione." *Europeo*, June 25, 1983. (In Italian.)

"Robert Venturi is Eighth Sullivan Award Winner." *Trowel*, Summer 1983, pp. 4–13.

"Robert Venturi Wins '83 Sullivan Award." *The Journal of the International Union of Bricklayers and Allied Craftsmen*, July 1983, p. 1.

Russell, Beverly. "The Neocon Winners." *Interiors*, August 1983, p. 95.

Scalvini, Maria Luisa. "Learning from Princeton." *Domus*, December 1983, pp. 18–23.

Stephens, Suzanne. "Gordon Wu Hall, Butler College, Princeton University, Princeton, New Jersey." *Vanity Fair*, October 1983, pp. 135–136.

"Sullivan Award: Robert Venturi Wins the Bricklayers' 1983 Honor." *Memo* (Newsletter of the American Institute of Architects), August 12, 1983, p. 5.

Swenarton, Mark. "Venturi in Princeton." *Building Design*, December 2, 1983, pp. 14–16.

Tea & Coffee Piazza by Officina Alessi. Crusinallo: Shakespeare & Company, 1983.

"Tea and Coffee Piazza." *L'Architecture d'Aujourd'hui*, November 1983, pp. 99–101.

Tickell, Simon. "An Interview with Denise Scott Brown." *Penn in Ink*, Spring 1983, pp. 18–20.

Upton, Dell. "The Power Things: Recent Studies in American Vernacular Architecture." *American Quarterly*, vol. 35, no. 3, bibliography 1983, pp. 262–279.

"Venturi, Rauch & Scott Brown." *Progressive Architecture*, January 1983, pp. 122–123.

"Venturi, Rauch & Scott Brown Announced as Designers of New Laguna Gloria in Austin." *Texas Architect*, May/June 1983, pp. 18–19.

"Venturi Shares Approach, Predilictions for New Laguna Gloria in Austin." *Texas Architect*, July/August 1983, pp. 23, 25.

1984
Adams, Brooks. "Architects at Tea." *House & Garden*, May 1984, pp. 52–60.

"American Living Monuments." *Connoisseur*, July 1984, pp. 96–101.

"Architects' Product Designs." *Avenue*, April 1984, pp. 141–145.

Bletter, Rosemarie Haag. "Transformations of the American Vernacular: The Work of Venturi, Rauch & Scott Brown." *Venturi, Rauch and Scott Brown: A Generation of Architecture*. Exhibition catalog, traveling exhibition co-sponsored by Krannert Art Museum and the School of Architecture, University of Illinois at Urbana-Champaign, March 1984, pp. 2–19.

Brenner, Douglas. "Petrie House, Wainscott, New York, by Venturi, Rauch and Scott Brown." *Architectural Record Houses of 1984*, Mid-April 1984, pp. 92–95.

Brown, Kim. "Living Theater," *Diversion*, September 1984, pp. 241–244.

Carmody, Dierdre. "Debut for the Westway Park Plan." *The New York Times*, June 21, 1984, p. B1.

Davis, Douglas. "Mr. Post-Postmodern." *Newsweek*, July 9, 1984, pp. 78–80.

Dean, Andrea Oppenheimer. "Cerebral Campus Center that Abounds in Contradictions." *Architecture*, May 1984, pp. 200–203.

"Design Awards/Competitions." *Architectural Record*, May 1984, pp. 92–95.

Filler, Martin. "The Architectural Tabletop." *House & Garden*, October 1984, pp. 96, 98, 104.

Filler, Martin. "Past with a Future." *House & Garden*, July 1984, pp. 46–50.

Filler, Martin. "Personal Patterns." *House & Garden*, January 1984, pp. 90–99.

Filler, Martin. "Traces of Greatness." *House & Garden*, October 1984, p. 250.

Gandee, Charles K. "Profiles in History." *Architectural Record*, June 1984, pp. 166–170.

Giovannini, Joseph. "By Venturi: Something Borrowed, Something New." *The New York Times*, June 7, 1984, p. C10.

Goldberger, Paul. "A Critical Crossroads for Times Square Plan." *The New York Times*, July 5, 1984, pp. B1, B5.

Goldberger, Paul. "3 Design Plans Being Considered for Proposed Park Over the Westway." *The New York Times*, March 28, 1984, pp. B1, B4.

Goldberger, Paul. "Venturi's Willfully Eccentric Furniture." *The New York Times*, May 3, 1984, p. C12.

Goode, Ruth. "Frank Lloyd Wright: How He Looks to Architects Today." *MD Magazine*, April 1984, pp. 107–122.

"Gordon Wu Hall, Princeton University, Princeton, New Jersey." *Global Architecture Document 10*, May 1984, pp. 76–81.

"Gordon Wu Hall, Princeton University, New Jersey." *L'Architecture d'Aujourd'hui*, February 1984, pp. 92–94.

Goulet, Patrice. "La Troisieme Generation." *L'Architecture d'Aujourd'hui*, June 1984, pp. 2–9. (In French; English summary p. LXXVIII.)

Grabar, Oleg. "From the Past into the future: On Two Designs for State Mosques." *Architectural Record*, June 1984, pp. 150-151.

Greene, Elaine. "Extraordinary Ordinary." *House & Garden*, May 1984, pp. 158–165, 242, 244.

Hamm, Madeline McDermott. "Architect's Furniture Designs are Fat, Flat, Fun." *Houston Chronicle*, June 21, 1984, section 6, pp. 1–2.

Hine, Thomas. "The Diminishing Demand for Expressive Design." *The Philadelphia Inquirer*, February 19, 1984, p. 12–I.

Hine, Thomas. "His Chairs Aren't Just Furniture." *The Philadelphia Inquirer*, May 2, 1984, pp. 1D, 3D.

Hine, Thomas. "Laurels for Phila. Architects." *The Philadelphia Inquirer*, June 22, 1984, p. 1C.

"Interview: Jean Nouvel." *L'Architecture d'Aujourd'hui*, February 1984, pp. 3–14. (In French; English translation pp. XLVI–LII.)

Janjigian, Robert. "Contextual Credit." *Interiors*, January 1984, pp. 146–147.

Keenan, Margaret M. "An Architect's Tour of Wu Hall." *Princeton Alumni Weekly*, January 25, 1984, pp. 11–15.

Laine, Christian K. "Robert Venturi." *Neocon 16 Program & Directory*, June 1984, p. 92.

Macrae-Gibson, Gavin. "The Ironies of the Difficult Whole: Venturi, Rauch and Scott Brown's Gordon Wu Hall." *A+U*, January 1984, pp. 85–86.

Markoutsas, Elaine. "An Architect Borrows a Line or Two from the Classics." *Chicago Tribune*, June 10, 1984, section 15, pp. 1, 4.

Marinelli, Ursula. "Breaking Away." *Lawrence Institute of Technology Magazine*, Summer 1984, pp. 1, 2, 4.

McDevitt, Lorelei. "Special Report: Neocon 16 Review." *Designer's West*, August 1984, pp. 46, 48.

Miller, Nory. "Grandma Never Looked So Good." *Metropolis*, June 1984, pp. 24–28, 39.

Nannerini, Guiseppe. "Gordon Wu Hall for Butler, Princeton University, New Jersey." *L'Industria delle Construzioni*, May 1984, pp. 40–45.

Plumb, Barbara. "Living: One-of-a-Kind." *Vogue*, August 1984, pp. 256–258.

"Regenerative Approaches to Mosque Design: Competition for State Mosque, Baghdad." *Mimar 11*, January/March 1984, pp. 44–63.

Rights, Susie. "Women Designers: If You Are a Girl Wanting to be an Architect . . ." *The Sentinel*, August 24, 1984, p. 32.

"A Riverfront Park for New York is Proposed." *Architectural Record*, February 1984, p. 51.

Schmertz, Mildred F. "Design Competition Entry for the State Mosque, by Venturi, Rauch and Scott Brown." *Architectural Record*, June 1984, pp. 142–149.

Schmertz, Mildred F. "Izenour House, Stony Creek, Connecticut, by Steven Izenour of Venturi, Rauch and Scott Brown." *Architectural Record Houses of 1984*, Mid-April 1984, pp. 124–127.

Schwartz, Barth David. "Knoll International: The Revolution Revived." *Town and Country*, March 1984, pp. 223–234.

Stockman, Leslie Ensor. "Originals." *Builder*, August 1984, pp. 82–95.

Takase, Hayahiko. "Columbus, Indiana: Museum of Modern American Architecture." *SD* (Space Design), June 1984, pp. 27–41. (In Japanese.)

Taylor, Markland. "Stony Creek House Built to Sound Great." *New Haven Register*, May 20, 1984, p. F1.

Truppin, Andrea. "Neocon Preview: Two Way Stretch." *Interiors*, May 1984, pp. 228–258.

Viladas, Pilar. "Remembrance of Chairs Past." *Progressive Architecture*, June 1984, p. 24.

Vogel, Carol. "Home Design: Design Trends 1985." *The New York Times Magazine*, August 26, 1984, pp. 44–50.

Walsh, Michael. "Venturi's New Chairs are Tongue in Chic." *Chicago Sun-Times*, June 13, 1984, p. 47.

Weinraub, Judith. "Breaking Boundaries: Robert Venturi's Unorthodox Designs." *The Washington Post*, May 24, 1984, Home Section, pp. 1, 22–23, 30, 32.

"Wu Hall Honored." *Princeton Alumni Weekly*, June 1, 1984, p. 22.

Writings by Robert Venturi

1953
"The Campidoglio: A Case Study." *The Architectural Review*, May 1953, pp. 333–334.

1960
"Project for a Beach House." *Architectural Design*, November 1960.

1961
"Weekend House." *Progressive Architecture*, April 1961, pp. 156–157.

1965
"A Justification for a Pop Architecture." *Arts and Architecture*, April 1965, p. 22.

"Complexity and Contradiction in Architecture." *Perspecta 9–10*, 1965, pp. 17–56.

1966
Complexity and Contradiction in Architecture. New York: Museum of Modern Art and Graham Foundation, 1966. (Translated into Japanese, 1969; French, 1971; Spanish, 1972.)

1967
"Selection from 'Complexity and Contradiction in Architecture.'" *Zodiac 17*, 1967, pp. 123–126.

"Three Projects: Architecture and Landscape, Architecture and Sculpture, Architecture and City Planning." *Perspecta 11*, 1967, pp. 103–106.

"Trois batiments pour une ville de l'Ohio." *l'Architecture d'Aujourd'hui*, December 1967/January 1968, pp. 37–39.

1968
"A Bill-Ding-Board Involving Movies, Relics and Space." *Architectural Forum*, April 1968, pp. 74–76.

"On Architecture." *l'Architecture d'Aujourd'hui*, September 1968, pp. 36–39.

1975
"Architecture as Shelter with Decoration on It, and a Plea for a Symbolism of the Ordinary in Architecture." Unpublished, 1975.

1976
"Alvar Aalto." *arkkitehti*, July/August 1976, pp. 66–67. (Reprinted in *Progressive Architecture*, April 1977, pp. 54, 102.)

"The Installation of the Special Exhibition: 'Philadelphia: Three Centuries of American Art' at The Philadelphia Museum of Art." Unpublished, 1976. (Printed in notice for Conference of Society of Architectural Historians, 1976, Philadelphia Museum of Art.)

"Plain and Fancy Architecture by Cass Gilbert at Oberlin." *Apollo*, February 1976, pp. 6–9.

"A Reaction to Complexity and Contradiction in the Work of Furness." *Pennsylvania Academy of the Fine Arts Newsletter*, Spring 1976, p. 5.

1977
Complexity and Contradiction in Architecture (revised edition). New York: Museum of Modern Art, 1977. (Translated into Spanish, 1977; German, 1978; Greek, 1978; Italian, 1980; Chinese, 1982.)

"Forum: The Beaux Arts Exhibition." *Oppositions*, Spring 1977, pp. 171–172.

Global Architecture, December 1977, pp. 160–167.

"Plain and Fancy Architecture by Cass Gilbert at Oberlin and the Addition to the Museum by Venturi and Rauch." *Allen Memorial Art Museum Bulletin*, vol. 34, no. 2 (1976/1977), pp. 83–104. (Also published in *Arquitectura*, January/February 1978, pp. 66–74. A portion of this article appeared in *Apollo*, February 1976, pp. 6–9.)

1978
"A Definition of Architecture as Shelter with Decoration on It, and Another Plea for a Symbolism of the Ordinary in Architecture." *Architecture and Urbanism*, January 1978, pp. 3–14. (Also published in *l'Architecture d'Aujourd'hui*, no. 197 (June 1978), pp. 7–8.)

1979
"The Campidoglio: A Case Study." *Stanza*, Spring 1979, p. 27. (Reprinted from *Architectural Review*, May 1953, pp. 333–334.)

"Learning the Right Lessons from the Beaux Arts." *Architectural Design*, January 1979, pp. 23–31.

"Une Galerie d'Art a Oberlin, Ohio." *Werk-Archithese*, January/February 1979, pp. 31–32, 96.

1980
"Donald Drew Egbert–A Tribute." In Donald Drew Egbert, *The Beaux-Arts Tradition in French Architecture*, Princeton (N.J.): Princeton University Press, 1980, pp. xiii–xiv.

1982
"Diversity, Relevance and Representation in Historicism, or Plus Ca Change . . . plus A Plea for Pattern all over Architecture with a Postscript on my Mother's House." *Architectural Record*, June 1982, pp. 114–119.

"Diversity, Relevance and Representation in Historicism, or Plus Ca Change . . ." *l'Architecture d'Aujourd'hui*, October 1982, pp. 94–101.

"Il Proprio Vocabolario." *Gran Bazaar*, February 1982, pp. 152–157.

"RIBA Discourse, July 1981." *Transactions 1. RIBA Journal*, May 1982, pp. 47–56.

Shore, Stephen. *Uncommon Places*. Jacket note by Robert Venturi, New York: Aperture, 1982.

1983
"On Aalto." *Quaderns 157*, April/May/June 1983, p. 55.

"A Pluralism of Tastes." *Advertising Age*, August 8, 1983, p. M–12.

"Proposal for the Iraq State Mosque, Baghdad." *L'Architecture d'Aujourd'hui*, Sept. 1983, pp. 28–35.

Writings by Denise Scott Brown

1962
"Form, Design and the City." *Journal of the American Institute of Planners*, November 1962.

1963
"City Planning and What It Means to Me to Be a City Planner." Unpublished, March 1963.

"Report on the Neighborhood Garden Association." Unpublished, March 1963.

1964
"Natal Plans." *Journal of the American Institute of Planners*, May 1964, pp. 161–166.

1965
"The Meaningful City." *Journal of the American Institute of Architects*, January 1965, pp. 27–32. (Reprinted in *Connection*, Spring 1967.)

1966
"Development Proposal for Dodge House Park." *Arts and Architecture*, April 1966, p. 16.

"Will Salvation Spoil the Dodge House?" *Architectural Forum*, October 1966, pp. 68–71.

1967
"The Function of a Table." *Architectural Design*, April 1967.

"Housing 1863." *Journal of the American Institute of Planners*, May 1967.

"The People's Architects." *Landscape*, Spring 1967, p. 38.

"Planning the Expo." *Journal of the American Institute of Planners*, July 1967, pp. 268–272.

"Planning the Powder Room." *Journal of the American Institute of Architects*, April 1967, pp. 81–83.

"Teaching Architectural History." *Arts and Architecture*, May 1967.

"Team 10, Perspecta 10, and the Present State of Architectural Theory." *Journal of the American Institute of Planners*, January 1967, pp. 42–50.

1968
"The Bicentennial's Fantasy Stage." *The Philadelphia Evening Bulletin*, March 8, 1968.

"Little Magazines in Architecture and Urbanism." *Journal of the American Institute of Planners*, July 1968, pp. 223–233.

"Mapping the City: Symbols and Systems." *Landscape*, Spring 1968, pp. 22–25.

"Taming Megalopolis." *Architectural Design*, November 1968, p. 512.

"Urban Structuring." *Architectural Design*, January 1968, p. 7.

"Urbino." *Journal of the American Institute of Planners*, September 1968, pp. 344–46.

1969
"On Pop Art, Permissiveness and Planning." *Journal of the American Institute of Planners*, May 1969, pp. 184–186.

1970
"Education in the 1970's–Teaching for an Altered Reality." *Architectural Record*, October 1970.

"On Analysis and Design." Unpublished, 1970.

"Reply to Sibyl Moholy-Nagy and Ulrich Franzen." Unpublished, September 4, 1970.

1971
"Learning from Pop" and "Reply to Frampton." *Casabella*, nos. 389/390 (May/June 1971), pp. 14–46. (Reprinted in *Journal of Popular Culture*, Fall 1973, pp. 387–401.)

1974

"Evaluation of the Humanities Building at Purchase" (with Elizabeth and Steven Izenour). *Architectural Record*, October 1974, p. 122.

"Giovanni Maria Cosco, 1926–1973." *Rassegna dell'Istituto di Architettura e Urbanistica* (University of Rome), August/December 1974, pp. 127–129.

1975

"On Formal Analysis as Design Research, With Some Notes on Studio Pedagogy." Unpublished, 1975.

"Sexism and the Star System in Architecture." Unpublished, 1975.

"Symbols, Signs and Aesthetics: Architectural Taste in a Pluralist Society." Unpublished, 1975.

1976

"House Language" (with Elizabeth Izenour, Missy Maxwell, and Janet Schueren). *American Home*, August 1976.

"A House is More than a Home" (with Steven Izenour, Dian Boone, Missy Maxwell, Robert Venturi, Elizabeth Izenour, and Janet Schueren). *Progressive Architecture*, August 1976, pp. 62–67.

"On Architectural Formalism and Social Concern: A Discourse for Social Planners and Radical Chic Architects." *Oppositions 5*, Summer 1976, pp. 99–112.

"Signs of Life: Symbols in the American City" (with Elizabeth Izenour, Steven Izenour, Missy Maxwell, Janet Schueren, and Robert Venturi). Text for Bicentennial exhibition, Renwick Gallery, National Collection of Fine Arts, Smithsonian Institution, Washington, D.C., 1976.

Signs of Life: Symbols in the American City (with Steven Izenour). New York: Aperture, No. 77, 1976, pp. 49–65. (Exhibition catalog)

"Suburban Space, Scale and Symbol" (with Elizabeth Izenour, Missy Maxwell, and Janet Schueren). *Via* (University of Pennsylvania), 1976.

1977

"Forum: The Beaux Arts Exhibition." *Oppositions*, Spring 1977, pp. 165–166.

1978

"On Architectural Formalism & Social Concern." *Werk und Zeit*, January 1978, pp. 34–40.

"Ordinances Design Neighborhoods" (with Mary Yee and Frances Headley [Hundt]). *HUD Challenge*, September 1978, p. 22.

1979

"Die Stadt als 'Zeichensystem.'" *Werk-Archithese*, nos. 33–34 (September/October 1979), pp. 33–39, 67–68.

"Highboy: The Making of an Eclectic." *Saturday Review*, March 17, 1979, pp. 54–58.

"On Formal Analysis as Design Research." Search/Research, *Journal of Architectural Education*, vol. xxxii, no. 4 (May 1979), pp. 8–11.

"Learning the Wrong Lessons from the Beaux-Arts." *Architectural Design*, Profiles 17, 1979, pp. 30–32.

1980

"Architectural Taste in a Pluralistic Society." *The Harvard Architecture Review*, vol. 1 (Spring 1980), pp. 41–51.

"Erhaltung historischer Bauten und wirtschaftliche Neubelebung" (with Frances Hundt). *Archithese*, March 1980, pp. 20–24.

"Revitalizing Miami." *Urban Design International*, January/February 1980, pp. 20–25.

"Judges' Comments." *Interiors*, January 1980, pp. 80–102 *passim*.

"Main Street is Almost All Right." In *The Arts and City Planning: Making Cities Livable*. New York: American Council for the Arts, 1980, pp. 102–108.

1981

"Competition Feature: Venturi, Rauch and Scott Brown." *Architectural Design*, December 1981, pp. 124–129.

"Denise Scott Brown." In Lynn Gilbert and Gaylen Moore, *Particular Passions*. New York: Clarkson N. Potter, Inc., 1981, pp. 311–323.

"Historic Jim Thorpe" (with Frances Hundt and David Marohn). *Solutions*, Fall 1981, pp. 31–32.

"With People in Mind." *Journal of Architectural Education*, vol. 35, no. 1 (Fall 1981), pp. 43–45.

1982

"An Urban Design Plan." *Design Quarterly*, vol. 117, 1982, pp. 12–23.

"Between Three Stools: A Personal View of Urban Design Practice and Pedagogy." *Education for Urban Design*, pp. 132–172. Purchase (N.Y.): Institute for Urban Design, 1982.

"Drawing for the Deco District." *Archithese*, 2–82, March 4, 1982, pp. 17–21. (In German and English.)

"The Drawing of Buildings," for the Exhibition "Buildings and Drawings, Venturi, Rauch and Scott Brown." New York: Max Protetch Gallery, 1982. Unpublished.

1983
"Changing Family Forms." *Journal of the American Planning Association*, Spring 1983, pp. 133–137.

"Interview." *Penn in Ink* (annual review, Graduate School of Fine Arts, University of Pennsylvania), Spring 1983.

"Invention and Tradition in the Making of American Place." Paper presented at conference on "American Architecture: Innovation and Tradition," April 1983.

1984
"A Worm's Eye View of Recent Architectural History." *Architectural Record*, February 1984, pp. 69–81.

Writings by Robert Venturi and Denise Scott Brown

1968
"Significance for A&P Parking Lots, or Learning from Las Vegas." *Architectural Forum*, March 1968, pp. 37–43ff. (Reprinted in *Lotus*, 1968, pp. 70–91.)

1969
"Der Parkplatz von Atlantic & Pacific oder: Was lehrt uns Las Vegas?" *Werk*, no. 4 (April 1969), pp. 257–266.

"Learning from Lutyens." *Journal of the Royal Institute of British Architects*, August 1969, pp. 353–354.

"Mass Communications on the People Freeway, or, Piranesi is Too Easy." *Perspecta 12*, 1969, pp. 49–56.

1970
"Reply to Pawley–'Leading from the Rear.'" *Architectural Design*, July 1970, pp. 4, 370.

1971
"Some Houses of Ill-Repute: A Discourse with Apologia on Recent Houses of Venturi and Rauch." *Perspecta 13/14*, 1971, pp. 259–267.

"Ugly and Ordinary Architecture, or the Decorated Shed." Part I, *Architectural Forum*, November 1971, pp. 64–67; Part II, December 1971, pp. 48–53; discussion, January 1972, p. 12.

"Yale Mathematics Building." Unpublished, 1971.

1972
Learning from Las Vegas (with Steven Izenour). Cambridge (Mass.): MIT Press, 1972.

1973
"Bicentenaire de L'Independence Americaine." *l'Architecture d'Aujourd'hui*, November 1973, pp. 63–69.

1974
"Functionalism, Yes, But . . ." *Architecture and Urbanism*, November 1974, pp. 33–34. (Reprinted in *Architecturas Bis*, January 1975, pp. 1–2.)

1977
"Funktionalismus ja, abe . . ." *Werk-Archithese*, March 1977, pp. 32–35.

Learning from Las Vegas, The Forgotten Symbolism of Architectural Form (with Steven Izenour, revised edition). Cambridge (Mass.): MIT Press, 1977. (Translated into Japanese, 1978; Spanish, 1978; French, 1977; German, 1979.)

1980
"Interview, Robert Venturi and Denise Scott Brown." *The Harvard Architecture Review*, vol. 1 (Spring 1980), pp. 228–239.

1982
Interview with Barbaralee Diamonstein for "American Architecture Now–II," to be published.

Writings by Denise Scott Brown and Robert Venturi

1968
"On Ducks and Decoration." *Architecture Canada*, October 1968, p. 48.

1969
"The Bicentennial Commemoration 1976." *Architectural Forum*, October 1969, pp. 66–69.

"Venturi v. Gowan." *Architectural Design*, January 1969, pp. 31–36.

1970
"Co-op City: Learning to Like It." *Progressive Architecture*, February 1970, pp. 64–73.

The Highway. Catalog for exhibition, Institute of Contemporary Art, Philadelphia, 1970.

1971
Aprendiendo de Todas Las Cosas. Barcelona: Tusquets Editor, 1971.

Writings by Others at Venturi, Rauch and Scott Brown

1970
Izenour, Steven. "Education in the 1970s–Teaching for an Altered Reality." *Architectural Record*, October 1970.

1971
Izenour, Steven. "Civic Center Competition for Thousand Oaks, California; Entry by Venturi and Rauch in Association with Steven Izenour and Tony Pett." *Architectural Design*, February 1971, pp. 113–114.

1972
Carroll, Virginia, Denise Scott Brown and Robert Venturi. "Levittown et Apres." *l'Architecture d'Aujourd'hui*, no. 163 (August/September 1972), pp. 38–42.

1973
Hirshorn, Paul and Steven Izenour. "Learning from Hamburgers: The Architecture of White Towers." *Architecture Plus*, June 1973, pp. 46–55.

1975
Carroll, Virginia, Denise Scott Brown and Robert Venturi. "Styling, or 'Three houses are exactly the same. They just look different.'" *Lotus 9*, 1975. (In Italian and English.)

1977
Headley, Frances (Hundt). Series of articles on historic Philadelphia buildings. *Arts Exchange*, 1977-1978.

1978
Headley, Frances (Hundt) and David Marohn. "The Comic and Fantastic Bosses at the Quad." *Arts Exchange*, May/June 1978, pp. 12–17, 35.

1979
Hundt, Frances. "New Light on Neon." *Portfolio*, December 1979/January 1980, pp. 38–40.

Izenour, Steven (with Paul Hirshorn). *White Towers*. Cambridge (Mass.): MIT Press, 1979.

Matheu, Christine. "Aldo van Eyck: Both/And." *Skyline*, April 1979, p. 7.

Schwartz, Frederic. "Future McDonalds" and "The American T-Shirt." *Society for Commercial Archeology Journal*, November 1979.

1980
Hundt, Frances and Denise Scott Brown. "Erhaltung Historischer Bauten und wirtschaftliche Neubelebung." *Archithese*, March 1980, pp. 20–24.

Matheu, Christine. "Architecture as a media event." *Architectural Record*, November 1980, pp. 43, 45, 50.

Schwartz, Frederic. "Design for the City." *CRIT 8, The Architectural Student Journal*, Fall 1980, pp. 12–13.

Schwartz, Frederic, associate ed. "Beyond the Modern Movement." *Harvard Architecture Review*, vol. 1, no. 1. Cambridge (Mass): MIT Press, 1980. (See also interview with Robert Venturi and Denise Scott Brown, pp. 228–239.)

1982
Hundt, Frances. "Vernacular Architecture: The Ordinary Has Its Value." *Cities: The Forces That Shape Them*, New York: Smithsonian Institution, 1982, p. 41.

1983
Izenour, Steven. "La Ville Americaine et ses Portes." *Les Portes de la Ville*. Paris: Centre Georges Pompidou/CCI, 1983. (In French.)

Izenour, Steven. "Review of *Dunroamin: The Suburban Semi and its Enemies*, by Paul Oliver, Ian Davis and Ian Bentley." *Journal of the Society of Architectural Historians*, March 1983, pp. 81–82.

Runyan, Stanley. "The Metropolitan Lobby: From Grime to Glamour." *Landmarks*, July 1983, pp. 2, 3.

The Editors

Peter Arnell and **Ted Bickford,** who were educated at Columbia and Princeton universities respectively, are partners in the New York advertising and design firm of Arnell/Bickford Associates. Their recent publications include monographs of the work of Robert A.M. Stern, Michael Graves, James Stirling, Charles Gwathmey and Robert Siegel, Aldo Rossi and Frank O. Gehry, and a new collection of photographic collages by David Hockney. In addition they are the senior editors of an ongoing series documenting architectural competitions. Arnell and Bickford contribute articles to such major design publications as *Architectural Record, Casabella* and *Vogue,* and are the American collaborators for Italian *Gran Bazaar* magazine.

Catherine Bergart was educated at New York University. For Arnell/Bickford Associates she has edited monographs on the work of Charles Gwathmey and Robert Siegel, Aldo Rossi and Frank O. Gehry, and is the associate editor of the series documenting architectural competitions. She has recently completed work on *An American Adventuri,* a multimedia presentation of Robert Venturi's furniture designs for Knoll International.